Design First

for 3D Artists

by Geoffrey Kater

Library of Congress Cataloging-in-Publication Data

Kater, Geoffrey.
   Design first for 3d animators / by Geoffrey Kater.
      p. cm.
   Includes index.
   ISBN 1-55622-085-5 (pbk., companion CD-ROM)
   1. Animated films—Technique.   2. Drawing—Technique.   I. Title.
   NC1765.K38 2005
   741.5'8--dc22   2005029771

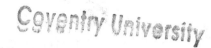

ISBN-10: 1-55622-085-5
ISBN-13: 978-1-55622-085-2

10 9 8 7 6 5 4 3 2 1
0510

All inquiries for volume purchases of this book should be addressed to Wordware Publishing, Inc., at the above address. Telephone inquiries may be made by calling:

(972) 423-0090

To David Solon, who gave me the courage and the guidance
to write this book... This book is dedicated to the man who
taught me the value of value.

(RIP 1928-2004)

Contents

Foreword xi
Acknowledgments xii

1 Why This Book? 1
Introduction 1
Who Am I? 2
What You Will Learn 3
What Is Design? 4
Anyone Can Do This 6

2 2D Exercises: Drawing Foundations First 7
Sketching and Illustration 7
"If You Can Draw the Four Basic Shapes, You Can Draw Anything" 8
Construction Explained 10
Line Drawing 13
Lighting the Four Basic Shapes 20
   Indirect Light 22
Value 32
A Quick Perspective on Perspective 34
Do a Sketch a Day 36

3 Design Basics and Observation 39
Contrast Rule 39
What Is Composition? 40
Get Graphic 41
Focal Point 44
Tension 46
Read the Flow 48
Tangents: The Good, the Bad, and the Ugly 52
Color Opposites Attract 56
Warm and Cool 60

Proportion. 68
An Odd Relationship 72
Contour 80
Observation 86

4 Designing Your Own Ideas 91
A Non-Boring Intro 91
Gesture Drawing 91
Inspiration and Design Themes 96
  Step 1: Find Your Inspiration 99
  Step 2: Apply Your Inspiration. 99
Drawing in the Rough and Overlay Techniques. 102
Advanced Construction 108
  Construction Drawing 110
Connecting Construction 112
The KISS Rule. 114
Verbal Communication 116
Get a Good Pair of Headphones 117
You Are Unique 117
Quick Non-Boring Review 118

5 Research and Presentation 119
Introduction 119
Client Guidelines 120
Who's Your Audience?. 122
Gather Reference Material 124
Define Your Concept. 132
  Concept 1 (Arcade). 132
  Concept 2 (Giant Phone). 135
  Concept 3 (Dance) 137
Presentation 138
  Printed Booklet. 138
  Digital Format 138
  Thank You Note 140
Ultimately the Client Knows the Business 140

If They Like Your Ideas 140
If They Don't Like Your Ideas 140
Review. 141

6 Your Project 143
Introduction 143
The Assignment. 144
Character 146
Inspiration for Story 150
My Inspiration 152
Story, Story, Story 153
Breakdown: What Is Your Design Focus? 155
Design Direction. 156
My Design Direction 158
Design It — Make It Fresh, Different, and Inspiring 160
Bleep 164
Angus. 168
The N4CER 171
Keep the Gesture 174
Refine Your Designs. 176
Color: Choice and Application. 178
Color Phase 1: Gather Color Reference Material 179
Color Phase 2: Determine a Few Colors of Interest. 179
Color Phase 3: Create Your Color Palette 179
Color Phase 4: Apply Your Color Palette. 181
Color Phase 5: Compare and Contraste Designs 183
Rewrite: How Visuals Influence Story 184
Rewrite Changes 184

7 Thinking Your Project Through. 191
Introduction to Storyboarding. 191
Words into Pictures 192
Shot Breakdown. 192
Subnumbering 195
Storyboarding: Your Road Map to Success 196

Contents

Technique. 196
Flow 198
Composition 201
Transitions 202
Getting a Response. 207
    Close-up. 207
    Wide Shot 207
    Long Shot 207
    Medium Shot 207
    Behind. 207
    Over the Shoulder. 207
    Extreme Close-up. 209
    Zoom 209
    Aerial 209
    Cut. 209
    Dissolve 209
    Fade 211
Storyboard Timing. 212
3D Model or 2D Replacement? 214
Render Time... Recognize the Enemy!. 216
    Composition 216
    Image Quality. 217
    Model Only What You Need 217
    Lighting. 217
    2D Replacing 3D 217
    Compositing 217

8   2D Translation into a 3D World. 219
A Translation Solution. 219
Three-View Basic Shape Drawing. 222
    Front View 222
    Side View. 224
    Top View 224
    Analysis. 226

Three-View Orthographic Drawing 227
Scan It 230
   3D Models 230
   Image Maps. 232
   Storyboards. 234

9 **Animation Production** 235
Introduction 235
3D Modeling 236
   Use a Three-View Basic Shape Drawing as Reference 239
   Model in Halves 241
   Check Your Proportions 244
   Contour 247
   Observation and Final Adjustments 250
   Detail 253
   Color 255
   Texturing 256
   The Power of Sublety 259
   BGs 263
   Finalized 3D Model. 263
3D Animation 264
   Stick to Your Boards! 264
   Animate for Composition. 266
   Who's Going to Notice? 266
Lighting 268
   Contrast 268
   Warm and Cool Lighting 271
Rendering 271

10 **2D Shortcuts for 3D** 273
Use Traditional Design to Save on Render Time 273
   Environments 273
   Textures 278
   Lighting. 279
   Reflections 282

Composite for Effect. 283
   Blurs 283
   Fake Depth of Field. 283
   Quick Backgrounds. 284
   Edge Blur. 286
   Motion Blur. 286
   Soft Render. 286
   Glow 286
   Lens Flares 286
   Brightness/Contrast 286
   Color 289
   Grain 289

11 Execution 291
Introduction 291
Critique Thy Work. 291
Delivery 294
Execution 295

12 Industry Tips 297
Introduction 297
What Studios Want: "Calling All Designers!" 297
Demo Reel Do's and Don'ts 299
   The Harsh Reality of Demo Reel Submission 299
   How to Improve Your Chances of Getting Hired 299
   Demo Reel Returns 300
   How Long Should You Wait? 301

Index 303

Foreword

Good design is an illusive beast. It's rare. Prized. Endangered. Sadly, it is not something that we encounter on a regular basis, so we might not recognize it when we do. It can be unfamiliar. It will surprise us. We have to train ourselves to recognize and understand it.

Sometimes design hides in plain sight, choosing to reveal itself only when being touched or held. The handle of a toothbrush, the placement of the buttons on a telephone, the balance of a coffee cup might signal the presence of design.

Design might envelop us before we are aware of it. We sit in a chair and sense its support and comfort. Its elegance. Its simplicity. We run through the controls and gauges of a new car to test their functionality while we sense the intuitive intelligence of their placement.

Design is not serendipitous or, worse, an accident. It is calculating and precise, the byproduct of imagination. Its antecedents are function and aesthetics, materials and intent. The Navajo rug, the Japanese gravel garden, the iPod are cousins.

Design brings with it not only the expectation of how something "looks," but how we interact with it in three-dimensional space. True design doesn't react; it anticipates. When it is at its very best, we barely notice it.

The lessons and ideals of design are present in nature and revealed through observation. The greatest asset a designer has is not how to execute but how to see. What we see, we must also feel, in the most elemental way. Our job is not to outthink nature but to let it reveal itself to us. In the end, design is the means by which we unravel the world, sort out its intentions, and make them our own.

To understand design, we must let the world shape us. We must allow the lessons of the world to inhabit our imaginations and transform our experiences into shape, form, and function.

Design, as always, has morphed and been modified into new and exciting forms. Old reliables like product, fashion, automobile, interior, and type design have been augmented by relative newcomers like entertainment design, including games, movies, and animation, interface, web design, and toys. The opportunities for intelligence and elegance exist in all these categories. The horizons are endless.

Geoffrey Kater has enthusiastically and intelligently embraced the challenge of demystifying design. He offers us a variety of methods and techniques, providing a much-needed path into the complex nature of design.

Read this book.
The beast awaits.

Dan Quarnstrom
Designer/Director, Rhythm & Hues

Acknowledgments

First off, I'd like to thank the tremendous staff at Wordware Publishing for believing in my passion about the subject, design first, and then taking a chance to let me author such a book. Special thanks to Wes Beckwith, who was the lighthouse in the fog. I consider you a colleague, a confidant, and a friend.

I'd like to thank Dan Quarnstrom, who was my tech editor for this book and who had an incredible influence on how I thought about the information I was trying to convey. Dan has been in the animation business for many years and serves as one of Rhythm & Hues most senior designer/directors. He has influenced the look, feel, and content of countless animated films and commercials. I've worked with Dan on a couple of projects over the years and we instantly bonded as friends. I think very highly of Dan and in many ways consider him a mentor. Dan, your input as tech editor on this book has been invaluable to its growth, and your tireless words of design wisdom have changed me as a designer, a director, and an artist for the rest of my career. Thanks again.

I'd like to thank Larry Le Francis, my business partner and friend. Thank you for doing editorial on "Feed the Dog" and helping me put it into script form. I would also like to thank you for suggesting that you read through the manuscript to make sure it conveyed my sometimes sarcastic and straight shooter personality. You know I think the world of you and appreciate your help and support during this whole process.

I would also like to thank my loving girlfriend, Cheryl, to whom I owe more dinners and weekend trips than I can even count. Thank you so much for supporting me with your beautiful smile and all the love in the world. I cherish the ground you walk on. I would also like to thank you for composing and performing the music for "Bleep's Kata"… the drums are great!

Thanks to John Novak, my good friend, my neighbor, and the owner of my inspiration, Angus. Thanks, Angus — you big spaz.

Last but not least, I'd like to thank my mother and father who raised me to follow my dreams and be nothing less than proud of myself. Your praise and support for this latest endeavor has been invaluable; thank you for being there. Mom, yes, you will see me more often so we can cook together. And, yes, Dad, you will get a free copy.

Why This Book?

Introduction

The most important element in any animated film is story and, as they say, story is king. The goal of a story is to take the audience on a journey through the lives and experiences of the characters within. Whether that journey is cerebral, emotional, or physical, the characters in that world should give the audience a point of view that is unique and compelling.

As a designer, your role within a production is as an aesthetic problem solver who is there to support the story. As a 3D artist/animator, your role is to solve problems, but comes after the design process. Design and animation are two different disciplines that problem solve in two different ways, yet each has the same goal. What if we combined these disciplines into a single role that uses design to influence animation throughout the entire 3D process? This book is about that very thing. For those who are open minded about learning a valuable skill like design, this book will not only improve your animation work, but will improve your worth as a 3D artist.

Production design for 3D animation is the process of using traditional drawing techniques to create characters, props, environments, color, lighting, compositions, and storyboards. Each design detail needs to be laid out and problem solved long before any animation is produced. The designer's job is to address all of the aesthetic challenges of the project and design solutions to those challenges. For example, the response to the aesthetic challenges of *Batman Begins* is in the form of dark visual themes like the deep moody lighting of Gotham City, the dynamic steep camera angles, and the mysterious-looking off-road industrial battle tank called the Batmobile. A designer is there to solve the aesthetic pieces of the project, to see what fits and what doesn't, and then offer at least one solution, if not a variety, to those problems.

A 3D artist or animator who acquires the skill of design brings more value to a production through his or her ability to problem solve intellectual and abstract concepts by using design as a guide. For example, a designer/animator not only controls the look of the Batmobile, but is also able to highlight the characteristics that make it a great design through the way it animates and functions within each scene. As a 3D artist, you should be in tune with what design is, how it functions, and how it can benefit your work. It's not something that just traditional artists can do; it's something everyone can do. Animation studios thirst for 3D professionals who have a traditional design background, so why not expand your skill set, enhance your work, and improve your professional worth.

Who Am I?

I started my career as a traditional designer, studying automotive design at Art Center College of Design in Pasadena, California. I soon left the world of car design, getting my first job at DIC Entertainment working as a prop designer on *Where on Earth Is Carmen Sandiego?* I spent many years in production behind the pencil, pumping out futuristic cars, spaceships, and environments for action adventure shows like *The New Avengers*, *Diabolique*, and *Silver Surfer*. It was on *Silver Surfer* that I took my first crack at 3D. As the lead spaceship designer, I had the ultimate job of designing, modeling, and animating space battles for that show. It was this crossover into 3D that changed my career forever. I loved having the control over my designs by drawing them first, then building and animating them in 3D.

Many years have passed and I now co-own a computer animation studio named S4 Studios, LLC, located in Hollywood. We've been in business for nearly six years and I've designed and produced animation for countless trailers, television shows, commercials, feature effects, and online webisodes. I employ numerous animation professionals, intimating every detail and direction on animated projects, and it is this day-to-day, from-the-field attitude that I'm employing in this book. Writing *Design First for 3D Artists* is one of the greatest undertakings of my entire career, but because I feel so passionate about the marriage of traditional design and 3D, I've outlined my journey, my thoughts, and my techniques for the purposes of improving our valued industry. I certainly don't have all the answers; in fact, this book is more of a starting point for those who want to get a glimpse of how design can improve their animation work. There are an enormous number of resources for design, animation, and filmmaking, and it works in your favor to learn as much as you can. So start with what you like and then take it from there.

What You Will Learn

You're going to learn to reach for the pencil before the keyboard. On many levels the keyboard technique is important, but you can easily overlook many crucial design phases that will improve your final animation. Design encompasses a wide variety of stages that include inspiration, research, story, sketching, color, modeling, and animation. This book will teach you how to get inspired, do research, sketch your ideas, finalize your designs, create storyboards, and animate your concepts with a focus on design first. It sounds a little overwhelming, but there is a tried-and-true process to learning all of this. For now, your focus should be on understanding what design is and how to use it.

You may have looked on in admiration of those who can draw and previsualize their ideas on paper, and some of those artists have probably looked over your shoulder in bewilderment as to how you make those cool animations. As an experienced production designer and CG director I understand how 3D artists think, so my design exercises will be conveyed in terms of getting through to the 3D artist's mind. For example, a lot of foundational drawing exercises encompass the use of simple shapes, like the cube, sphere, cone, etc. These are the same simple shapes used in 3D programs, so my drawing exercises have you starting with simple shapes that you're already familiar with. I bet if I asked you to draw a cube, you could do it on the spot. You'll find out later that just like a 3D cube can be transformed into a skyscraper or computer monitor, so can a traditionally drawn cube. It's all about technique. Throughout this book you will learn various techniques in sketching, graphic design, lighting, color, research, story, and how to translate all of this into your 3D project. You'll also learn several cool 2D tricks used as shortcuts for compositing, visual FX, and lighting.

The fun design exercises in this book will teach you about your strengths and weaknesses, and understanding your strengths will go a long way into helping you adopt a design process that is unique and solely your own. I fully understand that every artist has his or her own processes, so I want you to adopt these new techniques in ways that work for your personality. You can learn from others, but always interpret that into what works best for you.

What Is Design?

This question can only be answered by saying that design is what it means to you. Each of us has our own likes and dislikes as they relate to film, cars, furniture, fashion, etc. Understanding why you like what you do and how a designer created a combination of forms and function that appeals to you is the first lesson in understanding design.

I will now digress to a boring definition first and then go on to some very exciting examples that might put things into perspective...

"To create, fashion, execute, or construct according to plan." The definition of design is incredibly broad because it permeates everything, everywhere, and all of us. It is applied to our world through methods like industrial, graphic, production, and environmental design, filmmaking, lighting, fashion, architecture, photography, cinematography, and the list goes on forever. Even though each of these design applications varies greatly by trade and application, they have one thing in common: problem solving.

Much like a 3D animated element must address specific requirements like story, composition, lighting, interaction, movement, and so on, almost all things that are designed have been fashioned to solve a specific problem. For instance, let's say you're working on a very dramatic film and the script calls for an atmosphere of fear. Your first problem would be to define what aesthetic elements you need in order to create an atmosphere of fear. The solution could be dark contrasted lighting, characters in silhouette, low scary music, and edge-of-your-seat camera movement. Or the solution could be a super-saturated, grainy colored image with only the sound of a heartbeat and blurry chaotic camera movement. Solutions to the aforementioned problem are as varied as there are people in the world — there is no perfect solution, nor is there only one solution. This is where you can really start to learn the definition of design because it's all very personal.

Not only does design differ according to its chosen discipline, such as architecture vs. graphic design, but even within each discipline, let's say just architecture, there are a variety of techniques, styles, philosophies, and applications. For instance, Frank Lloyd Wright and Santiago Calatrava are two very famous architects and both have designed countless structures ranging from bridges to skyscrapers, apartment buildings to museums, and music halls to terminals. They are both architects and they both address the same problems, but their solutions, styles, and philosophies differ drastically. Wright is known for designing the Guggenheim Museum in New York City, which could be described as a giant ribbon that spirals toward the sky, almost spring-like in its appearance — it's a magnificent structure. Calatrava is known for designing the Quadracci Pavilion at the Milwaukee Museum of Art, another magnificent building. This structure could be described as having giant 250-foot multidirectional sails that tower high into the air like the wings of an albatross and are held together with sailboat-like rigging. Both structures serve the same purpose and both are considered incredibly beautiful, but what makes them different is style. Personal style is what separates all designers and all people, because personal style is your own unique expression through whatever medium of design you choose. For some it's through the way they dress or decorate their home; to others it's a hobby like ceramics, painting, or model making. For those who make design their profession, it becomes a life-long pursuit of innovative problem solving and the wisdom that unique design can make someone's life better or more exciting.

Other good examples of the same discipline but different personal style can be seen by looking at works by Syd Mead and Moebius, both industrial design futurists but with distinctly different visions of the future. Mead is known for designing some of the greatest production sets of all time, like *Blade Runner*, *2001*, and even *Tron*, and could be considered the godfather of slick, organic futuristic functional and social industrial design. Works by Moebius look like some kind of retro-future world filled with oddly colored exotic characters, flying animals, and earthy-organic buildings. Moebius' work is by far more surreal and dream-like, but has the same grounded quality of reality and style that Mead shows in his work. Mead's polished, clearly delineated, huge beasts and giant futuristic cities respond to the same design challenges, yet envision the future in a completely different way.

Jesse James of *Monster Garage* and Paul Teutul of *American Chopper* are both vehicle designers. James blends old school hot rod with a contemporary thread, and Teutul designs themed choppers akin to sculptures on wheels.

George Nakashima and Charles Eames were furniture designers. Nakashima used the cracks and knots to his advantage to reveal a single piece of furniture that embodies the soul of the tree. Eames, on the other hand, supplied our nation with some of the most iconic modern industrial furniture by using bent wood technology and revealing the tree in a technological fashion. Each designer was a powerful contributor to our world; they just differed in their approach and solutions.

John Lasseter and Martin Scorsese make films that have a lot of heart. Lasseter, whose expression through animation has redefined modern animated storytelling with some of the most funny, heartfelt, whimsical moments in animation history, is truly a gift to our world. Scorsese, who tells it like it is through gritty, dramatic live-action tales of human struggle and perseverance, is one of the most influential and highly revered directors ever.

What draws us into the work of these designers? Is it their use of shape and color or could it be the metaphors about life and passion that are woven into the fabric of their work? Whether it's based on a vision of the future or a reaction to our current world, each designer examines problem solving with a personal touch. Understanding that personal style is nothing more than one person's take on design brings you one step closer to understanding what design is.

I've given you plenty of examples of designers that I think represent the best work in their chosen field, but what do you think is the best in any of those given fields? Maybe you think *Blade Runner* is kind of old school and really like the designs from Unreal Tournament. Perhaps a bronze Cadillac Escalade with 24" spinners is your cup of tea, while to me a bright green 1970 Plymouth Barracuda 440 is the baddest thing on the street. Maybe you admire the work of a certain video game designer or love collecting a specific comic book. Who are these designers? What do you like about their work? How do you go about defining the

elements that make a design good? The answer to these questions is *observation*. Observation is the first step in training your design eye. Your design eye is what distinguishes the difference between good and bad design and, like anything worth pursuing, can only benefit from training and proper application. Start the training with observing the things in your life that you feel are examples of good design. Ask yourself why. Why is this a good design? Could it be the colors, shapes, size, or function? Then ask yourself what could be improved. Does it feel cold and uninviting,

and if so, why? What makes it cold and uninviting? Could it be its hard- edged steel exterior? Maybe this design could benefit from softer edges and warmer colors. Through the process of observation, you'll learn to decipher the good and the bad in design and make mental notes that will eventually apply to your work. Observation means to be interested and open to everything and learning from everything. As a designer you cannot limit yourself; you have to walk into the world with your eyes wide open and learn from other designers and your own experiences.

Anyone Can Do This

I once had a professor who said, "Everyone comes up with at least one good idea in their lifetime." I always sat there hoping I'd come up with a lot more than that, but he was generalizing to make a point. His point was that your chances of coming up with some new radical concept that no one's ever thought of before is rare. Since design can be so subjective, your best bet is to

start with what works, and then improve upon it from there, all the while incorporating good design skills into your work ethic. Improving upon what already exists or giving it a new spin can be almost as fulfilling as creating something no one has ever seen before.

Anyone can do this because learning how to design can be taught; it's your

ideas that matter the most. We're going to take those ideas and, over the course of this book, you'll be focusing on two very important things: learning observation and improving your animation work with simple yet powerful traditional design techniques. So turn your computer off and get your pencils sharpened and your paper stacked up. We're going to do some drawing.

Chapter Two

2D Exercises: Drawing Foundations First

Sketching and Illustration

Sketching and illustration are the foundations of the commercial art industry, and mastering these techniques can take a long time. Even today, I'm still learning new ways to improve my drawing technique and how to express my ideas through media in unique and artistic ways. Much like the world of 3D animation and visual effects, the learning process never stops. Sketching and illustration classes are offered at most colleges and trade schools, which are

great if you have the time, but my job is to get you learning to sketch as quickly as possible. In my years of teaching, I've developed shortcuts that will give you enough insight into the world of illustration and design to affect your work in a positive way. I know that the following easy-to-learn drawing exercises will improve your work and give you the confidence to pick up a pencil before you touch the keyboard or stylus. Before you get started, I want

you to keep in mind that the drawing concepts and exercises I have developed are to get you drawing quickly. They are by no means the all-encompassing drawing exercises you'd get from five months in an art class, but rather shortcuts designed for what I feel are the day-to-day challenges of designing first as it relates to an animation project.

"If You Can Draw the Four Basic Shapes, You Can Draw Anything"

The four basic shapes being the cube, sphere, cylinder, and cone. This was a theory taught by one of my first art professors, Orrin Shively of Walt Disney Imagineering, and I find this basic rule to be true. The **"you can draw anything"** rule, as I like to call it, mostly has to do with light, shade, and shape, because understanding how light and shade interact with the most basic shapes is directly related to how light and shade interact with the most complex shapes.

How does this apply to the work we do in 3D? 3D simulates the interaction of light, shade, and shape, and it is from these fundamentals of 2D application that most 3D programs give you a choice to start your model with a cube, ball, disc, or cone. They know that the foundation of every good design starts with at least one or a combination of the four basic shapes, these

being the root shapes of your design. Knowing the root shapes of your design in 2D first makes it that much easier to later model in 3D. Since modeling in 3D can be a labor-intensive process, drawing gives you the opportunity to experiment with a myriad of factors including proportion, value, color, volume, and concept before you turn on your computer.

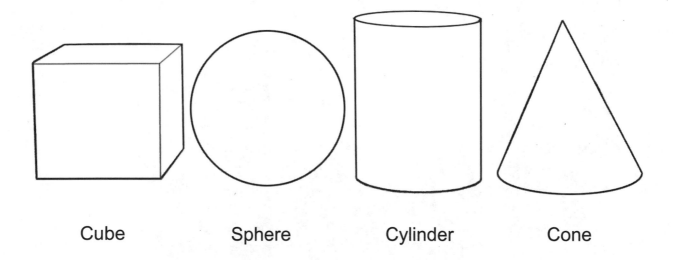

| Cube | Sphere | Cylinder | Cone |

The four basic shapes

Construction Explained

The four basic shapes — the cube, sphere, cylinder, and cone — are the most primitive and simplistic shapes in our culture, hence we have another name for them — *primitives*.

2

3D Primitives

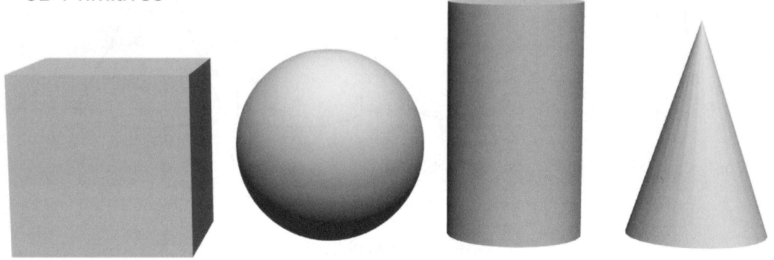

Some good examples of using primitives in design are the wheels of a car, which can be attributed to a cylinder; a computer monitor, which is essentially a cube; and a lightbulb, which is mostly spherical in shape.

The real question is, how do you get from a simple primitive like the sphere to a human head? The answer is "construction." *Construction* is defined as just that — constructing your design using simple shapes first, then creating more complicated shapes using the primitives as a guide. It's kind of like a road map to your final design.

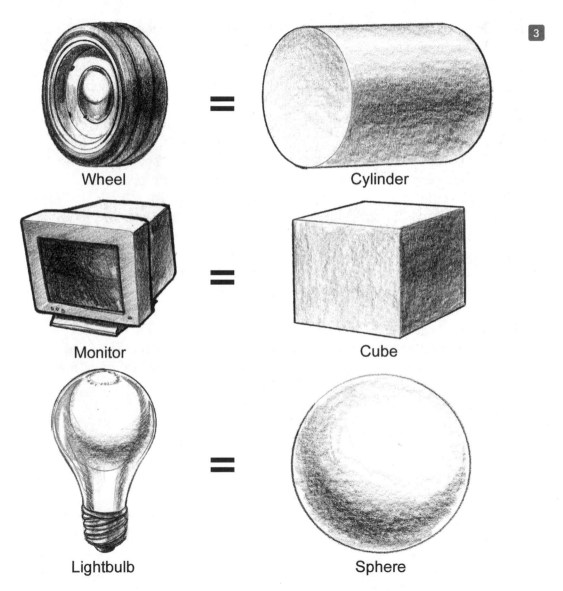

Wheel = Cylinder

Monitor = Cube

Lightbulb = Sphere

11

The quintessential example of using construction as a road map is Mickey Mouse's head. At first glance the most obvious shapes are three primitives — one big sphere for his head and two small flat cylinders for his ears. With further examination, there are a lot more details like his eyes, nose, mouth, and hairline, each represented by a basic shape. Since the foundation for his design was conceived using these three primitives, whenever a designer draws Mickey's head, he or she starts with these three primitives to get overall proportion, then adds the detail. Not only do the primitives serve as a road map for Mickey's head, but the use of these simplistic shapes is what has made Mickey Mouse a classic design that has stood the test of time and his head one of the most recognizable icons in the world. Mickey Mouse is a fairly easy example to understand. The human head is much more complicated with lots of volume and subtle detail, but all in all the process of using primitives for construction is the same.

Before we can start constructing anything, we need to focus on drawing primitives; then we can get to more complicated shapes. The following sections focus on using exercises to improve your drawing skills. That way, when we get to the design section, drawing will feel more comfortable and won't become a distraction.

Just a general rule about the exercises in this book: do them over and over again until they become easy. Diligence is ultimately your best friend and it will show in your work.

Line Drawing

Note: Use a #2 pencil and 8.5 x 11-inch paper for these exercises.

Line drawing is exactly that — using lines to draw your subject matter. Kind of like a wireframe 3D model, it doesn't include shading or shadow, but is merely the beginning of the illustration process. There are two key elements in line drawing: the drawing itself and what is called "line weight" or line thickness. In these first exercises (1-4) I want you to use a consistent thickness of line until we get into line weight later in this section.

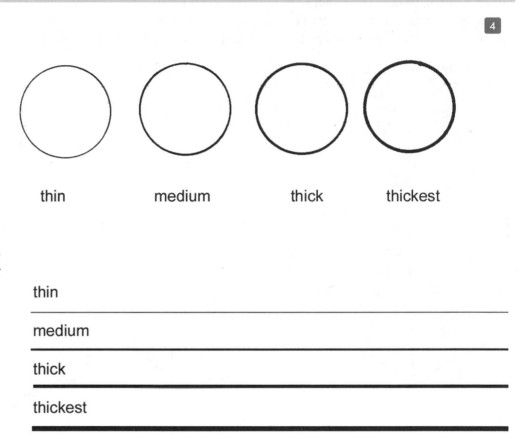

thin medium thick thickest

thin

medium

thick

thickest

In image 5 I've drawn the four basic shapes using lines only. Note that I've drawn the four basic shapes so that our camera angle is looking down onto the top of the objects, otherwise known as a top-down view.

The **viewing angle** is one of the first design elements you'll learn.

Ask yourself, "From what angle am I viewing my subject matter?" It can be from the side, top, bottom, behind, far away, close up, etc. (image 6). Decide this first, then draw.

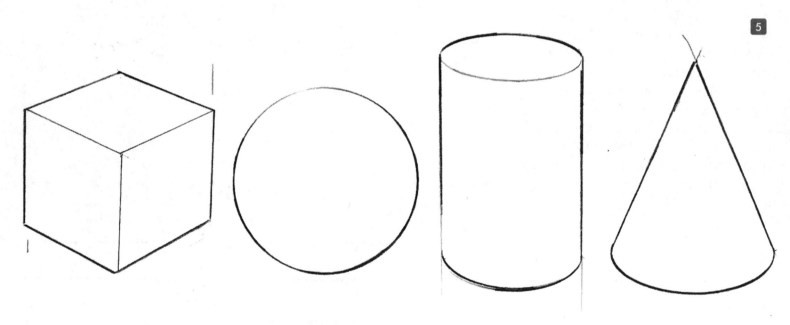

5

Top-down view of shapes

Viewing angle

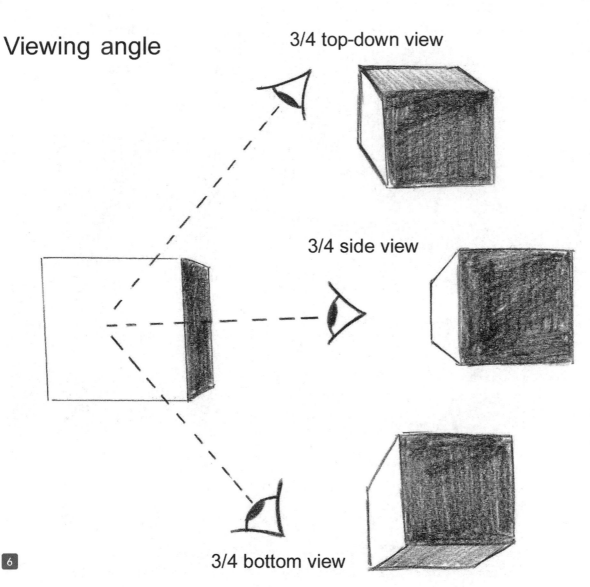

3/4 top-down view

3/4 side view

3/4 bottom view

Back to my example. A cube should be drawn showing three sides of equal size. The sphere is easy; it's just a perfect circle. The cone is a combination of a rounded or semicircular bottom with lines that converge to a point at the top. The cylinder is what looks to be a squashed circle, otherwise known as an ellipse, with lines extending to a semicircle at the other end.

Exercise 1: Copy my basic shapes drawing as shown in image 5.

6

My next example (image 7) shows several different takes on the cube through the use of size and viewing angle.

Exercise 2: Draw each primitive at least 10 times on its own page, experimenting with size and viewing angle.

7

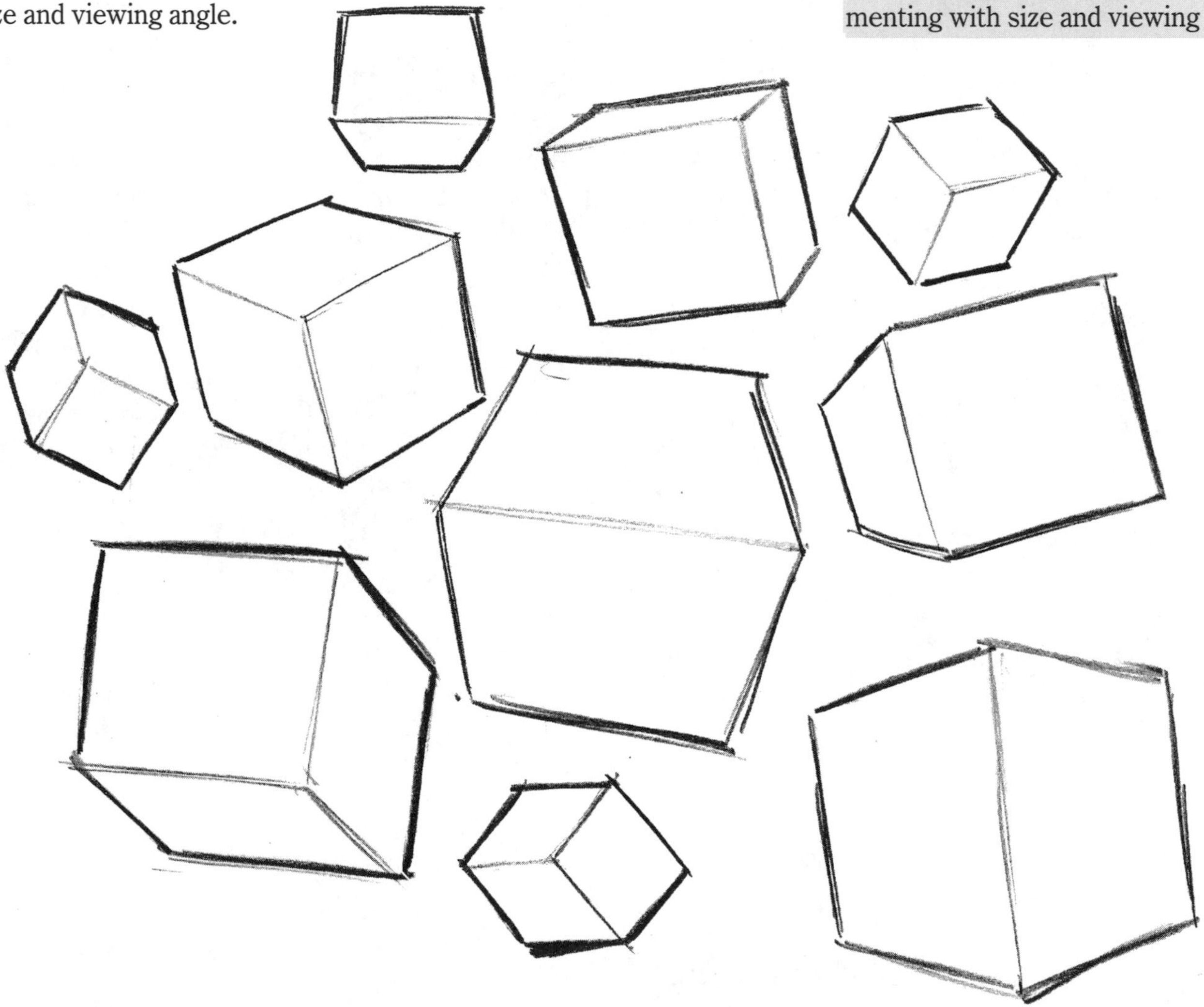

Now that we've got that exercise out of the way, let's put the primitives into some sort of composition (image 8). I've now rearranged the objects onto a surface or ground plane, indicated by the line behind them, and put the sphere and cone as the two objects closest to camera, otherwise known as foreground elements. The cube and cylinder are in the back, farthest from camera, and are known as the background elements.

Exercise 3: Copy my drawing.

Exercise 4: Create the same drawing, but use the cube and cylinder as the foreground elements and the sphere and cone as the background elements.

8

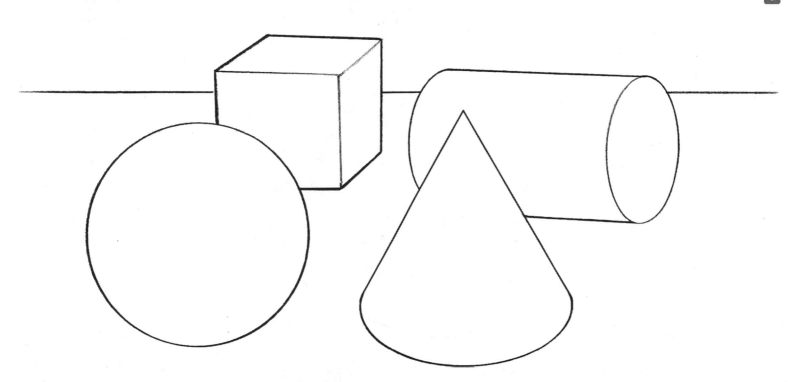

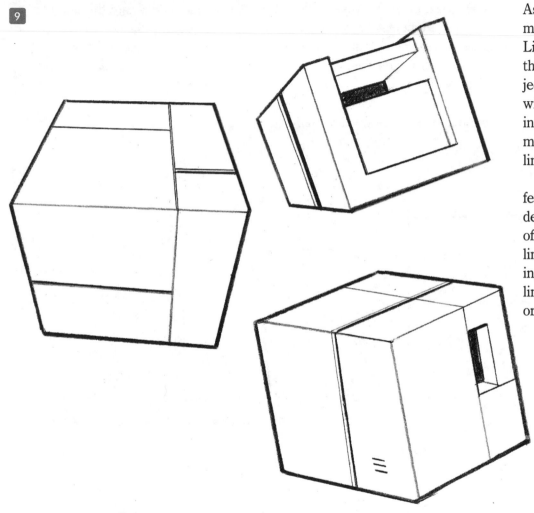

As stated earlier, the second key element in line drawing is line weight. Line weight is another tool in drawing that allows us to further define our subject matter by contrasting thin lines with thick ones. This is especially used in traditional cartoon animation, where most of your definition comes from a line, not shading.

Image 9 shows a new drawing with a few floating cubes that have some inner detailing. Notice that the outside lines of each cube are thick and the inside lines are thin. In this case we are outlining the edges of our cubes with thick lines to emphasize their overall shape or silhouette.

A silhouette is the outline of an object (image 10). Filling this outline in with black and putting it on a light-colored surface would be the true silhouette of our cube. You see this a lot in film to create a creepy mood or a more graphic approach to the scene, where an actor is backlit so you only see the silhouette.

Drawing is about defining your subject matter, and in this case using a thick line to create a silhouette further defines our cube and brings attention to its overall shape. The other reasoning would be that thick lines on these types of edges help create the illusion that

there is a change in the radius, or turn, of a surface from what is visible to us to what is not visible. As you can see, the thick line gives weight to our cube, really defining its foreground presence. The inside edges have been treated with a thin line weight because those thin edges define a shared border. Shared border areas usually are the detail areas of an object and in turn should not compete with the silhouette for attention, so using a thin line that is less prominent will avoid that situation. Unless you're doing some sort of technical schematic, varying line weight

creates a kind of visual contrast that makes your drawings more appealing.

There is a rule in 2D animation that objects closer to camera have thicker lines than those farther away, so your line weight should vary depending upon how close your object is to camera.

Exercise 5: Create a composition of four floating primitives with inner detailing that uses varied line weights to define the objects.

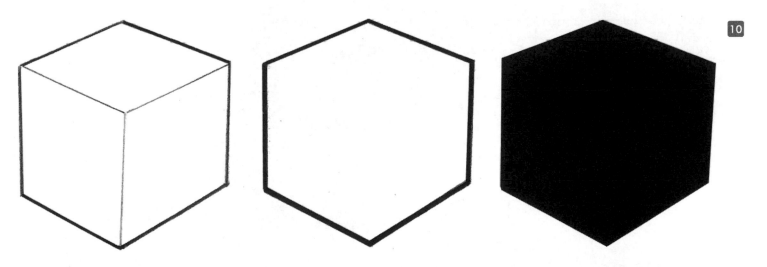

10

Lighting the Four Basic Shapes

Now that we've done some primitive line drawings, let's take it to the next level. First we will start with drawing a cube using a basic "single light setup." As you can see in the example (image 11), this setup consists of three elements: one distinct light source or key light, a cube, and a ground plane that our cube will rest upon.

If you look at our cube, there are three visible sides, of which the top side is the lightest because of the position of our key light. If we shade the sides from lightest to darkest, we will give the lightest a value of 1 and the darkest a value of 3. A shadow will always lighten in value the farther it gets from the object casting it, so for our cube, the shadow will naturally graduate to a soft edge.

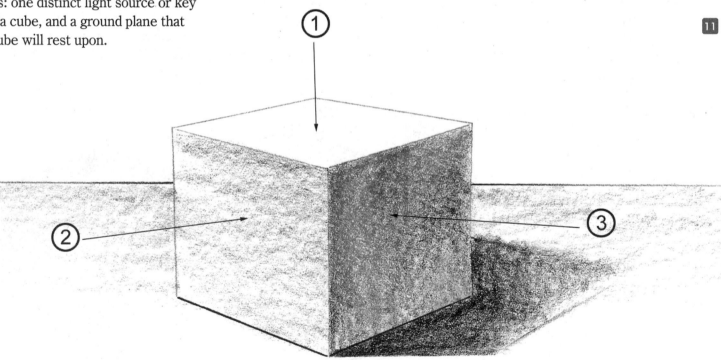

11

For learning purposes, I've included several examples of our cube that illustrate the changes in key light direction (image 12).

Now I'd like you to try.

Exercise 6: Copy my cube example and feel free to try some multiple views.

The sphere is a little more complex in that it is a round object that contains no straight edges (image 13). This rounded shape adds a whole new dimension to how we shade the object, but before I get into a shading explanation, I must first explain indirect light.

Indirect Light

Most objects are lit directly from a key light or main light source; however, there is another light source at work called *indirect light*. This indirect light comes from other places such as the sky, the background, a ground plane, even other objects. Light that comes from the sky or background is called *reflected light* because it is, in a sense, reflecting onto the surface of our object. Indirect light that comes from a ground plane or another object is called *bounced light*, because light rays literally bounce off those items back up onto our key object. The combination or mixture of direct light and indirect light causes hot spots and banding across all objects. The easiest way to understand

13

Sphere

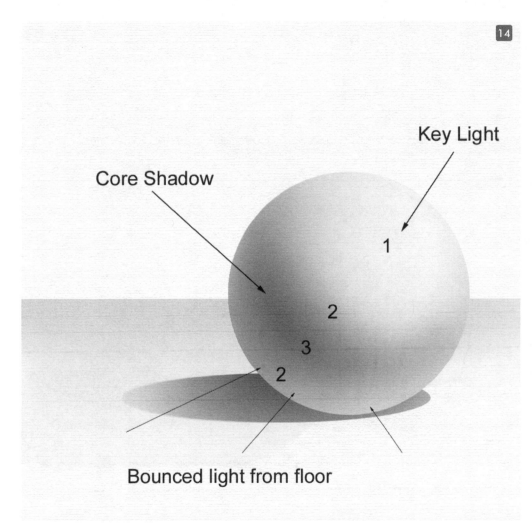

Key Light

Core Shadow

1

2

3

2

Bounced light from floor

this effect is to observe our sphere. The sphere has a band of darkness where the key light and bounced light have affected the value of shading. This band is otherwise known as the *core shadow* (image 14).

The key light is responsible for the #1 area. The bounced light is responsible for the #2 area. They are both equally responsible for the #3 area, which meets somewhere in the middle and creates the core shadow. To create an accurate representation of the sphere, it's easiest to start drawing the core shadow first and then gradate slowly out to your #1 and #2 spots.

Now it is your turn.

Exercise 7: Copy my sphere example (image 13).

Exercise 8: Now do a composition that includes a cube and a sphere. Focus on key light direction for accuracy within your drawing.

A cylinder is a combination of a cube and a sphere in that it is an object with flat areas (cube) and rounded areas (sphere). Flat areas react to light in the same way a cube would react. Similarly, areas that are round react like a sphere would react. The rounded areas have a core shadow and contain reflected light from both the background and the ground plane (image 15).

Now you try.

Exercise 9: Draw a composition of two cylinders, one on its side and the other upright (image 16).

15

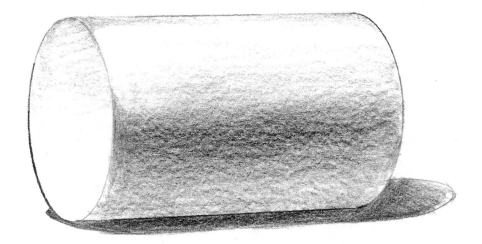

Cylinder

The cone is nothing more than a cylinder with a decreasing diameter along its length until it finally reaches a point. Note that the lighter areas and core shadow of the cone will become more compact as they converge toward the end point of the cone (image 17).

Cone

Exercise 10: Draw a composition of two cones, one on its side and the other upright (image 18).

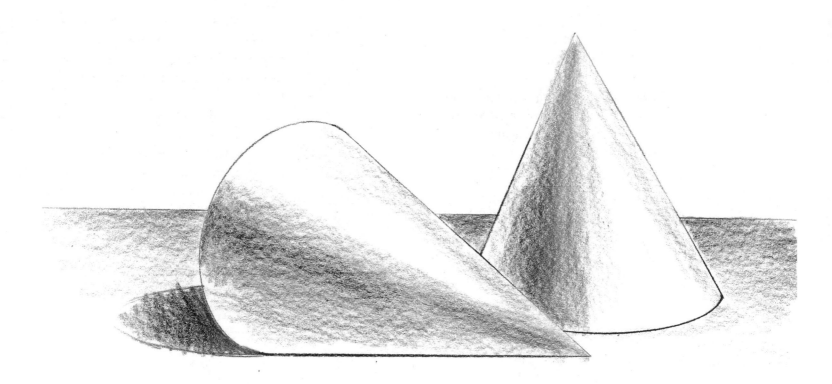

The final phase of this lesson is combining these shapes together into a single composition. As you can see in image 19, I have arranged two of the shapes to interact with each other and two on their own.

You can see how the shadow of the cylinder extends to hit the sphere, riding up the radius of the sphere and then slowly tapering off, finally dropping back to the ground plane and combining with the sphere shadow to create a combined shadow area. Understanding how the interaction of the shapes affects each other is essential, so doing this exercise a couple of times will really go a long way into helping you with your drawing skills.

Exercise 11: Draw a composition using all four basic shapes. Note how the shadows are plotted against each object's surface.

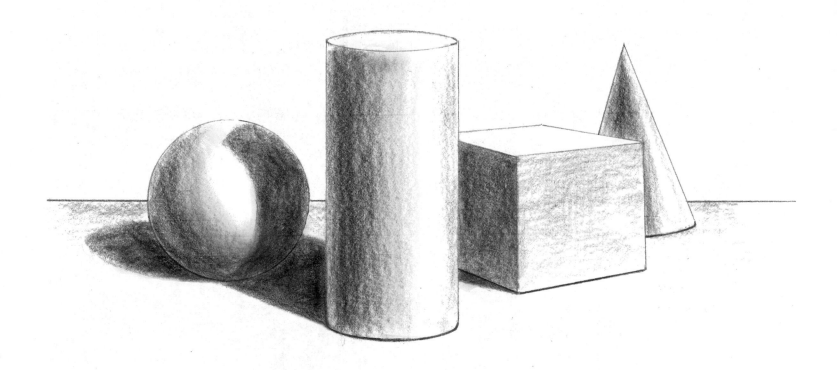

Primitives composition

Going back to construction, our next composition is of a single object (image 20). Note the lighting, shadow, and reflected light. Using Photoshop, I've done a highly detailed illustration of a single object comprised of three of the basic shapes.

Exercise 12: Draw a single object comprised of all four basic shapes.

A myriad of factors influence light and shadow as they relate to your object, like value (a light or dark surface), reflectivity, multiple lights, surface texture, transparency, specularity (shininess), and environment. Let's

add a reflective property to one of our shapes and I'll do the same composition (image 21).

Note how the sphere reflects not only the other objects, but the world around it, including what is unseen by our camera. It is your job to create a reflection that makes sense for your composition. In this case I've used a

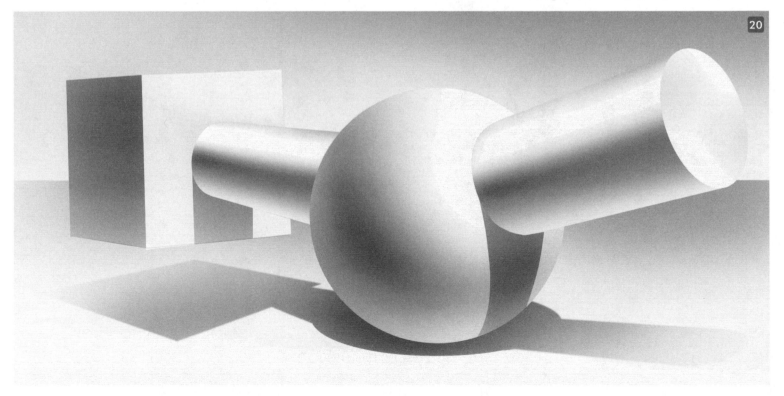

20

simple horizon and the three other shapes. Note how the sphere distorts its reflection as it creeps away from the camera, and the surface area mostly facing the camera has very little distortion. In contrast, a cube would have no distortion as it has flat sides like a mirror. A nice little trick is to put a thin edge of highlight around your reflective object in order to create the illusion that its back-facing surfaces are taking the background reflection and compressing it so much that it turns into a thin edge of light. This will really help your reflected objects look real and give them contrast.

Exercise 13: Draw a reflective cube and a non-reflective sphere in the same composition.

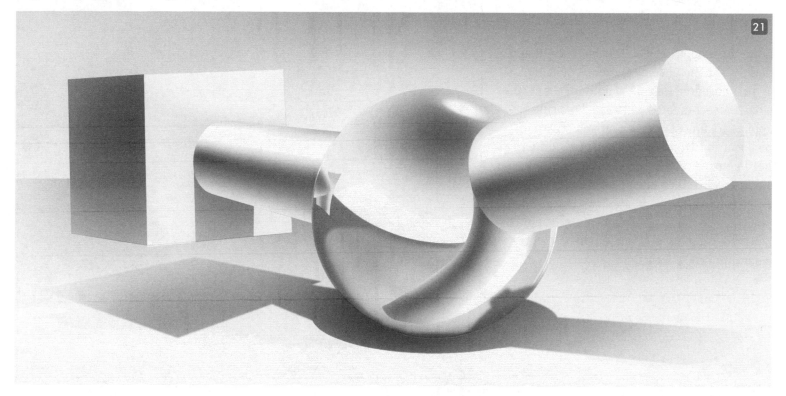

Value

Value is the relationship between light and dark colors to create contrast. Contrast is defined as "the obvious dissimilar qualities in shape and value of objects as they relate to each other." Since contrast is not just about light and dark but also about shape, proportion, size, movement, etc., I have written a whole section on the "contrast" rule in Chapter 3, "Design Basics and Observation." For now, our emphasis is on the use of light and dark or the increase or decrease of value.

Just as a general rule, a light object against a dark object creates contrast. This rule applies to almost everything you create on paper or in 3D. It can be used in a subtle manner like my first example (see image 22) or in a dynamic manner like my second example (see image 23). I've created two sample compositions containing the same subject matter, but through the use of value have created a clear difference between the two.

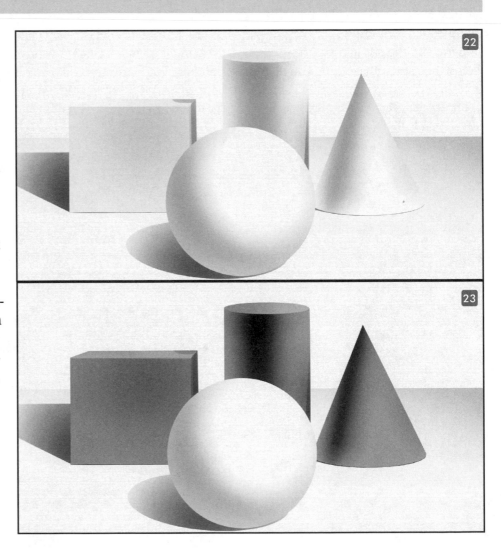

Using our four basic shapes, I've arranged the first example in a way that is straightforward and basic (image 22). There's no dynamic feeling of lighting or mood... the shapes just sort of sit there looking simple and undefined. This undefined feeling is caused by four simple white shapes sitting on a white background, with even lighting and simple placement.

Our second example uses the same shapes, but the use of dark objects against our white sphere has created a high-contrast environment (image 23). This kind of composition has a lot more energy and focus and feels well defined and more interesting.

I could write an entire chapter about contrast and value, but the best way for you to learn is to do it. Over time you'll start to use high or low contrast to increase or decrease the focus of objects within your compositions. When you get to that point, you'll be doing pretty well.

Exercise 14: Create a composition using the four basic shapes by utilizing value to create contrast between the cylinder and the rest of the shapes. Remember, it could also be a dark object against light shapes.

A Quick Perspective on Perspective

Perspective is an incredibly intense subject that is far too broad for me to dabble in. The only thing I can do is recommend a few books that you might try or suggest you take a class. In this section I'll give a brief explanation and example of perspective and then I'll move on.

In short, perspective is what gives us a sense of distance and scale and includes the physical law that as an object recedes toward the horizon, it appears to become smaller. This physical law applies to lines as well, and creates what is called *line convergence*. 3D programs do a great job of creating perspective, so they make it easy to learn through experimentation. Try creating the primitives in a 3D program, render out a frame, and then trace them by hand to learn exactly how they are constructed. Here, I've created a quick example of what I mean by line convergence and the use of scale to create distance (image 24).

Books I recommend:

Perspective Made Easy, by Ernest Norling, Mineola, NY: Dover Publications, 1999.

Perspective Without Pain, by Philip W. Metzger, Cincinnati, Ohio: North Light Books, 1992.

Creative Perspective for Artists and Illustrators, by Ernest W. Watson, New York: Dover, 1992.

Draw 3-D: A Step-by-Step Guide to Perspective Drawing, by Doug C. Dubosque, Columbus, NC: Peel Productions, 1998.

Perspective Drawing Handbook, by Joseph D'Amelio, with illustrations by Joseph D'Amelio and Sanford Hohauser, Mineola, NY: Dover Publications, 2003.

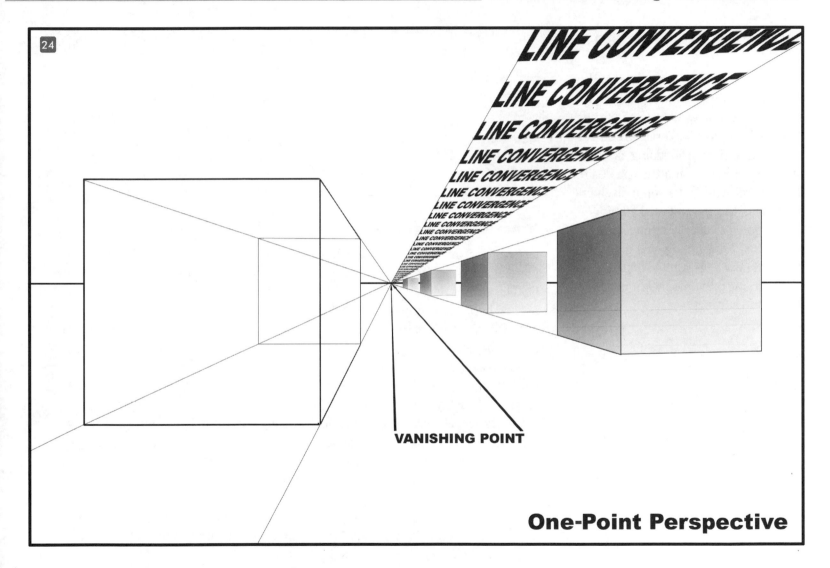

VANISHING POINT

One-Point Perspective

Do a Sketch a Day

Now that you understand some of the most fundamental drawing techniques, I want to take you away from all of these "do it at your desk" exercises and get you out into the world, doing sketches of whatever subject matter you desire. This exercise will take some discipline because of the amount of sketching you're going to do. Sketching what you see, or *still life drawing*, will give you further knowledge into how all of our basic artistic principles work in a real-world setting.

Your first assignment:

Go to a local art supply store and buy yourself a small sketchpad, about 4" x 6". This size is perfect to fit in a jacket pocket, book bag, purse, or whatever, but will give you plenty of room to draw. The assignment is, using a #2 pencil, pick out at least one piece of subject matter per day and sketch it. Remembering to make your subject matter the focal point, start with small things at first, like soda cans, erasers, CD cases, pencils, remote controls, boxes, fire alarms, light switches, clocks, books of matches, bottle caps, coffee mugs, door handles, bars of soap, candles, utensils, etc. Anything that's small and simple will be the best choice. Don't worry so much about how good your drawing looks; instead, worry about looking at all the subtle details in your subject matter. Try to observe subtle changes in direct lighting, bounced light, value, proportion, and shape. Vary your line weights and apply good shading techniques. Really take time to study the shapes, especially curves and intersections, and reflective and matte materials. Do your best to accurately draw what you see and take your time. After many sketches you'll see your accuracy improve and your design eye become more trained to see the subtleties (image 25).

Chapter Three

Design Basics and Observation

Contrast Rule

The word "contrast" at first makes you think of light and dark or how light and dark contrast with each other, but it is a very broad term that applies to nearly every type of design and art principle. For example, there can be a contrast in size — big head, little body; color — orange against blue; or movement — fast versus slow. In fact, contrast motivates every design decision you make as it relates to your 3D models, animations, and composites. I like to call it the "contrast" rule and I use it as a gauge for whether or not the animation I'm creating is compelling and unique

imagery that leaps off the screen with an aesthetic that supports the story. If it leaps off the screen and tells the story that has been intended, then I've done my job. Asking yourself the simple question, "Does this scene have enough contrast?" will allow you to dissect and refine your design intent into something visually astute and appealing. It just takes a few tweaks here and there. "Is the color contrasted enough?" "Are the shadows helping to define my object?" "Is there too much contrast between the fast movement in the beginning and the slow movement

near the end?" "Are my designs doing their job to support the character's environment?" Remember that your job is to engage the audience through the use of visual imagery, whether it be designed objects or cinematic camera movement. Anything that adds more aesthetic appeal and is in direct support of the characters will help the audience comprehend the story's intent. Any way you slice it, examining your animation using the contrast rule will give you better, simpler, and more exciting animations.

What Is Composition?

Composition is an extensive subject with about a million different rules, styles, and approaches. It is like a visual puzzle with the subject matter, color, value, perspective, and spatial relationships being the pieces. It's all of these puzzle pieces combined that make up a composition. A successful composition is a planned piece of work that guides the viewer's eye as it absorbs and accepts the subject matter it is trying to relate.

I'm going to follow this section with some tried-and-true exercises that will give you basic tools for good composition. After completing this chapter, do your own research on art that you feel embodies good compositional qualities. You'll know what to look for and in turn will continue to learn more about the foundation of visual storytelling. Some of my favorite artists include Syd Mead, Jack Kirby, Bill Watterson, Alex Toth, Will Eisner, and Degas. Their use of color, value, spatial relationships, and subject matter are second to none and have taught generations of artists sophisticated compositional principles that have stood the test of time.

Get Graphic

An essential part of creating anything visually exciting is the understanding of graphic design. Uuugggghhhh...... I know it conjures thoughts of text-laden layouts full of blurred images, and a million oversized avant-garde icons somehow crammed onto a 4 x 5 flyer for some local band. Fortunately not in our case.

Bear with me on this one. Graphic design is defined as "the art or profession of using design elements (as typography and images) to convey information or create an effect." As it pertains to this book, graphic design is the relationship of shape, value, negative space, and color working together in a two-dimensional medium to produce a visually exciting composition.

"Visually exciting" and "two-dimensional" are the key words, because our final product should be just that. The medium that we are working in is intended to produce images for television or film, both of which are considered two-dimensional media, and in this case graphic design is used to guide the viewer's eye into reading a scene or composition in a way that best helps to convey a mood and message.

A good example is the opening scene in *Star Wars* (image 1). The viewer is watching the vast reaches of space, when the camera slowly pans down to a few planets in the distance and one nearby planet fills the lower third of the screen. At this point our eyes are exploring the composition, but mostly wondering what this giant planet is all about… when all of a sudden a Rebel ship comes in from the top of the screen, blasting away at something behind it. At this point all we see is the Rebel ship and the planets. Our eyes are drawn to the Rebel ship. As we examine it, we feel curious as to what they are shooting at, when súddenly a huge, triangular Star Destroyer roars in from above, pursuing the fleeing Rebel ship. Our eye immediately travels up to the Star Destroyer, which seems to go on forever and now our curiosity is at an all-time high. "What is this enormous ship?" The Star Destroyer now fills the upper third of the screen and our eyes are searching and examining every detail as it fires laser blasts at the Rebel ship. To add to the graphic impact of the scene, the Star Destroyer is triangular in shape, which literally looks like an arrow pointing at the Rebel ship and saying, "I'm coming after you." When it finally passes overhead, our eyes are led to its massive glowing blue engines and we are left with a feeling of awe. There is no doubt that our fleeing Rebel ship is in real danger with such a huge Star Destroyer behind it. When looking at the scene as a whole, we felt many things, including curiosity, "What is this?"; awe, "Whoaaa! My mind is blown, because this is the biggest thing I've ever seen in my life!"; and fear, "Uh, oh… that little ship is doomed!"

The scene composition used shape and contrast to guide our eyes to the most important object at the time and one by one introduced us to each element that comprised the scene. When you think about it, the blackness of space served as the perfect backdrop to contrast the gray Rebel ship and the gray triangular Star Destroyer by focusing our eyes on the brightest object in the scene at the time. This use of contrast and shape gave our eyes just enough information so that we knew what was taking place without really having to think about it.

Sticking to the contrast rule, creating a scene like this that can be understood even on the most basic level was achieved through the contrast of value, size, shape, and movement. Using all of these tools, the filmmakers were able to direct our eyes to wherever they wanted us to look, which for 3D animators is the ultimate goal… creating a focal point.

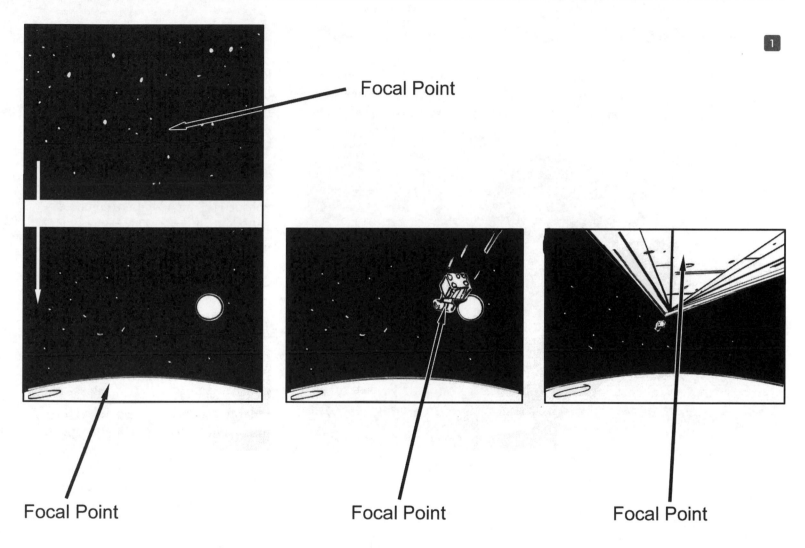

Focal Point

Focal Point

Focal Point

Focal Point

Focal Point

The focal point is the most important design element in any composition. It is the focus of your composition and should take center stage among all other design elements in order for your design to be a success. For example,

2

let's say that you've decided to do a drawing of a beach with a lone palm tree swaying in the wind. If the focus of your drawing is the palm tree, then it should be the first element your eye focuses on. All other design elements, such as the ocean, sand, and sky should enhance the mood but not compete with the palm tree. This can easily be accomplished through the use of value, tension, perspective, and color (image 2). Note how the palm tree is the center of attention, using light and shadow to stand out from the rest.

Before you start on any composition, ask yourself these questions: What is the focus of my composition? What other design elements are necessary in order to support and help define this focal point? What story am I trying to tell? Write your answers down to use as a reminder while you're designing your composition. The use of notes related to your projects can help you stay focused until completion.

Exercise 1: Create a composition using a simple piece of subject matter (bottle, pen, phone, soda can, palm tree, etc.) and two other elements that will enhance your composition and drive your message home. For example, draw a wallet as the focal point with two quarters laying next to it, or a candle as the focal point with a pack of matches and a burnt match.

Tension

Tension is defined as, "A balance maintained in an artistic work between opposing forces or elements." In the case of our lone sphere among the other shapes, we seek to define our focal point even more by arranging our shapes in such a way that their direct spatial relationship to each other gives a feeling of tension or claustrophobia. In the examples in image 4, note how the rearrangement of the shapes works together to force your eye into reading the sphere first.

Exercise 2: Create a composition using the four basic shapes by utilizing tension and value to create a focal point.

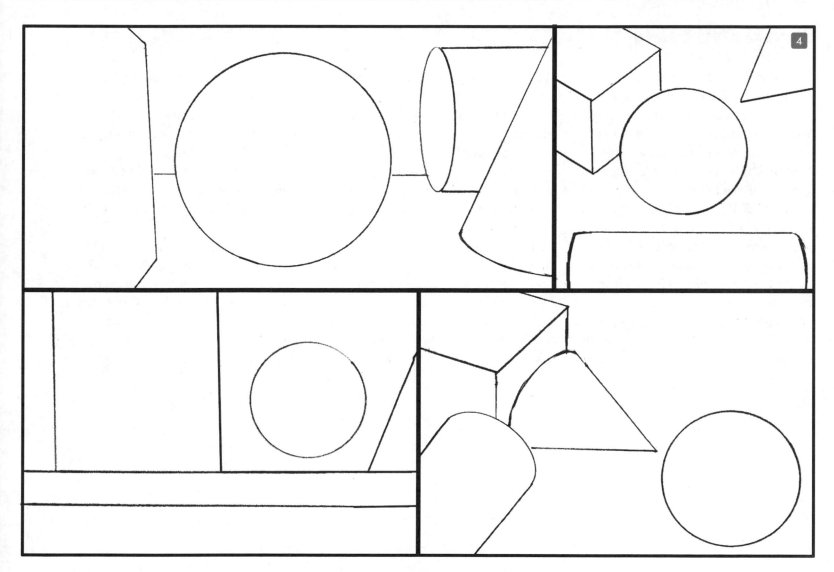

Read the Flow

The "read" is the way your eyes perceive visual information as it relates to "the flow" of a composition. The flow is kind of like an arrow that points to our subject matter saying, "Look here!" It should be a very natural feeling that guides the eye to our focal point, and then at will, the viewer's eye can casually wander throughout the composition, soaking up the rest of the details.

A very basic example of flow is that in the U.S. we read text from left to right. It is so much a part of our culture and our training that our eyes feel most at ease when absorbing information or design elements that start on the left-hand side and end on the right. This natural tendency for our eyes to move from left to right is capitalized upon by all sorts of visual media such as print ads, commercials, television, film, and so on. For example, if during a car commercial the car enters from the left side of the screen and exits to the right, we feel more at ease with this movement than if the car enters from the right and moves across to exit stage left. The exit stage left technique creates a certain amount of tension in our eye movement. In some cases this kind of tension is good and helps to pique visual interest, but in the name of selling a product, an easy read is better than a confusing one. An easy read is a highly effective compositional technique that allows for quick absorption of the subject matter.

Creating the flow of your composition can be achieved through the use of value, color, graphic impact, and tension.

Note my example (image 5). This is a very simplistic use of shapes and values to lead your eye to our focal point — the sphere. Note the use of random shapes at the top of the drawing that sort of force your eye past them to our focal point.

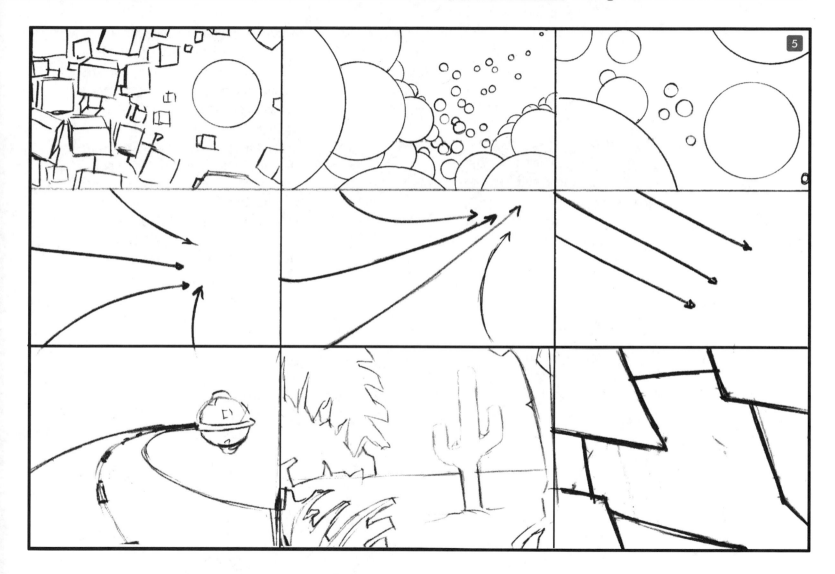

Exercise 3: Create a composition using any simple graphic shapes by utilizing tension, value, and flow to create a focal point.

A more sophisticated use of the flow technique is seen in the second example (image 6). Notice the use of large foreground shapes; the wheels and suspension, one after the other, descend upon and lead your eye up to the pilot in the cockpit. As you can see, even though the cockpit is the focal point, the other elements are just as important because they are controlling the flow. Also note how the cockpit contrasts with the white background, thereby putting more attention onto our focal point.

6

JOFFREY KATER

Tangents: The Good, the Bad, and the Ugly

Knowing a little about tangents will improve your work dramatically, so I'm going to show you a few examples first, then explain the good and the bad. In its most simplistic explanation, a *tangent* is when two lines meet at a single point (image 7).

As related to your artistic work, what you see in the upper example is called a bad tangent and should be avoided. Why? Because it creates a feeling of discomfort and visual tension that detracts from the overall composition, since the two lines are fighting for attention. Note how the triangle looks as if it's piercing the circle and how the big circle looks cramped in the space between the edge of the composition and the other elements. In the lower example I've redone the composition using good tangents only and have relieved that cramped feeling by moving the circle away from the edge of the composition, and have provided a feeling of depth by moving the triangle behind the circle. In examining this second composition, all I did was move the shapes around until all of the bad tangents were gone and simultaneously lessened the tension and created depth.

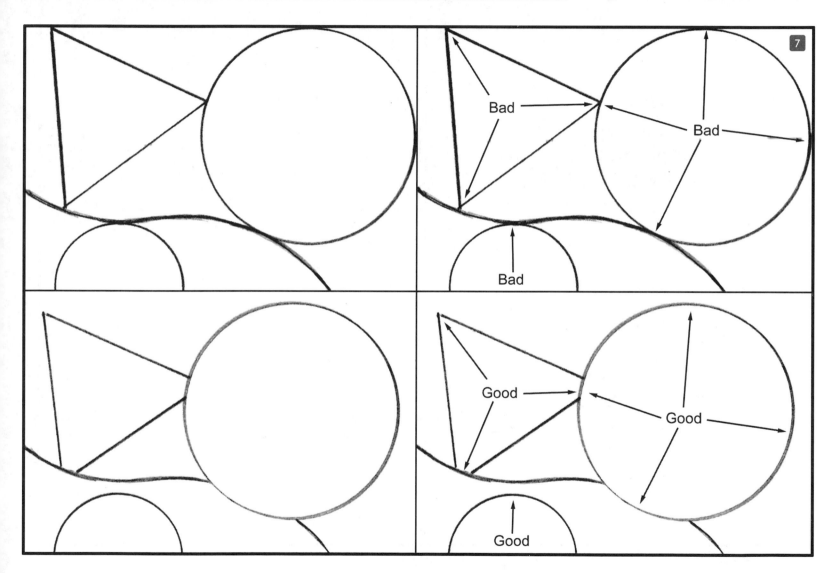

Avoid bad tangents by either separating or overlapping your objects.

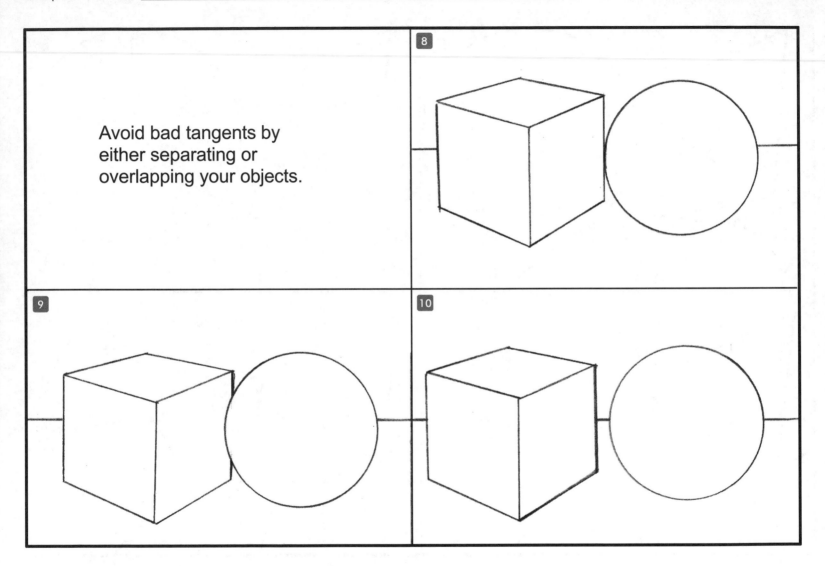

As another example, let's take two objects — a cube and a sphere (image 8). Note how the cube and sphere look cramped together, kind of uncomfortable. This is an example of a bad tangent, as it creates a form of tension that unless directly related to your project goals is visually unpleasant and negative. There's no sense of perspective or depth and the composition feels flat.

A solution would be to add a slight distance between the two objects (image 10), as shown in the lower right drawing. Now our composition feels more open and less cramped, like it can breathe. This is a lot better, but it still lacks a certain amount of depth and perspective. Overlapping the two objects (image 9) has now created a great feeling of depth and perspective, a much more desirable result. In this example, there are no bad tangents and so our objects have great spatial relationship and contrast.

Keep in mind that the bad tangent rule really only applies to objects within your composition that should have either some kind of overlap or none at all. Unless you purposely create bad tangents as an integral part of your design concept, as a general rule stay away from them.

Color Opposites Attract

This is an extremely brief overview of color; in fact, it's more of a shorthand into the understanding of how each color has an opposite color. Whenever I work on animations, color is obviously a major part of my overall design aesthetic, so without ever really focusing too much on color theory, I use the relationships of colors and their opposite colors to add contrast to my projects. Although certain projects dictate specific color choices, using color to control the flow and focal point of your compositions will add a sense of realism and depth that goes a long way.

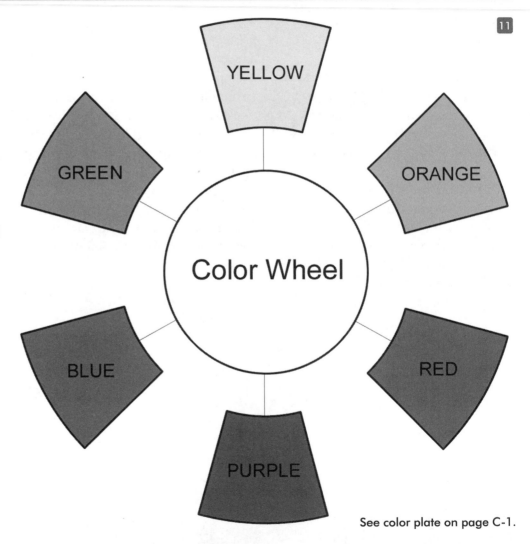

See color plate on page C-1.

Opposite colors give more value and depth by contrasting with each other. The color wheel (image 11) provides a quick visual understanding of how colors are related and can be used as reference for designers when mixing or applying color to their projects. This is an example of a color wheel with only primary and secondary colors. The three primary colors are red, yellow, and blue. The three secondary colors are orange, green, and purple. In looking at the color red, we can see on the color wheel that its exact opposite color is green. Yellow's opposite is purple, and blue's opposite is orange.

In the same way that we understand that light and dark objects contrast with each other, two opposite colors that overlap each other will create an obvious difference, adding further contrast to your composition. In fact, when two opposite colors are put together in the same scene, they are actually competing for attention with the viewer's eye. Using only the primary and secondary colors, here are a few examples of how opposite colors can work against each other but in favor of your animation: red ornaments hanging on a green Christmas tree; an orange muscle car in front of a blue sky; a yellow bicycle in front of a purple garage door.

12

See color plate on page C-1.

As an example, I've created a simple composition (image 12) that clearly displays its focal point. (You'll have to imagine the color orange for the sphere and the color blue for the cube until you can flip to the color section of this book and see the colors I'm talking about.) Taking our sphere and cube, I've colored each with an opposite color. The sphere pops off the page due to its light value and color of orange. Its relationship is the direct opposite to that of the cube, which is darker in value and the color blue. Since the background of our composition is a light blue color, it further assists in making our sphere the focal point. The opposite color design technique works great for making foreground objects separate themselves from the background and can be used in a variety of ways.

This is very important: When using any color, just know that all of these theories only work when our colors are used in a subtle manner. What I mean is that you should do your best to look at the world around you and notice how subtle color can be. It will be those slight shifts in color that will add realism and depth to your work. Really look at a red apple and notice all the subtle shifts in red. You may find the color yellow, but all in all it's a red apple. I think you get my point — subtlety.

Again, this section just gives you a basic understanding of color. If you're interested, take it upon yourself to further your education through art books and art classes; you'll learn a tremendous amount and the results in your work will be noticeable.

Now that you have a little more knowledge on this subject, look at other artists' works to see how they use these basic rules of color to create a focal point. From now on, use opposite coloring to your advantage on your animation projects.

Exercise 4: Create a composition using any simple subject matter utilizing the theory of opposite coloring.

Warm and Cool

I know this is a lot to absorb, but bear with me on this one — it's worth it. Colors are also classified as warm and cool. Warm and cool denote temperature, like a hot sunny yellow day for warm and a freezing cold blue winter for cool, so from this point on when I say there's a difference in the temperature of a color, you'll think warm and cool. Warm colors as they relate to our color wheel would be red, orange, and yellow, kind of like the warm glow of the sun, a wooden bench, or a brown carpet. Cool colors as they relate to our color wheel would be blue, purple, and green, kind of like the color of the sky, mountains, or plants.

Since our world is not made up of just bright saturated colors, it's essential that you understand how important the color gray is to design. As far as I'm concerned, the most frequent application of warm and cool tones is to that of the color gray. From city streets, architecture, and home furnishings to electronics, fashion, and so on, gray is by far the most used color and fills our surroundings everywhere we look. Just go outside one day and look at the overwhelming amount of gray out in the world, but look at how vast the range of grays is. From light grays to dark grays, warm grays to cool grays… you get the point, but its importance and range of use within our animations is crucial.

WARM COLORS

COOL COLORS

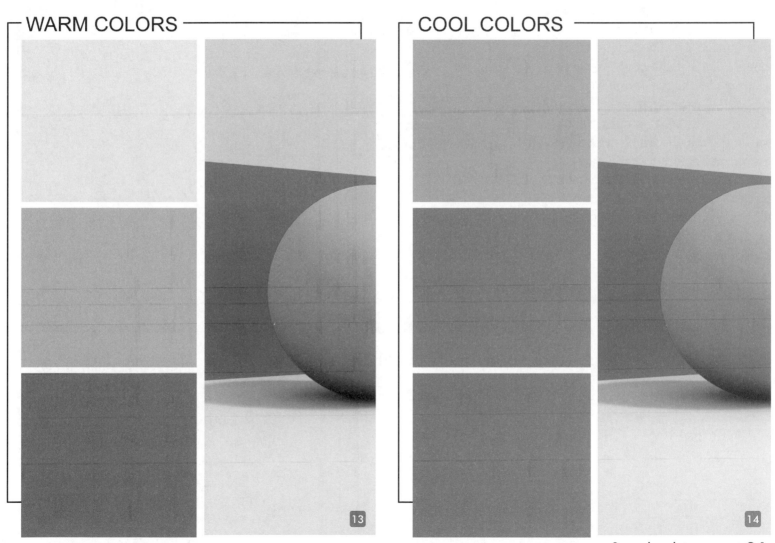

See color plate on page C-1.

Take a look at the grayscale I created so you can get a good idea of what I mean (image 15). The first grayscale shows a single value of gray with a vast temperature change. It ranges from cool gray to warm gray, or blueish to yellowish, with what is called neutral gray in the middle, which is neither cool nor warm. The other three grayscales, cool, neutral, and warm, range from a dark value of gray to white. Look at what an incredible difference there is, yet they all come from the same basic color and value.

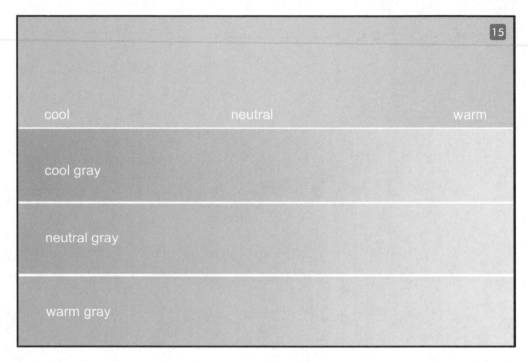

cool   neutral   warm

cool gray

neutral gray

warm gray

See color plate on page C-1.

Let's apply this to our sphere and cube, making them the same value but using different temperatures of gray (image 16). I've colored our foreground object, the sphere, a warm gray and I've colored our background object, the cube, a cool gray. Look at how they're both the same value, but the difference in temperature puts them in stark contrast with each other.

See color plate on page C-2.

16

How this relates to our animation work is simple: warm and cool is related to lighting. The most significant influence on how your animations will look is the lighting. Using warmly lit objects against cool ones will give your work a sense of realism and depth, because in nature things that are closer to us are generally warmer in tone, whereas objects farther away tend to be cooler in tone. It's a fairly complex topic, so without going into too much detail about the subject… the Earth is round and the sky is blue and as things recede into the distance, they tend to become more blue because of the haze on the horizon, which is made up of air that is dense that also makes things look whiter, bluer, flatter, and less detailed. So when things are close they look detailed and warm and things in the distance look cool and flat, whereas shadows and shade tend to be cool from a warm light like the sun, because they are capturing bounced light from the blue sky and so tend to look blue. Go outside and stare at the horizon, sky, and things in front of you and test this theory as much as you want… whewww… get it?

See color plate on page C-2.

In general, most light sources are warm in nature, so they create comparatively cool shadows and shade areas. This is really going to work in your favor because you'll be using the opposite color theory: warm versus cool. Some 3D packages have render engines that do the lighting naturally, with bounced light, cool shadows, and the whole bit, but more often than not most 3D packages don't give you all the subtle details, so you might have to dial in the shadow color to be more of a cool gray if you're using a warm to neutral colored light. Again, depending on what your application is, you can usually stick with this theory.

I've created a composition of warm and cool lighting schemes (image 18). The first image is of a robot in a warm setting. Stylistically this works, but the red graphics in the background and the orange robot colors are competing for your attention. With a quick adjustment to the background, I can enhance his readability by changing the second image to use a combination of both warm and cool colors and have now clearly made my robot the main focal point. I'm also enhancing the focal point by making him the only object in the foreground and using a little cool reflected light around the far edges of his body to increase contrast with the background. I've also included several variations on this theme to show you some additional color combinations (image 19).

On the next sunny day, go outside and see how blue the shadows on the ground can be — it's absolutely amazing. Most people don't notice this, but once you do it will help you in lighting your scenes more realistically. Also experiment with your own drawings and animations to make them read better and give depth by using warm and cool lighting and opposite coloring. Using shadows and shading, warm light, cool light, tension, and contrast will make your animations stand out.

Exercise 5: Using warm and cool grays on our primitives, create a composition that has an obvious focal point.

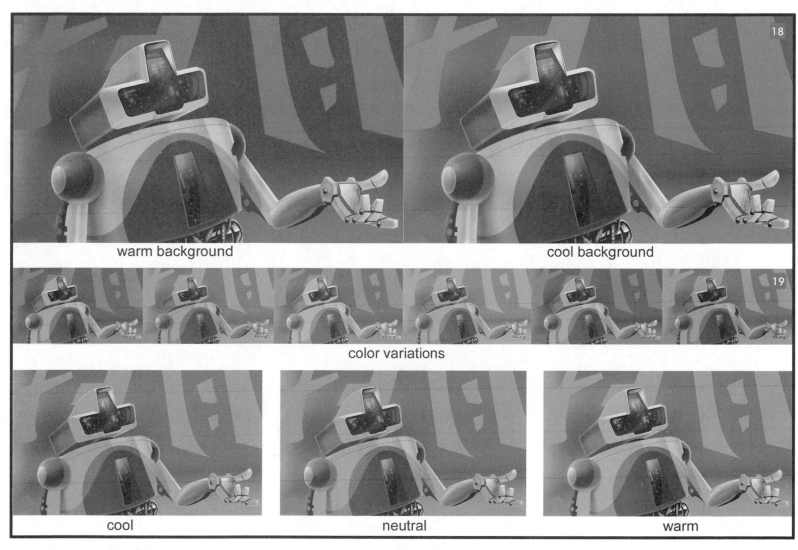

warm background

cool background

color variations

cool

neutral

warm

See color plate on page C-3.

Proportion

This is a short section about proportion. In order to get you thinking about what proportion means, I must digress for a moment. I want you to think back to our most basic tool in design — contrast. I have talked a lot about contrast thus far as it relates to value and color, but understanding that *contrasts within proportion* will improve the look of your designs is at the heart of this section. Our definition of contrast is: "one thing that is strikingly dissimilar to another or the use of opposing elements such as color forms or lines in proximity to produce an intensive effect in a work of art."

That definition is perfect, because contrast is not just about light and dark but is also about volume, shape, and proportion. A thin line against a fat line or a large muscular superhero with a huge chest, thin waistline, and small head. It's that contrast in size that makes subject matter interesting to look at or quirky. Knowing when to use odd or even proportions within your designs will help give your projects the unique qualities of originality and personality (image 20).

Design is all about projecting a mood or personality. The more interesting or unique your designs are, the more your audience will pay attention, and the longer you hold their attention, the more success you will have within your profession.

"Contrasts within proportion will improve the look of your design."

21

Proportion is defined as "the harmonious relation of parts to each other or to the whole; balance, symmetry."

What we define as having good proportions is a little subjective, but as a society we mostly agree on certain tangible qualities that define what is and what is not attractive. Two contrasting examples of attractiveness would be a supermodel and a baby (image 21). What makes the supermodel attractive? Is it the relationship between her long legs, curvaceous hips, and thin waistline? Maybe her face has great proportions with big blue eyes, voluptuous lips, long hair, and a small cute nose. It's the proportion (big versus small) of her physical assets as they relate to each other that make her attractive.

Now let's look at the baby. Babies are quite the opposite of a supermodel in proportion. They have a fat little tummy, chubby short legs and arms, a big head, fat cheeks, no teeth, and a smidgeon of hair. Yet somehow the baby is considered cute. How is that? Again, it's all about proportion, but the extreme thereof. The extremes to which a baby's arms, legs, and head are completely oversized for its body somehow registers as cute. Personally I think it's because a baby is so small in comparison to a full-grown adult, the exaggeration of its body parts is attractive. What if we gave the baby proportions similar to our supermodel? Somehow I don't think she'd make the cover of *Glamour* magazine. That is, unless supermodels with big heads, no teeth, and a smidgeon of hair somehow become the new trend.

Proportion is all about the size relationship between shapes and a balance of these existing within the proper context. A big-headed supermodel is out of context for what we perceive as attractive; the same goes for a baby with legs three feet long.

Controlling proportion as it relates to your designs and animation takes a long time to master, but fortunately for you I have a few tricks up my sleeve. I've titled the following section "An Odd Relationship" because it encompasses a more hands-on approach to proportion with cool design shortcuts, tricks, and exercises relating to this subject.

An Odd Relationship

Ever wonder why most car rims have an odd number of spokes? The odd relationship rule establishes the idea that an odd number of design elements or accoutrements (details) is more interesting to look at than an even number.

To be even more literal, asymmetry looks more interesting than symmetry. This rule must, of course, be used in context. For example, a car usually has four wheels, humans usually have two arms, an airplane has two wings, and so on.

As long as your idea of using an odd number of design elements doesn't go against the basic logic of your audience, you will successfully conceive a good design. What I mean is that your human may have two arms, but his shirt may have five buttons or he may have three earrings. It's the odd number of elements that makes his overall appearance more interesting to look at. I'm not saying that a shirt with five buttons is an intensely interesting design element, but it is better than four buttons (image 22).

Here's why: For whatever reason, our eyes perceive an odd number of objects or oddly proportioned objects as being more visually interesting, mostly because it gives our eyes many types of contours and shapes to look upon, rather than just a few that are the same size and shape. For example, take two candles of even height and width sitting in the middle of a table (image 23). As it stands, two candles of even size go against our rule of odds, so if we add just one more candle (image 24), somehow our drawing looks a lot more interesting and the composition is more aesthetically pleasing. It also has a bit to do with placement, but overall it's more interesting to look at. To take it another direction, let's say that instead of adding a third candle we just shorten one candle (image 25) so that the candles have a size contrast. Again, we've managed to make the composition more interesting because two oddly sized candles are more interesting than two evenly sized ones.

Some good examples of this rule are applied in many forms of industry, including automotive design, cinematography, photography, architecture, fashion, landscaping, and animation. In automotive design, oddly proportioned shapes are applied to get the most visual impact out of cars. A great example is the 2005 Volkswagen Beetle and the Audi TT.

They both share the same chassis and have a similar rounded appearance, but what makes them different? If you look at the Beetle, it is fairly symmetrical as far as the body and cabin are concerned. The Audi TT has nearly the same size body, but the cabin has been reduced in height, giving it a more aggressive, streamlined look. The automotive designers at Audi used an unevenly proportioned body to cabin to increase the car's visual appeal.

26

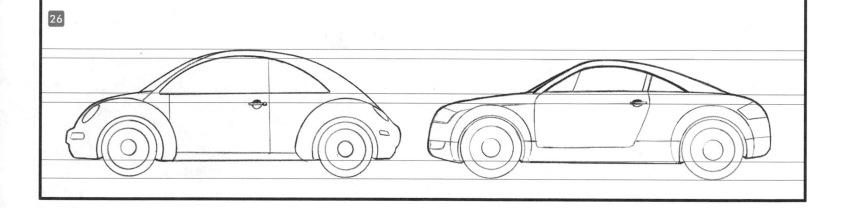

Staying with the theory that odd looks better than even, take a car's wheels, for example (image 27). These are drawings of the same car but with three different wheel treatments. The first has four-spoke wheels, which look boring, even, and plain. The second car has five-spoke wheels, which make it look more aggressive and sporty. Sticking with an odd number, the third car has seven-spoke wheels, which make it look a little more classy and upscale.

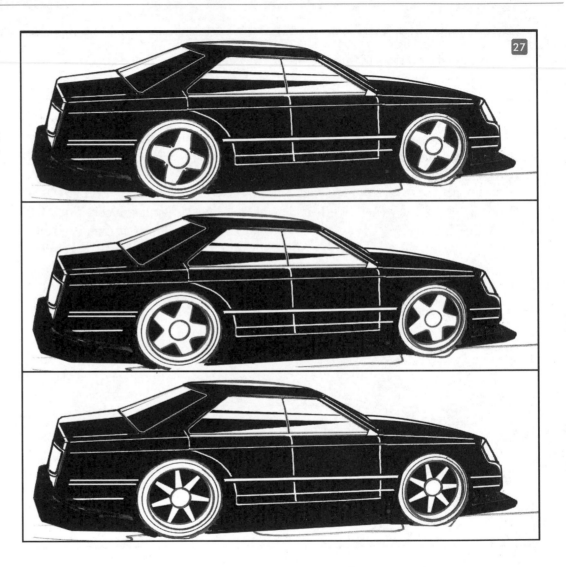

I suppose the theory is that by adding more spokes, you're increasing the number of details, kind of like a ring with a single diamond versus the same ring with three diamonds — the more you have, the more upscale it seems. Psychologically speaking, in most societies, more is better, so the more spokes you have on a wheel, the more it is perceived as being upscale. All of this must be taken into context, so when it comes to new rims for your Bentley, you want to use 7, 9, 11, or even 13, because it matches the personality of the car — wealth. How about putting the same rims on my Honda Civic? No! Why not? Because it's out of context. The Civic is a small economy car meant to get you from point A to point B, and it exudes that personality. Putting expensive multi-spoked rims on a car of that nature is too much detail; it should be simplistic like the car itself.

So for all you Civic owners out there, Kater recommends five. No more, no less. Too many looks gaudy and too few looks wimpy. This, of course, is my opinion and perhaps some of you don't agree, but all in all if you stick with an odd number, you'll be better off.

Some more examples of odd numbering that can be used to your advantage are:

- Five buttons on a shirt instead of six.

- Three big trees in front of a house instead of two.

- Five rivets on the side of a space ship instead of four.

- Seven shelves instead of eight.

- Three eyes instead of two… for creatures only.

- Three seats in a car instead of four.

- Three windows on the front of a house — two on one side, and one on the other.

And so on…

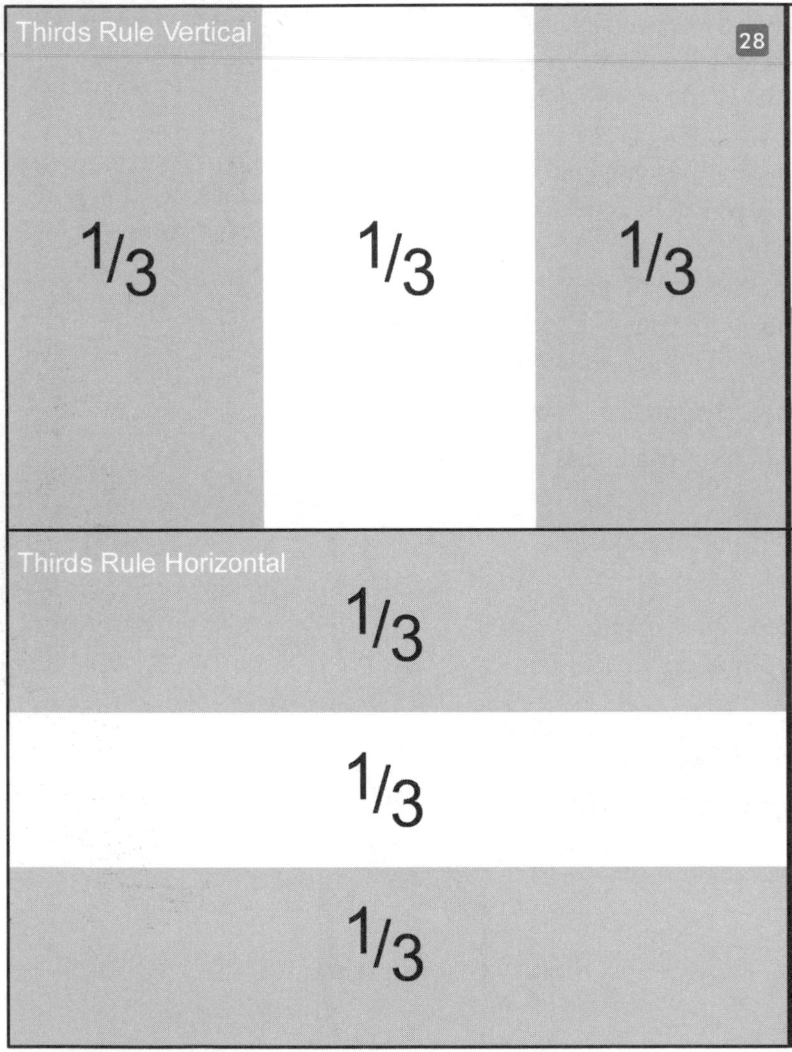

Thirds Rule Vertical

28

$1/3$ $1/3$ $1/3$

Thirds Rule Horizontal

$1/3$

$1/3$

$1/3$

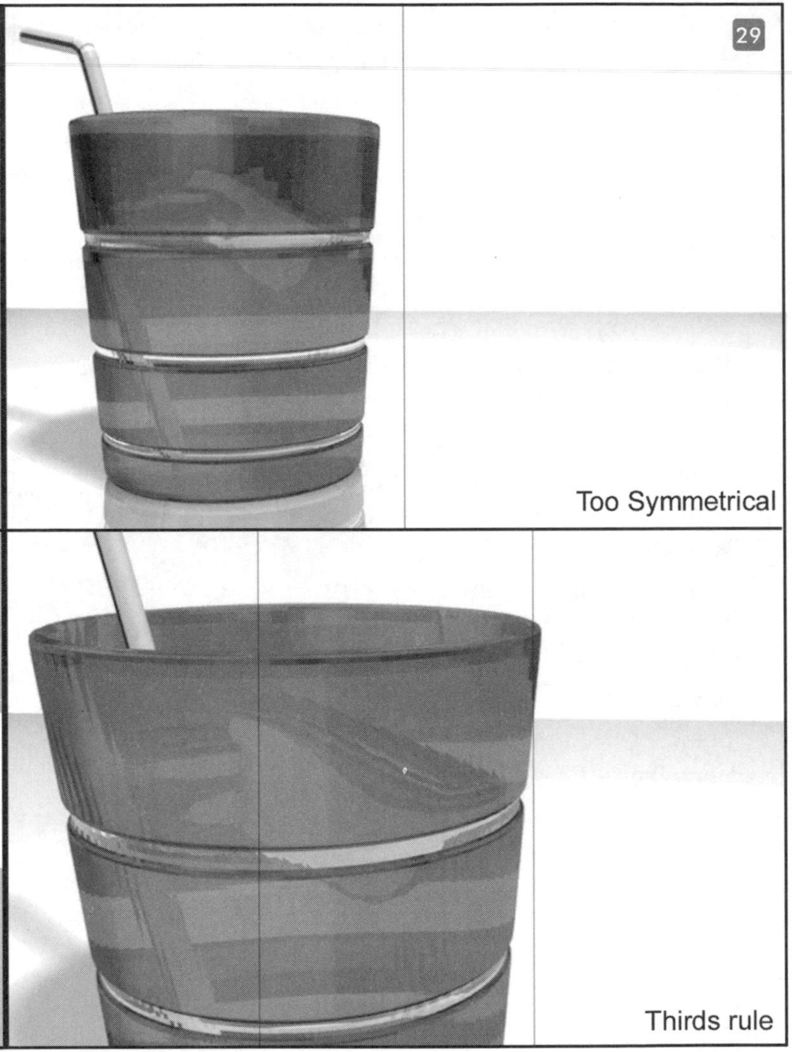

29

Too Symmetrical

Thirds rule

This brings me to the rule of thirds. The rule of thirds is used mostly in cinematography and photography. The rule being that your field of view (whatever the camera sees) should be divided into thirds on the horizontal or vertical (image 28). The application of this rule is to divide your image so that the focal point takes up one-third of the screen or two-thirds of the screen, never half (image 29). This will, of course, change within the movement of your shot, but establishing the shot by utilizing the rule of thirds adds the contrast of odd is better than even. Notice how in the upper example our subject matter takes up half the image area. With a slight reframing of the image, the lower example looks more interesting.

I've drawn a few more examples to show you how this works (image 30). By giving each image a little asymmetry, I've made them more interesting to look at. Of course, this is a basic approach to the rule of thirds, and some might argue that you can do whatever you want when it comes to framing. I would agree with that, yet there is a reason that time and time again the rule of odd proportions has been used by professionals and that is because it is a tried-and-true rule that adds visual interest to projects. There are many scenarios that use symmetry effectively; just keep in mind that as long as it is a stylistic choice that brings the best result out of your work, symmetry is good. Remember to keep it in context of what you're trying to accomplish and the use of either will yield a good result.

Contour

The contour of a design is the outline of irregular surfaces and shapes, with one flowing into the next. Examples of contour in design would be a person's neck flowing into his shoulders, the sides of a water bottle flowing into its top, the roof of a car flowing into its windshield, the flow of your eyelid into your forehead, etc. (image 31).

Contour is simply one surface transitioning into another surface. How contour applies to what we do in design is important and learning how to control those contours in order to increase your design's appeal is paramount. This section is going to teach you what contour is, how it's used, and how to control it.

If you look at the figure, I've illustrated what a contour is. In the car, the contour is the line that transitions from the roof of the car into the windshield. That's the easy part — identifying the contour. The next question is how is it used? In the case of the water bottle, contour defines the shape and the transition from one shape into the next. Notice that the contour of the bottle's side is an arc that slowly curves toward the center as it makes its way toward the top. That arc just kind of slowly makes its way with no abrupt changes in movement, sharp turns, etc., until it reaches the top, where it sharply undulates to create the transition between the side of the bottle and the top of the bottle. I've drawn a close-up of that transition so you can get a better idea of what I'm talking about. That sudden

transition in movement suddenly increased the energy of that line. It was slowly meandering toward the top, then it rapidly changed direction and undulated back and forth until it hit the top. The energy of the contour changed from mellow and easygoing to abrupt and determined.

All of this sounds a little subjective, but understanding how contours transition from one kind of energy to another is a great tool for design. It's this keen understanding of the energy of a line that allows us to know what makes a shark look fast and a turtle look slow. A shark has sharp transitions from one contour to the next that fly at mach speed across the body, undulating up and down and in and out of every shape to create vicious teeth, a sharp dorsal fin, and hugely triangular tail.

Contour

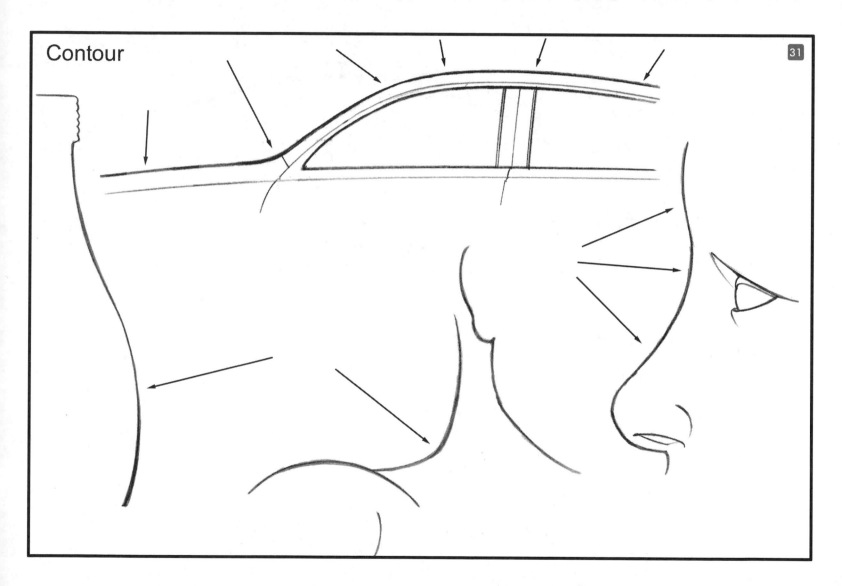

Think of the energy in a contour like a rollercoaster track. If the coaster starts off slow and goes over a hill that slowly rises and then slowly descends, the coaster goes slow. If the coaster goes slowly up the track, but then sharply goes down the other side, you have a fast coaster, hence a lot of energy (image 32).

The same goes for design. An energetic or non-energetic line has just as much to do with its purpose and appeal as proportion or color — appeal being the operative phrase. How contour is used has a huge amount of influence on appeal by its ability to add energy, flow, and transitions that make a design compelling. As to the "how it's used" portion, let's move on to control.

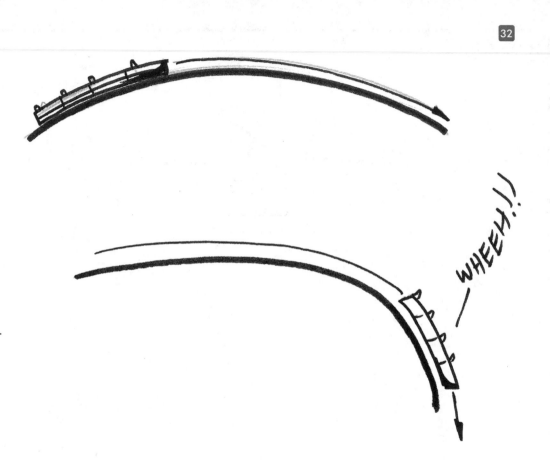

WHEEH!!)

32

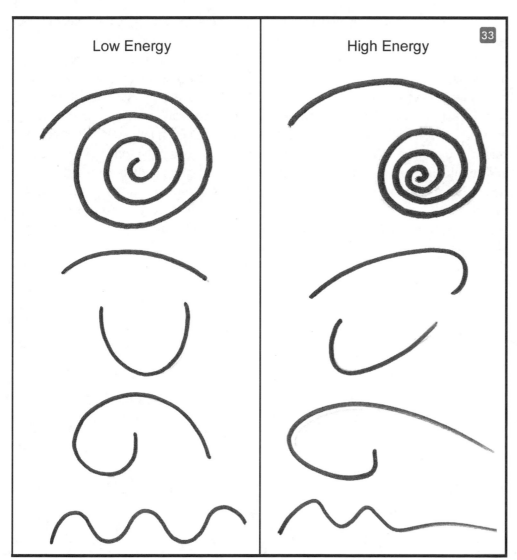

Low Energy | High Energy

Controlling contour contributes to a design's aesthetic and energetic appeal. I've created an image with the most basic contour-like shapes (image 33). They are simple curves that have a spiral flow. Notice how the low-energy contours are slow to move toward a spiral; their movement is even and uninteresting. In contrast, the high-energy lines seem to start off slow, but then speed up rapidly, spiraling toward the center into a much tighter ball. That rapid change in movement is a more energetic application of the line, feeling lively and interesting.

It's sort of the same principle as the "odd relationships" theory discussed earlier. There's an odd relationship between the movement from the beginning of the curve until its end. Just because a line doesn't have high energy doesn't mean it's bad — it's all about the proper context. Like I said earlier, a turtle looks slow because it is slow. It would look a little silly if a sleek and sharp-edged shark were as slow as a turtle.

We now know how to create an energetic and non-energetic line, but how do we control them as they transition from one into the other? The answer is with precision. Precisely plotting one contour into the next is the *art of the transition*. I like to make each transition as purposeful and controlled as possible. There are two kinds of transitions: smooth and abrupt (image 34). The smooth transition is just that — smooth movement from one curve into the next, gracefully joining two curves on a single contour. The abrupt transition is a sharp edge or rough contour with sudden movement or change in direction. Either of these can be appropriate to a design — it's just a matter of what you're going for.

This kind of observation and application of energetic and non-energetic contours is part of making good design decisions. Control over energetic movement is the same kind of application of design that makes an animation exciting to look at or boring. Applying this kind of energy takes some thought and should be applied in the proper context. A good example of an awkward use of energy would be if you were watching a Kung Fu action movie and all the camera work was a wide shot that moved around at a snail's pace. Action movies need camera work that has the same energy as the characters involved in the action, not the opposite. Again, it's all subjective, so maybe a few snail-paced shots might wake up the audience, only because they're expecting a fast-moving camera with quick cuts from one scene to the next. Just use good judgment and a design eye that keeps it all in context.

As for contours, we now know what they are, how they're used, and how to control them. You'll find that as we get into 3D modeling later in the book, controlling contours will be just as crucial as the model itself.

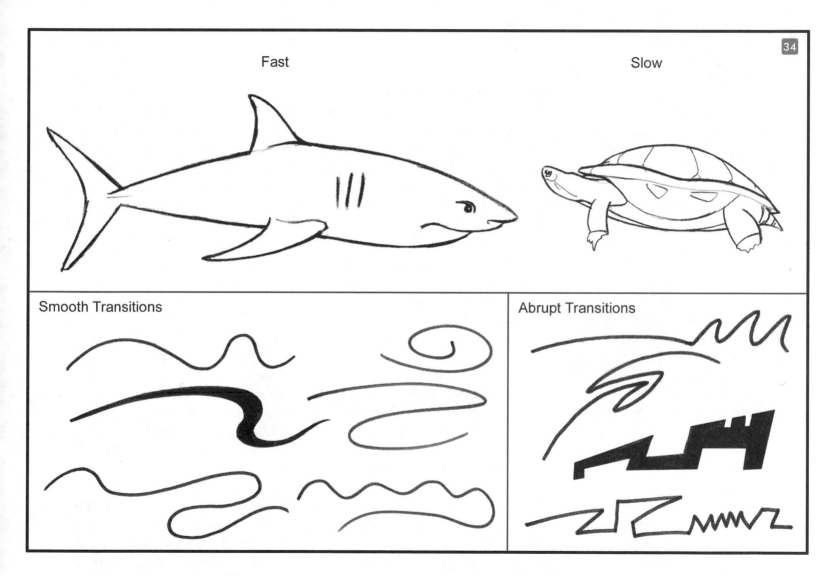

Fast

Slow

Smooth Transitions

Abrupt Transitions

Observation

This next assignment is an easy one. It will give your hand and eye a chance to get to know the world around you and help you develop a more critical eye for design. The critical eye is developed by critiquing either your own design work or others' work. Over time you'll start to notice what is good and bad design. This can only come out of careful *observation* of many designs over time and making mental if not written notes of the good, the bad, and the ugly. Observation is the keen awareness of what you are examining, and noticing design elements, such as proportion, contour, size, color, concept, and function, that make that design a success or failure. In layman's terms, use observation and critique so you don't make the same mistake twice, and notice any mistakes others have made. You learn from good design by applying it to your work.

Critiquing your own work is very important to learning the observation process, but for starters, let's critique others. In your sketchpad, devote at least a few pages to doing this next exercise. I want you to look at cars, buildings, people, trees, flowers, fashion, furniture, jewelry, store displays, and sculpture and analyze the characteristics that make them unique. Is the design perfect for what it does? Does it stand the test of time? Does it have mass appeal? At the top of the page, list your object and the design elements that make that object look cool, interesting, quirky, ugly, etc. List all the attributes that make up its physical appearance. This list should consist of design traits that you think are responsible for its identity, whether good or bad.

Take a mobile phone, for example. If you think it's an attractive phone, perhaps it's the cool aluminum case, smooth round buttons, and huge LED screen that make it feel modern and hip. In contrast, maybe the mobile phone is unattractive because of its cheap green plastic case, squarish hard-to-read buttons, and small LED screen.

Using observation as your primary tool, examine each object and ask yourself what makes this good or bad. Design flaws that stick out like a sore thumb are easier to notice, so look for the subtle flaws, like a coffee mug handle that's too small, a picture hung too low on a wall, a beautiful curve in a household product, nice subtle lighting at a restaurant. Critique color, shape, quality, proportion, and ease of use. Ask yourself why you are drawn to certain design elements and make note of these.

If you are drawn to a certain consumer product, like Apple's iPod for example, what is it about the iPod that makes it so cool? Is it because its function and form is perfectly simple? It looks simple to use and it is simple to use, and it's that simplicity that permeates the product. Simply put, the iPod functions like it looks. It functions intuitively, looks stunning, and personifies cool. That kind of simplicity is the ultimate goal of any designer, but can only be achieved through trial and error, a keen eye for design, and careful observation.

All of this relates to production design and ultimately filmmaking. Once you have the hang of observation, find your favorite movie and really watch it this time. Use the scrutiny of your new critical eye to pick out color, movement, composition, and environment that make this movie a real success. If you pause your favorite scene and start to move through it frame by frame, you'll start to notice things about color, contrast, and composition that you never noticed before. With your newly acquired drawing skills and critical eye, you'll really be able to break down a shot and figure out what the cinematographer was trying to achieve from a graphic standpoint. Look at each shot as a graphic drawing, purposely composed with a focal point and flow. Ask yourself where the director wants your eyes to go. What graphic shapes are in the background that add a mood to the shot and makes it poignant or compelling? Study each shot as if it were a graphic design problem and make a mental or written note of all the things that you discover. Ultimately, this kind of careful observation and patient critique of others will lead you naturally to designing your animations with the same sensibilities and subtleties as found in your favorite films. I like to think of this kind of observation as a path of discovery that leads to a broadened sense of what good design is and the confidence to apply it to your own work.

I must digress briefly to tell you a story of observation that even today has left an indelible impression upon me.

I was on a flight from Los Angeles to Florida on a new Boeing 777, which is a huge airplane with all the modern amenities. I had read a lot about the 777's construction and was really excited about flying on this bad boy (well, any plane that has an engine the circumference of a 727's fuselage is a bad boy). Every person who boarded that day was greeted by the flight attendant saying, "Welcome aboard, please watch the Flight Attendant call button because it is located on the top of the armrest and it is easy to hit it with your elbow." As soon as I sat down I noticed the armrest had a recessed touchpad for telephone, TV, etc., and sure enough the call

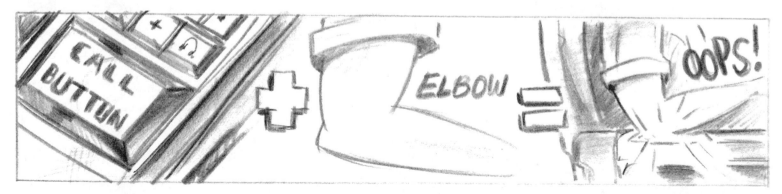

button was there. Instead of putting the keypad on the side of the armrest, some genius thought it would be more convenient to access the keypad from the top, which in plain English means a constant beeping sound over the PA. To make things worse, my seat was located right under a speaker, so my whole flight was nothing but hundreds of elbows hitting this call button, "bing, bing, bing, bing… pause… bing, bing," shortly interrupted with "ladies and gentleman, please remember that BING, BING, BING…."

The preceding is a true story and a great example of a design flaw. The real question for you is, "What kind of design flaw?" Understanding that there are different types of design will further refine your observation skills and improve your work by keeping things in context.

What I mean by "different types" of design are different studies within design, like industrial design, production design, fashion design, graphic design, photography, cinematography, architecture, lighting design, and interior design.

As a designer and 3D animator, your greatest tool for improving your work is to create a 3D world that is viable and believable. If your scenes contain elements of industrial design, lighting design, and graphic design, you want to accurately portray each of those design elements looking their best. A good example would be a short 3D film that I just saw. It was lit beautifully and had great character design, but the architectural elements were awful. I could tell that this filmmaker was really good at lighting, animation, and even character design but had no eye for architecture, so for the entire film I was distracted by this animator's lack of caring for such an important design element. In fact, there were times I cringed at how bad the designs were, to the point that I missed some of the dialogue and action… NOT GOOD!

In your own work, do your best to observe the good and the bad in all types of design, not just what interests you.

production design   photography   industrial design

graphic design   architecture   fashion design

lighting design   interior design   cinematography

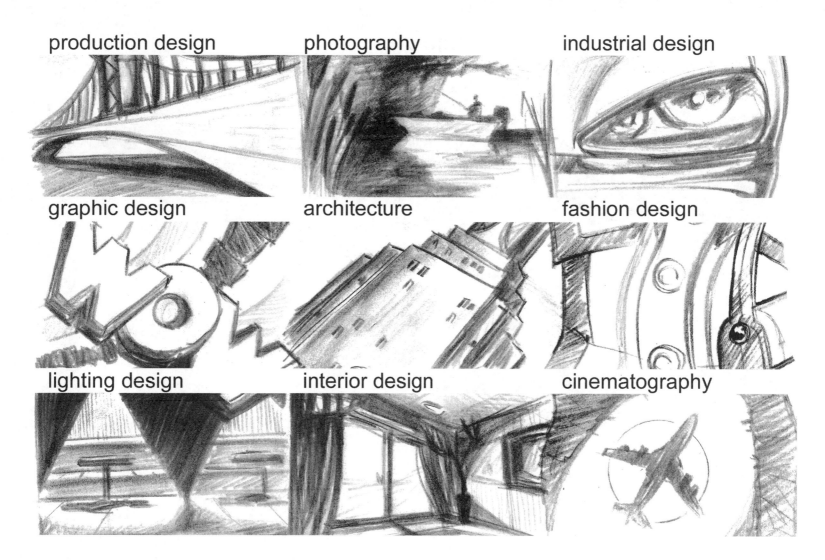

"The process of analysis is life long…start looking at everything in the world because observation trains your design eye."

— Dan Quarnstrom, 2005

Moving on, Chapter 4 is going to be fun! We're going to take all of the drawing, design, and observation skills we've been developing and start to create our own designs.

Chapter Four

Designing Your Own Ideas

A Non-Boring Intro

This chapter is about having fun, and the amount of fun you have is directly related to the knowledge you've gained in the previous chapters. I want you to feel confident that what I'm teaching you is really going to improve your work as a 3D artist or designer. The next exercise is to help you loosen up before we get into more advanced design themes.

Gesture Drawing

A gesture drawing is a drawing that captures the basic contours and details of your design and can be considered a sort of inspirational sketch that leads to a more refined drawing. Gesture drawing, a tried-and-true technique of figure and still life drawing, is usually done within a time limit, like 10 seconds, 30 seconds, and so on. The idea is to train your hand to instantly sketch what you see and capture as much of the shapes and details as possible. If I gave you a pineapple and told you to draw it 10 times and all I gave you was 30 seconds each time, I bet by the time you reached drawing 10 you'd really know what that pineapple looked like. I also bet if I asked you to draw that pineapple the next day without looking at it, you probably could. This exercise promotes great hand/eye coordination and will help you to sketch more confidently and accurately. When using this technique, you should focus on trying to capture the shape and proportion of your design as loosely and quickly as possible. Once your pencil hits paper, you should barely lift it off the page as you swirl your pencil around, sort of defining and filling in detail as you go. Start first with the outline or silhouette of your object and then fill in detail. See my example of the teddy bear sketch (image 1).

The first panel indicates a rough outline of the shapes of the teddy bear; the second panel focuses on detailing his head, arms, and legs; and the third panel focuses on adding shadow. This whole process only took 30 seconds, but through the use of gesture drawing I was able to capture the overall shape, proportion, and detail of the teddy. To further define my teddy bear drawing, I would use an overlay technique to sharpen up the line, shadow, and silhouette.

Gesture Exercise 1: Get a bottle, vase, pineapple, teddy bear — anything simple. Using the gesture drawing technique, draw your subject matter five times as quickly as possible. Give yourself only 30 seconds for each drawing.

We only have a few sources for visualizing new ideas, such as inspirational material, printed material, and our imagination. Drawing something over and over again promotes what is called *imprinting*. Through the process of repetition, you are imprinting the shape, contour, and details into your memory. Imprinting comes in handy when you're given the task of designing a specific item that you're familiar with. Rather than doing research, you can just think about the item and come up with what you need. Focusing on things that you're familiar with is quite a luxury. In our work as 3D animators and designers, we're usually working on ideas or designs that don't exist in our memory. We must rely on our imagination, and the only way to harness our imagination is with our mind's ability to communicate that idea or vision to our hand. When gesture drawing a new idea, try to first picture it in your mind, then sketch quickly and loosely to capture the design.

Gesture Exercise 2: Using your imagination, choose a single subject matter and by using the gesture drawing technique, draw your subject matter 10 times as quickly as possible. Give yourself one minute for each drawing (image 2).

Inspiration and Design Themes

Inspiration is the motivation behind your work, and it is the spirit or aesthetic of this inspiration that should be apparent in your final design. Inspiration can come from almost anywhere, including manmade objects, music, film, and nature. It can be a classic film that inspires a modern film, an art deco inspired television show, or a field of purple and orange flowers that inspire a newly tiled bathroom. Inspiration can range from the simple, like flowers, to the complex, like love. A fantastic example of inspiration embodied in execution is the modern Volkswagen Beetle. Back in 1994, I had the incredible opportunity to hear a lecture by the automotive designers of the new Beetle while I attended the Art Center College of Design in Pasadena. Debuting in 1994 at the Detroit Auto Show, the new Beetle received an unprecedented amount of public interest and would go into production for release in 1998. The first Beetle had arrived in the U.S. in the late '40s and from the beginning it was defined as cheap, basic transportation. It wasn't until the late '60s and early '70s that the Beetle became the shining star in a new era of love and freedom, and it was this particular era that gave the designers of the modern Beetle their inspiration. The hippy generation, sometimes called flower children, adopted the Beetle as their own and turned it into something of an icon; in fact, it was nicknamed the "Love Bug." As a true icon, the Love Bug embodied the spirit of their most treasured beliefs, like simplicity, affordability, independence, freedom, and love for all things. The spirit of love for one's automobile is a theme that affects our hearts to this very day. Since most people buy a car based on love, the designers of the new Beetle capitalized on this human emotion through the use of nostalgia. Even though the car is modern, it contains those quintessential Beetle aesthetics that made the original so popular, like its fun-loving, smiling exterior with rounded fenders and bug eye headlights. The interior is welcoming and open to give a sense of freedom and simplicity. The designers even went so far as to put a flower vase in the dashboard to connect Mother Nature with automobile, in honor of the nostalgia associated with the flower children. Even with all the design variables and possible doubt that this car could ever succeed, the designers knew that if they stuck closely to their inspiration and executed their concepts without sacrifice, that people would accept and love this new interpretation of the Beetle. There's no doubt that their vision paid off — hundreds of thousands of new Beetles have been sold to a new generation of Beetle lovers and in the meantime they've helped to redefine automotive design and created an instant classic (image 3).

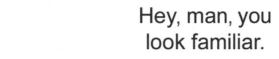

Almost anything that inspires your idea is fair game, but knowing how to harness and apply that inspiration is what this chapter is all about. It is a simple two-step process of finding and applying your inspiration.

Finding and applying inspiration.

Use visual cues like shape, contour, silhouette, and proportion to inspire your designs. In this case I've used things found in nature as my inspiration.

Tiger lily to inspire wheel design.

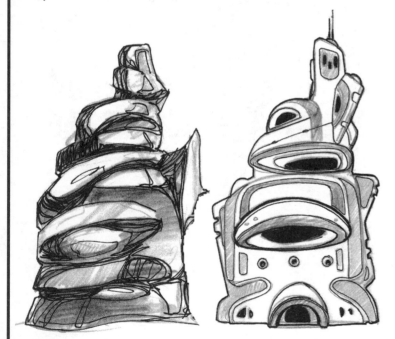

Rock structure to inspire futuristic dwelling.

Butterfly to inspire perfume bottle.

Step 1: Find Your Inspiration

There is no right or wrong way to find inspiration; it can come from any source that does the job. Go to a bookstore or magazine stand, surf the Internet, look at old pictures, listen to music, go for a drive, go for a walk, talk to someone — whatever gets you to that place. Look for whatever captures your interest. Look for colors, shapes, lighting, move-ment, personality, contrast, subtlety, patterns, lines, themes, art, architec-ture, fashion, products, commercials, nature, and on and on and on. There is no timeline, there is no simple answer — you are the only person who will know, because it will come to you in a flash and you'll say, "That's it, I've found it!"

Step 2: Apply Your Inspiration

Once you've found your inspiration, try to look at all of the applicable design qualities, like shape, color, proportion, mood, and so on. Once you've done this, interpret those shapes, colors, and so on into graphical elements that will work with your design (image 4).

Draw these little shapes and graphic elements in a sort of collage to give yourself a visual reference for your final drawing.

The process of choosing what to use for inspiration is called establishing a *design theme*. In the case of the animated series *Silver Surfer*, I used insect-like and reptilian shapes, colors, and proportions to inspire the design themes for the spaceships of the Skrull, a reptilian-like race. Borrowing design details like triangular, horn-like shapes for cockpits, organic beetle-like wings for the fuselage, and mosquito-like legs for landing gear helped establish themes from which I designed an entire fleet of ships. If I were to have interpreted my inspirations literally, I would have ended up with a mechanical insect. Instead I worked for weeks on interpreting those key shapes, colors, and proportions into something that looked like a spaceship but had an insect-like or reptilian feel (image 5). Plain and simple — pick your inspiration(s), then establish your design themes and apply them to your work.

5

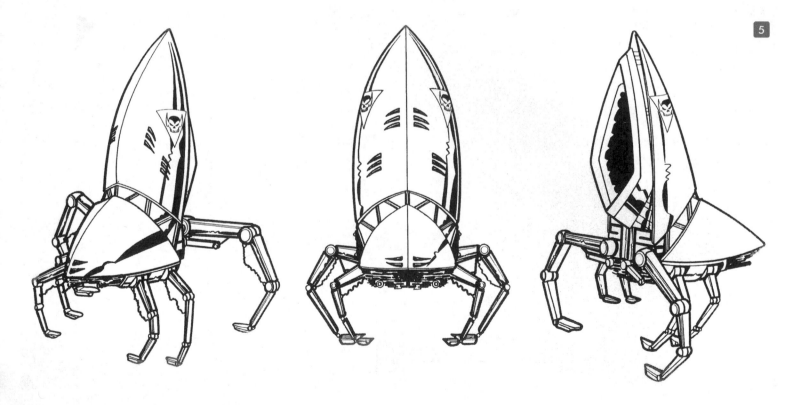

Design themes can also come in the form of objects. For instance, let's say you're designing the interior of a Gothic dance club and your inspiration is *Frankenstein*. Borrow all the design elements like stark lighting, stone walls, smoke, metallic surfaces, giant electrical gizmos, and chains to establish your design themes. Taking those themes, apply them to your design. The application as I see it would result in a dark, moody atmosphere colored mostly with shades of gray to emulate black and white film. All bartenders and waitstaff would have to wear mad scientist-type uniforms. Maybe the bar is made of rolled and dented aluminum, like it's been beaten with a hammer; to make it even creepier, it's suspended by chains. The smoke-filled dance floor is surrounded by dungeon-esque stone walls lit by balls of electrical light. Drinks would be served in large test tube-like glasses and the house would serve a bright green drink called "The Frankenstein," of course. In this case, the design themes are right at your fingertips, and with a quick list of the aesthetic qualities and mood of

Frankenstein's lab, I was able to apply those themes to our Gothic club (image 6).

In the work that we're doing, focus on finding what inspires your idea first, apply its core design themes, then work on carrying that inspiration through to

the end. All in all, it will be a great start to something unique.

Inspiration Exercise 1: Design a bottle of perfume that gets its inspiration from the Eiffel Tower in Paris.

Drawing in the Rough and Overlay Techniques

For this exercise, you'll need a 9" x 12" pad of tracing paper. The rough sketch is like a rough 3D model; it's the initial pass on your concept and it contains many design variables like proportion, size, composition, mood, and aesthetic, but it's not so concrete that you would call it your final design. It's a very forgiving stage of design with no time limit that allows you the opportunity to experiment with all the design variables and come up with something that fulfills your vision. Even after I have a final design and then scan it into the computer, I'm constantly experimenting with the design variables in 3D to see if I can make improvements. The tweaking and fine-tuning never stops until delivery, so giving yourself the opportunity to experiment with design details and achieve your concept is the fundamental process that makes your animations a success.

Not to scare you, but there are a million different ways that artists go about sketching. Some artists will only use a certain kind of pencil and paper, others need to draw a hundred little tiny drawings, and still others prefer to use a fat pen and fill the page with broad strokes to get their designs. How this applies to you is called *individuality*. It's crucial that you practice sketching techniques that others have shown you, then slowly adopt your own. Sketching is kind of like cooking, in that you start with raw ingredients, an empty pan, and some utensils and somehow through a process of your own you end up with a meal. If you're cooking spaghetti sauce, there are a million ways to make it and no two people make it the same, yet you've both made spaghetti sauce. Sketching is a means to an end, and hopefully with good inspiration and enough drawing you end up with a final design.

The approach to rough sketching can vary, so I'll show you a few techniques and you'll be on your way, but first we need a concept. The concept is to design a modern desk lamp that gets its inspiration from the huge vines that grow in the jungles of South America. In my mind, I've chosen a few design themes that will give me something to shoot for in the realm of shape and proportion. When I think of jungle vines, I think of a long skinny vine curled at the bottom with leaves sprouting out at different levels (image 7).

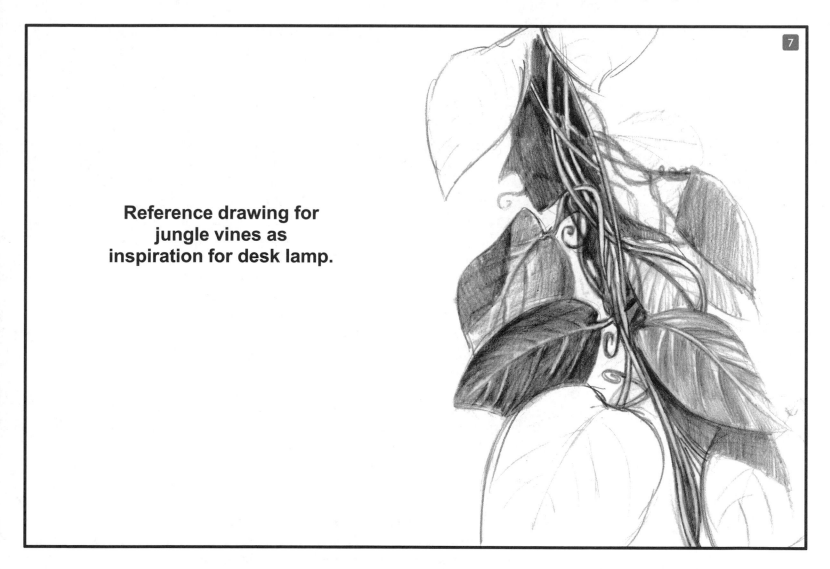

**Reference drawing for
jungle vines as
inspiration for desk lamp.**

Our design themes include long, skinny tendril-like shapes, curls, and leaf shapes. It's good to think of color and texture as well, but they're not applicable at this stage, so I'll save those thoughts for later. Our concept is a modern desk lamp, so it should have some sort of base or a way to connect to our desk, an appendage or arm of sorts that elevates the light above the desk, a switch to turn it on and off, and a place where the lightbulb goes.

The first phase of our concept creation will incorporate a simple overlay technique and is what I call "sketching the blob." This will be considered sketch #1. The best part about this technique is that you can be as messy and unrefined as you want. I'm going to use my personal favorite, a blue Col-erase pencil, and a 9" x 12" piece of tracing paper. Do not pull the paper out of the pad, but draw on the first page of the pad because it gives you a soft surface to work on. Now, keeping in mind that I'm designing a lamp, I just put pencil to paper and start drawing those long tendril-like shapes as loosely and organically as possible. I'm not worried about how this looks; I'm just trying to envision my design and get a feel for shape and proportion (image 8).

The appendage section of our lamp is well suited for the long skinny vine shape, and in keeping with my theme, I put a few leaf-like shapes along this section to indicate where lightbulbs might go. Since a vine can curl at the bottom, I use that shape to form the base of my lamp. My technique yields a super sketchy blob-like shape, but has plenty of information to further refine my design. If I like what I see, I can move on to the second phase. If I don't like what I see, I can choose to start over or refine my design.

I choose to refine, so I pull a clean sheet from the bottom of the tracing pad and put it on top of my design. By tracing my design, I can now make adjustments in proportion and shape. In this case, I didn't like how evenly spaced and sized the leaf sections were, so I moved them a little bit and changed their size to be more oddly proportioned (image 9). It's still a blob, but I'm happy enough with the result to move on to the second phase.

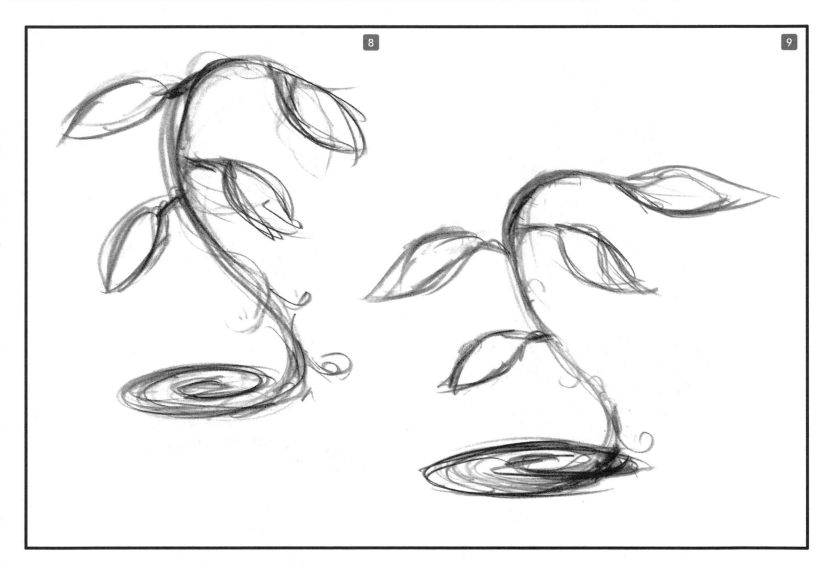

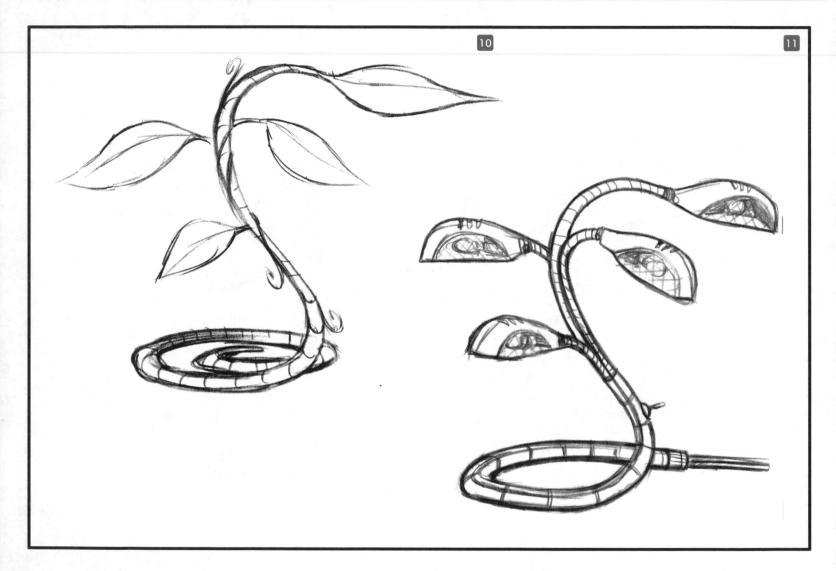

The second phase is all about refinement. I will now discard sketch #1 and, pulling yet another clean piece of tracing paper from the bottom, I put it on top of sketch #2. In this phase I'm going to concentrate more on final design, so using an outlining technique, I'll vary line weights to further define contours and detail (image 10).

It's looking pretty good, but I feel my lamp still looks a little too organic, kind of like a lamp made of vines and leaves. I pull out a clean piece of tracing paper and do further refinement. Since our lamp is modern, the shapes can be a little more architectural with harder edges leading into soft shapes, and with a more contemporary, functional aesthetic (image 11).

As you can see, the base is curled in shape but has a strong hard-edged quality, and the lights are leaf-like but have a more clam shell-like shape. I've also included swivel points for the lights and have designed an on/off switch in the base. The arm of our lamp is still rounded, but I've now included spiraling lines of detail to give it a more organic feel. What I have here is about as good as you need for a rough sketch. It defines our concept, inspiration, and design theme.

If I didn't feel that I had worked out enough of the details, I could do what's called a "detail drawing" (images 12 and 13) and further refine that design element.

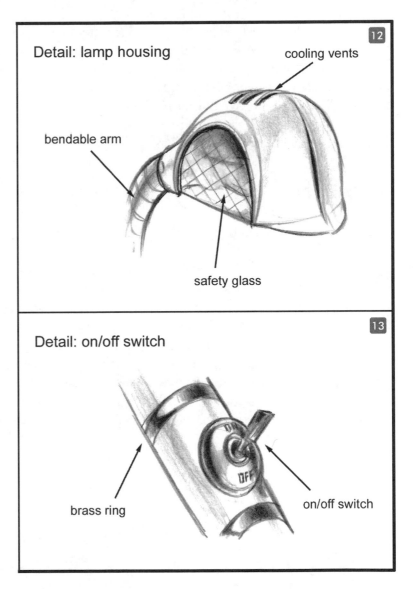

12

Detail: lamp housing

cooling vents

bendable arm

safety glass

13

Detail: on/off switch

brass ring

on/off switch

From this point, we would go into a final design phase, working out every little design aesthetic in the form of illustrations showing color, texture, and materials. For now, you have the basic understanding of the rough sketch technique, so it's time to do your own.

Rough Drawing Exercise 1: Rough sketch and refine a chair that gets its inspiration from a waterfall.

Rough Drawing Exercise 2: Rough sketch and refine a large floor lamp that gets its inspiration from an ocean plant.

Advanced Construction

Using construction is just one tool of many that can be used as a guide for 3D modeling. I covered construction a little in Chapter 2, but since you've advanced to this stage, I want to give a more detailed explanation of its application. When sketching a concept for a design, you typically start with a single view until you like what you see, but a single view is not going to give you the information you need to model your design in 3D. In our case, construction is the technique of breaking down your design into its most simplistic shapes for the purposes of 3D. We know what our primitives look like from every angle, so if you break your design down into a combination of several primitives, it will become a simple guide for constructing your character from several angles (image 14).

I've done a construction sketch of a simple character by using a combination of modified spheres, cubes, and cylinders to gain its overall proportions. Nearly all the shapes connect to each other in places where there would be a pivot or twist, so our construction model gives us a clear indication of how our character would animate. Let's do a direct translation into 3D (image 15). Our 3D model is a spitting image of its 2D cousin and I can now move the character around to get an even better sense of size and proportion (image 16).

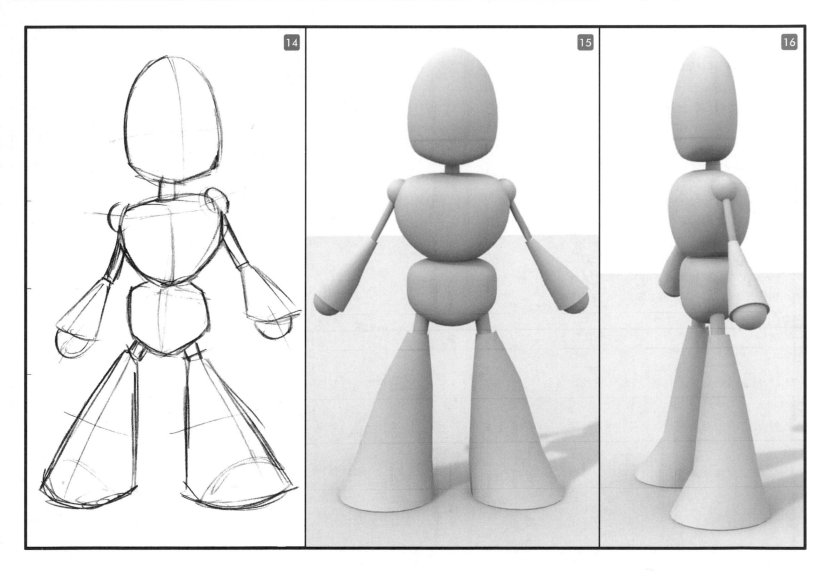

Construction Drawing

The construction technique works in the reverse order as well. I have a drawing of a simple tractor and, using an overlay, I've done a simple construction model to indicate its most basic shapes (image 17).

If drawing your design means doing the construction first, you'll need to connect those shapes with smooth contours and lines to get a more finalized design. I cover the connecting of shapes technique in the next section.

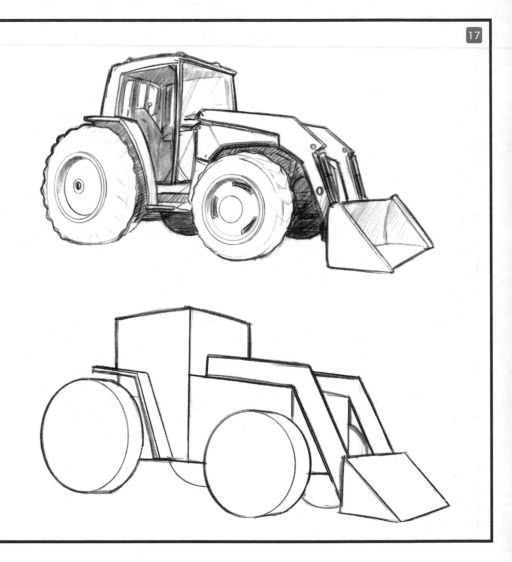

17

Construction

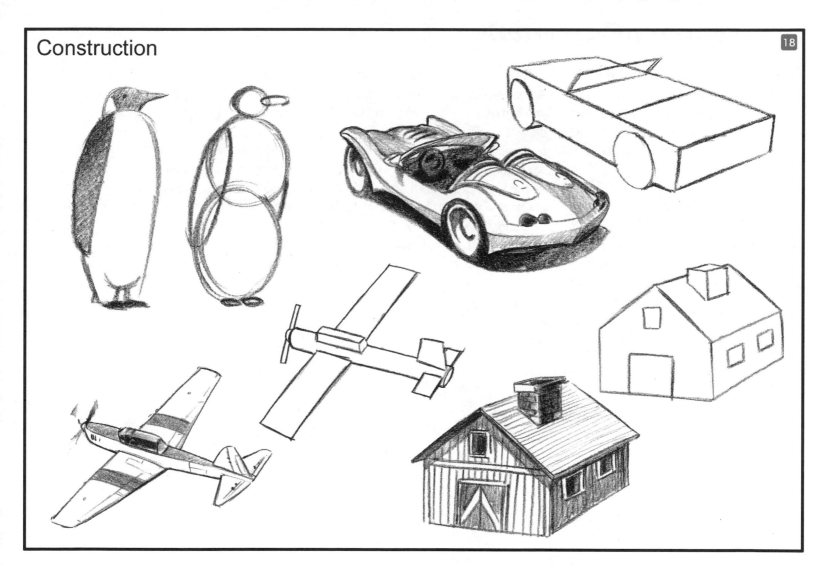

Connecting Construction

My process is to figure out my idea, do some rough sketching, and then do the construction on my design so I can get an idea of how to model it in 3D. Some people find it easier to do construction first because it gives them a guide they can stick to for rough proportion and shape. If your approach is construction first, the next step would be to connect those construction shapes with lines and contours to complete the design. If your process is to do a construction drawing after your design, that construction drawing will serve as a guide for your 3D model.

Taking our same construction character from the previous section, I've worked on sketching line work and detail that fill in the connective contours so that our character is more realized (image 19). At this stage, I would hardly call this a final design, but it's now starting to look like something.

Using the overlay rough sketch technique, I fill in more detail, shading, and shadow to get an even more complete character (image 20). Whenever I model in 3D, sometimes I want to get a quick idea of size and proportion, so I rough out my design using

construction, make adjustments if necessary, then using the 3D construction model as reference on a background layer, I start modeling the more sophisticated shapes.

Another technique is to design your object first, then using a three-view orthographic drawing, draw your model from three different views: front, top, and side. I'll teach the three-view orthographic technique later in this book.

Using the overlay technique, turn a rough sketch into a more detailed drawing.

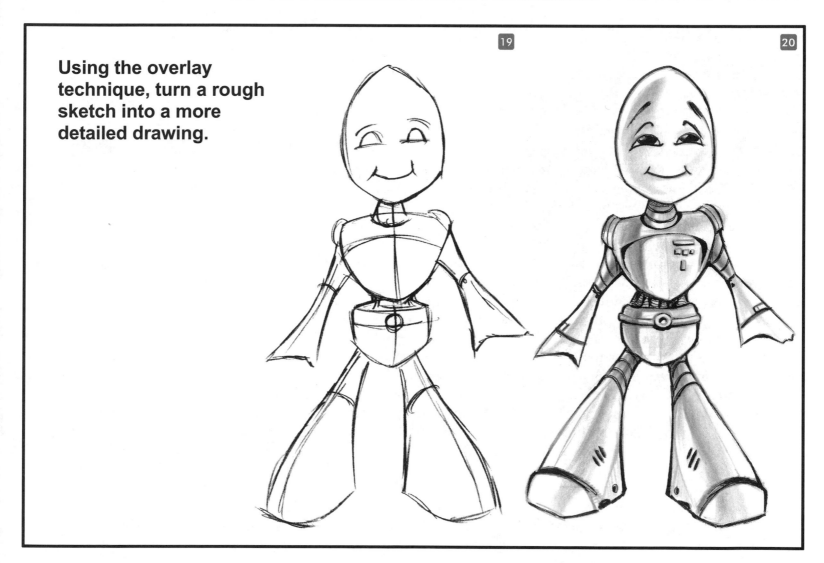

The KISS Rule

KISS is an acronym for "keep it simple, stupid." It simply means, keep the execution of your designs simple, straightforward, and easy to understand. It's sort of an equation that addresses the problem-solving aspect of design and takes into account human qualities like intuitiveness, perception, and patience.

A perfect example of the KISS rule in action is a pair of scissors. Scissors were invented to cut paper and are usually easy to use with a design aesthetic that embodies their function. In other words, the form and function are apparent upon review so that almost anyone can pick them up and use them effectively. In contrast, the remote control, one of the most utilized devices in our homes, can be a huge pain to figure out. There can be what seems like 50 different buttons that aren't labeled clearly or intuitively, the menu is confusing, or the shape feels awkward in your hand. The remote control is an over-designed product wherein most of its function

gets lost because most people don't have the patience to figure it all out. I'm not saying that there aren't great examples of simple, easy-to-use remotes, but in most cases, the designers overlooked the human quality of impatience and went for excess functionality. The goal of the KISS rule is all about having an idea that's as complicated as a remote control yet as easy to use as scissors, such as the iPod and the one-wheeled gyroscopic Segway.

How does this apply to us? The KISS rule should be something you keep in mind before you execute any idea. Let's say your goal is to design a cute robot character that is secretly a master of espionage. In fact, our robot — we'll call him "Bleep" — is so cute that no one takes him seriously and it kinda pisses him off. Just those few key descriptives like cute, pissed off, and robot are enough to conjure images of what he could look like. So in sticking with the KISS rule, let's address each key descriptive and start sketching. If

Bleep is cute, he should be small and maybe a little pudgy like a baby. We could give him a fat, rounded midsection, big head, big cute eyes, and one wheel. As for the pissed off part, that's all about expression and posing. If he's pissed all the time, we're going to take those big cute eyes and make them angry, and add a small frown and stiff posing to help give him attitude. Now that I've got my list of design qualities, I can sit down and sketch something out (image 21). As you can see, Bleep is definitely cute, but he's got major attitude and it's that overemphasis on the pissed off part that makes him even more cute. Poor Bleep can't win unless you really piss him off. With guns blazing he now fulfills his role as the master of espionage, because his design says, "Don't mess with me." Now, I could have gone way over the top from the beginning by designing him with guns, armament, electronic gadgets, antennae, and night vision goggles, but that approach is too confusing and it doesn't

KISS Rule Example

Key Descriptives:

Cute

Pissed Off

& Secretly a master of espionage.

Original "Bleep" thumbnail sketch

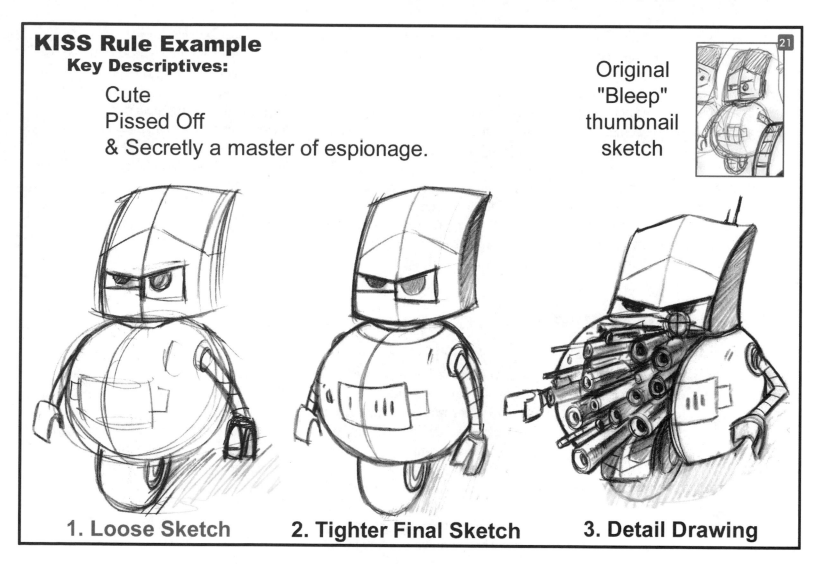

1. Loose Sketch

2. Tighter Final Sketch

3. Detail Drawing

say much about his personality except, "Don't mess with me." A cute robot that's pissed off is his personality and he exudes this. Giving a twist to the story, like making him a master of espionage, gives our audience something to look forward to and can be revealed at a later time. It's also important to mention that in the name of character development, if we as the audience can feel that a character reminds us of someone we know, it goes to further define our character's personality.

So, as you do the following exercises, I want you to stay focused on your inspiration and keep it simple.

Exercise 1: I'm going to give you a storyline and I want you to design for it, staying focused on the inspiration and keeping your design simple. Use reference material and draw this in whatever views you feel most comfortable. I want you to critique your work and then make improvements by resketching your design.

Story for KISS rule exercise 1: There is a bottle of ketchup whose name is Tom and he's a tour guide for the refrigerator. He's a happy-go-lucky kind of guy and since he spends more time in the refrigerator than most any other food item, he has lots of great information on the best places to visit.

Verbal Communication

Design as it relates to 3D is about visually communicating your ideas, but knowing how to back up your designs with a verbal explanation will allow you to communicate your ideas more effectively and successfully. For example, a day doesn't go by in which I'm not either pitching new ideas or explaining what I've created to a client. In your animation work, there will come a time that you have to explain your ideas to a client, and knowing why you chose your design themes will help you qualify their application and defend their existence. In other words, each design idea must have a reason for existing. For example, if you animated a scene that was to take place in heaven and you used a color palette of blues and white, you could rationalize that you chose blue and white because they seem spiritual and inviting. It's simple and it makes sense. Just think about your motivation and have a logical explanation to back it up. "Why are you doing this?" "Because of _____ reasons." Get it? Understanding the basic motivation behind your design work is essential from a visual and verbal standpoint.

Get a Good Pair of Headphones

What does this have to do with anything? Some people told me not to include this little section because they thought it veered away from the focus of the book. To them I say, "Who cares what you think? I know what works."

The fact is I love music. Many professional animators and artists will tell you that they listen to music while they work. Why? As an artist, I think music is the greatest complement to what I try to achieve visually, because it shuts out reality and provides a bed of sound to focus on my own world. It's there to inspire you and not for anyone else's benefit. So, buy a good pair of headphones and listen to music as you work; it's an investment in your career.

You Are Unique

This is an important section about recognizing and marketing the fact that you have a unique gift. Knowing how to define what separates you from everyone else is going to be the key to your success.

First I must digress for the purposes of example: When I attended art school, I was studying transportation design. The class that I was in was really small, like fewer than 40 students, as compared to some universities with hundreds. Our teachers were the best in the business and the atmosphere was incredibly competitive, with every student pulling all-nighters as the norm and with up to seven drawing and design classes, you were lucky to average five hours of sleep a night. This kind of non-stop pace would go on for about three years. The teachers were incredibly demanding and didn't like slackers, so if you slacked, you'd get an earful, like, "What is this!... Mr. Kater, do you really expect that with this kind of boring design direction that anyone in the world would ever buy it? Maybe you should reconsider your career!" I would just sit there with beads of sweat running down my face thinking, "I'm a loser... I'm done for... My dream is over." My teacher would say, "Come on!!! I know you can do better, give me something different, unique." I can thank him for the most severe tongue-lashing of a lifetime and the most life-altering moment in my career because he drove home the reality that being who I am makes me unique. My experiences, my thoughts, my ideas... if I could just tap into that uniqueness and exploit it, I would be good.

The lesson here is that even though I may be working on an idea that's been seen before, like a cartoon, sports car, or character, it has my own unique twist and execution. I analyze my work against others and look for the unique qualities that separate my work from theirs. I take a mental note and keep going. Don't settle for the norm —

push your work to the extreme, even if it's way radical, because you can always pull it back later. Believe me, a client would rather see one way far-out idea than a hundred mediocre ones.

On a similar note, I know people who savor every idea as if it were their last and hold onto it forever, hoping nobody finds out. As this applies to your career, you're supposed to offer up your unique ideas — that's what gives your work monetary value. In fact, you can define your career by the unique ideas you bring to each project because people will pay for them. If you're running out of ideas, then maybe this isn't the career for you. Put your ideas out there, learn from your mistakes, and don't look back. The fact is, the animation and visual effects industry thrives on unique ideas that can be marketed, so become the market trend. Bottom line, every company is pushing to be the best and most unique, so it's this quality of uniqueness that will make you a great hire. Knowing your worth in this industry is determined by the amount of money you can make for a company based on your ideas.

So for the sake of career, don't hold back, know what you're good at, and apply it to everything you create.

Quick Non-Boring Review

Hopefully you've spent the time to do all the exercises in this book so far, not only to amp up your drawing skills, but to give you the language of design. The language of design as it relates to what we're doing includes terms like contrast, proportion, inspiration, value, gesture, detail, and so on. This chapter was also about applying basic drawing techniques to your own ideas and the best ways to accomplish that task. Keep working on your rough sketching and gesture drawing, and remember to keep it simple, stupid. These fundamental exercises are bound to stick with you for the rest of your career.

Chapter Five

Research and Presentation

Introduction

What you learn in this chapter has an incredibly high value in my opinion, because without proper research and a successful presentation for any proposed project, you don't get the job. Since the goal is to spend your career getting paid for your ideas, you shouldn't let any opportunity slip by due to shoddy presentation material or disorganized research. No matter who you present your ideas to, whether it be a director, art director, executive, or a whole company, your ideas should be applicable to their project goals, be easy to understand, and look professional. This chapter will use a mock project for Nokia to illustrate proper research techniques and presentation styles, so let's begin.

Client Guidelines

A client to me is anyone who approaches you for the sole purpose of assigning or hiring you for a project. Whether you work as an employee or freelance artist, the person assigning you a project should be viewed as a client. I like viewing every assignee as a client because it establishes a more formal context from which I define my role as the hired artist. Ultimately the client is always right, because he is the one paying for the job, but knowing how to influence your client to accept your ideas is a skill directly related to service. Good service means doing your best to remain open and positive to all of your client's ideas, being there when he needs a good explanation of what you're doing, offering up as many solutions as necessary for the project, and making him feel confident that you're going to do a good job. This service is also influenced by circumstances like deadlines, budget, creative freedom, trust, personal taste, relationship, and so on. In the context of deadlines, success comes from a properly researched project, well-defined project goals, solid creative direction, and proper time for client input. No matter the circumstances, do your best to understand the client's needs, formulate a proposal, and then deliver what you promise.

Creative problem solving takes time. Make sure that you give your client ample notice of your needs as it relates to a schedule, and don't agree to show him something if you don't feel there's enough time to execute your ideas. Unless you're under the gun and the client wants an on the spot creative session, it's always better to give yourself a chance to absorb the project and come up with some ideas. Case in point: Whenever I ask any of the animators who work for me to make a change or come up with something new, they always respond with "No problem, check with me in an hour." I understand going into the situation that they need to work things out first, then once they feel comfortable with their creative choices, I get called in for a review of their work. A good client/boss will understand this, so take your time. Anything worth viewing is going to need some time for creative problem solving.

When coming up with ideas, I like to develop at least three different concepts. Why three? Simply put, variety. Everyone, including yourself, wants a variety of choices, so do your best to come up with a minimum of three different concepts for talking points. Perhaps your final project contains elements from all three or maybe just one, but all in all it bodes well for a well-researched presentation.

Mock Project: The client guidelines for the project we are going to research and present are as follows: Come up with a hip commercial idea for Nokia's new MP3 cell phone. It should appeal to teenagers and feature an animated cell phone.

1

Teenagers

Cell Phone

Music

Who's Your Audience?

Defining your audience is simply establishing the demographic or market appeal as it relates to your projects. The demographics for film and television are groups of viewers that are targeted with programming specifically because of their age, buying habits, income, family structure, education, and so on. It's simple — children's entertainment is created in such a way that children can relate and adult shows are created with adult themes and content. This targeting of specific groups motivates all forms of media so much that they will do almost anything to get your viewership. This is especially true with extreme reality shows like CBS' *Survivor* and NBC's *Fear Factor*. These shows are very popular and appeal to the 18 to 49 demographic, a core demographic that has a decent amount of discretionary income. It is for that reason advertisers spend millions on car commercials, beer commercials, movie trailers, and so on in order to get that demographic to spend. How consumers spend is the driving force behind marketing and so becomes the motivation for research into targeting these key markets. Since visual appeal plays a very important role within this context, design is influenced by the demographic as well.

Fortunately for us, our client Nokia has established the teen audience as our target market, and so our research should reflect an understanding of what appeals to teens. Our goal isn't to earn a Ph.D. in marketing to teens; it is to simply get a flavor for what they like. When given an assignment that needs some research, think about who you're trying to appeal to and keep that in mind as you gather reference material.

Teen Demographic

Gather Reference Material

Gathering reference material is easy and fun. It's the process of collecting images or video that reflect the taste and buying habits of your target market. It is also the process of collecting inspirational imagery that will inspire your design aesthetic, like colors, shapes, furniture, architecture, people, fashion, advertisements, and so on. This collection can be a group of images you found on the Internet, photocopies from a magazine, or video from a TV show. Whatever you use, you should collect what's needed and organize it for your project. When justifying your design themes to the client, you'll want to present this collection of images or video to show how your research has inspired your design choices.

Whenever you're doing research for a project, talk to your client first, because they may have already done the research for you. Through either a web site, brochure, or written material, most clients have something of value to add to the project. It could just be their opinion, but that opinion may give you a wealth of understanding about their business... in any case, the client is always right.

The first place to start to get information for our Nokia commercial would be from the people who assigned the project. Jot down their ideas first and then research the consumers they are targeting, in our case teens. If you know some teens, it would be great just to ask them what they like in the way of fashion, music, television, and so on. It's a win-win situation because you're actually talking to the target audience.

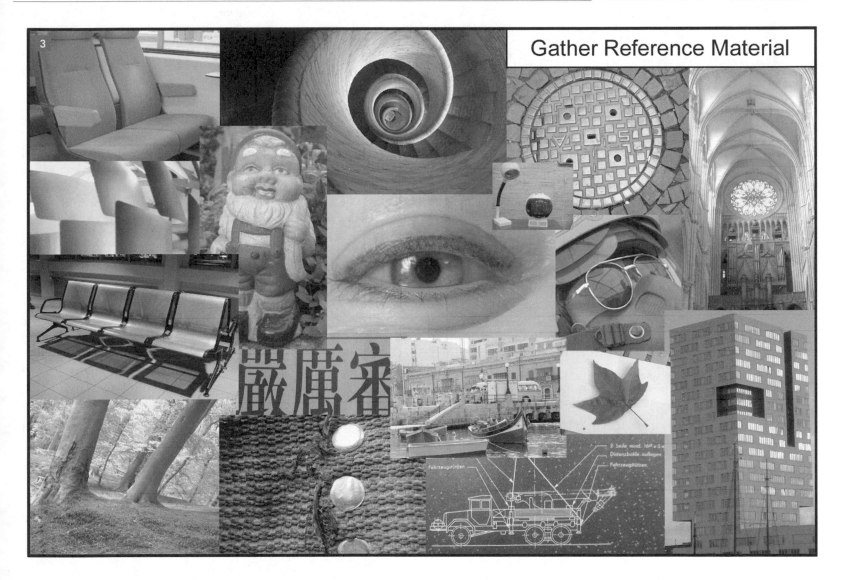

Gather Reference Material

A web site is another great resource. In our case, Nokia's web site is filled with an astounding amount of imagery and animation selling its products. Nokia has already spent millions on developing a web site that markets its products to the right people, so for the sake of our research, it's the best game in town. At first look, the web site may seem a little corporate, but with further research you'll find that each phone has its own web page. Each web page has been designed with an aesthetic appeal targeted toward that phone's core demographic, and if you look closely at the images, you'll see fashion, color, texture, graphics, and animation all used to entice the prospective buyer. This is exactly what we need. As I peruse the web site, I come across a phone that is marketed toward young people. It looks really hip and graphic, so I'll print some images for reference material.

I definitely get the feeling that Nokia sees itself as having a very hip and technology-driven product. Hip and technology are two great design themes that we can use as references for our project. At this point, I have a good idea of what Nokia thinks appeals to young people, but I want to look for a design angle that's different and cool, so I'm going to look for other sources of "teen" inspiration.

As my research continues, I want to look in the best place for observing the current trends in music, fashion, television, film, and advertising directed toward that teen demographic. When thinking about the best source for a collection of teen targeted imagery, I can only think of one — MTV. MTV is my old favorite, because it does a better job than anybody at appealing to a young audience through the use of dynamic animated visuals. Flip on MTV and watch for a while; you'll soon see the repeated use of color, music, celebrities, world events, fashion, sports, and so on in order to pique the viewer's interest. Make a list of these qualities like graphic shapes, text layout, motion, nostalgia, colors, and so on and if you're inspired by a specific image, draw the design themes like shape, proportion, and color to use for your research. Record a video or commercial that gives meaning to what you are trying to convey in the way of inspiration.

While observing MTV, I've noticed a recurring use of graphics, fashion, music, and color all inspired by iconic designs used during the '80s. I take note of what I like and I go online to gather printable reference material. The first thing I do is Google "trends in the '80s," and my search yields thousands of web sites dedicated to celebrating this era with details on fads, themes, music, and more. With an hour or so of searching, the most iconic theme I see repeated over and over again is that of classic arcade games, with titles like Donkey Kong, Asteroids, Frogger, Pac-Man, Defender, and Robotron. Yeah!

I was a kid in the '80s and nothing else existed for me after school except the local arcade. Even today I can't shake the video game bug. Now I feel that I'm onto something; in fact, '80s arcade games are so close to my heart that it will be a snap to come up with some cool ideas.

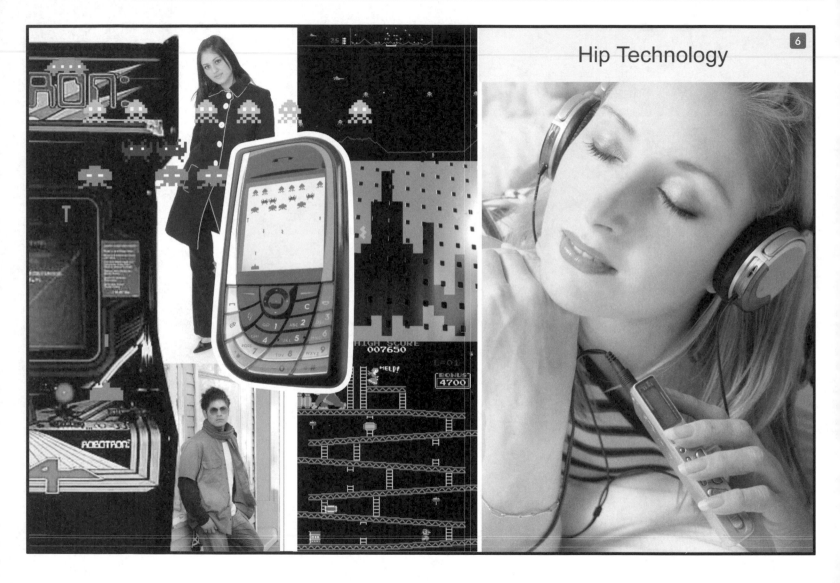

Hip Technology

6

My collection of reference material now includes images from the Nokia web site and images of classic arcade games. I spread the pictures out into a collage of sorts and try to get an idea of my design direction. With great inspirational images, somehow I see a cool fusion of hip technology and classic arcade games on the horizon.

"Great inspiration can come from just one source or a combination of many sources."

Define Your Concept

Defining our three concepts will consist of using all the reference material we've collected and examining it as a group. I feel like I should make a list of the qualities that are iconic to both my themes: hip technology and '80s arcade games. The hip technology angle uses a blend of contemporary colors, shapes, textures, and design that make it a fashion statement, with all of that applied to a fully functioning wireless phone with MP3 player, camera, video games, organizer, and so on. The '80s arcade games have a two-dimensional quality, with simplistic pixely shapes, dated sound effects, flat colors, simple designs, and linear game play that make them look really archaic, yet nostalgic. I'll create a list that clearly identifies the iconic design themes I think are the most useful for this project.

While I stare at both my images and my list, my inspiration comes to me in the form of three different concepts. Each concept addresses the need to appeal to teenagers through the use of retro-classic arcade themes and blends the hip technology angle that Nokia needs to sell.

It is now time to develop three scripts that describe our concepts.

Concept 1 (Arcade)

We open onto a black background and our camera is slowly pulling back to reveal simplistic '80s arcade game characters dancing to what sounds like a monophonic '80s video game version of hip hop. The camera is continuing to pull back and slowly the dancers turn into real teenagers dancing with headphones and Nokia phones in their hands. Our music slowly turns into full stereo hip hop. At this point we can see at least 20 teenagers. The edges of our Nokia's screen push past the edge of the camera to reveal that we've been looking at the Nokia's color video screen the entire time. The phone continues to float back until it settles, '80s arcade-style, and the text slowly dissolves onto its video screen and says, "MP3 ME." —Fade out.

Nokia Concept 1 "Arcade"

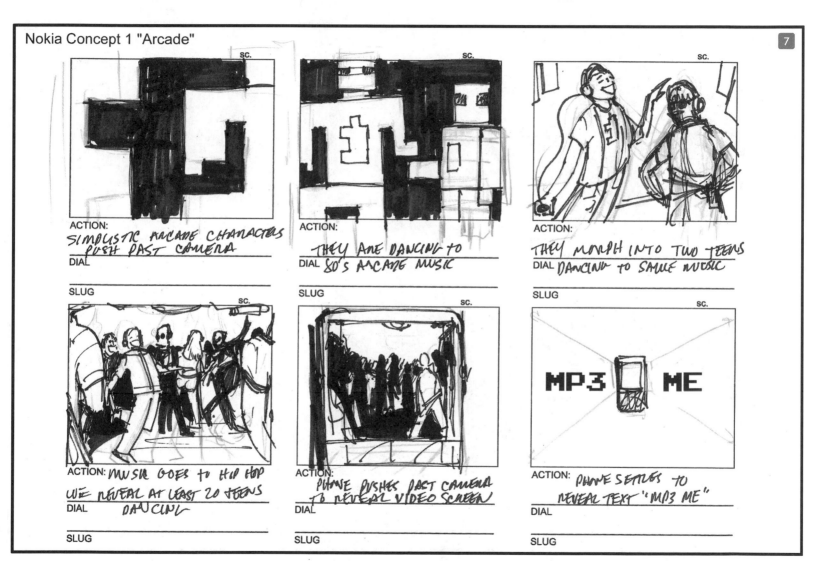

7

ACTION: SIMPLISTIC ARCADE CHARACTERS PUSH PAST CAMERA
DIAL
SLUG

ACTION: THEY ARE DANCING TO
DIAL 80'S ARCADE MUSIC
SLUG

ACTION: THEY MORPH INTO TWO TEENS
DIAL DANCING TO SAME MUSIC
SLUG

ACTION: MUSIC GOES TO HIP HOP WE REVEAL AT LEAST 20 TEENS
DIAL DANCING
SLUG

ACTION: PHONE PUSHES PAST CAMERA TO REVEAL VIDEO SCREEN
DIAL
SLUG

ACTION: PHONE SETTLES TO REVEAL TEXT "MP3 ME"
DIAL
SLUG

Nokia Concept 2 "Giant Phone"

8

ACTION: C/U KIDS DANCING

DIAL

SLUG

ACTION:

DIAL

SLUG

ACTION: PULL BACK TO REVEAL 20-30 DANCERS

DIAL

SLUG

ACTION: DANCING ON GIANT PHONE

DIAL

SLUG

CONNECTING

MUSIC

ACTION: TEXT DISSOLVES ON "CONNECTING MUSIC"

DIAL

SLUG

ACTION:

DIAL

SLUG

Concept 2 (Giant Phone)

We open with a low-angle shot, looking up at a few teenagers dancing to the monophonic video game music from Dig Dug. Our camera starts to rise and pulls back to reveal 20 or 30 more dancers. As we continue to pull back, we reveal that the dancers have been dancing on a giant Nokia phone. Buttons from the phone roll by and our dancing party ship slowly flies off into the distance. A classic arcade game looking text says, "Connecting Music" and fades off. This is a play on the real Nokia slogan, "Connecting People."
—Fade out.

ACTION: TEENS DANCING TO CORE SONG FROM 80's

DIAL

SLUG

ACTION: CUT TO GIRL DANCING

DIAL

SLUG

ACTION: CUT TO C/U GUY W/SHADES SMILING

DIAL

SLUG

ACTION: CUT TO SKATER KID DANCING

DIAL

SLUG

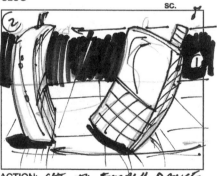

ACTION: CUT TO EMPTY DANCE FLOOR — NOKIA PHONE SLIDES IN.

DIAL

SLUG

MP3 IT

ACTION: PHONE DANCES AND GOES INTO BACKSPIN.

DIAL TEXT DISSOLVES ON "MP3 IT"

SLUG

Concept 3 (Dance)

We open up on a dance floor filled with '80s fashioned teens dancing to a song from The Cure with headphones in their ears connected to a new Nokia phone. The camera cuts from one person to another showing how much fun they are having. We then cut to an empty dance floor and suddenly a Nokia phone slides in and does a backspin… (like break dancing from the '80s). Text dissolves over our animation and says, "MP3 IT." —Fade out.

In the case of all three of these concepts I used animated visuals that would evoke the hip technology angle, then gave the visual design elements a nostalgic feel in the use of a classic arcade game text and characters. Along with my reference material, I've created the most basic storyboards on the planet… they're just enough to give the visual information I need to clearly illustrate my intent.

Presentation

There are many levels of presentation, whether it be very formal with a slide show and color booklets or informal with loose sketches and a brief explanation. Which level you choose depends upon your situation. In this situation, presenting our animation idea to Nokia is a simple, straightforward approach that doesn't require a formal presentation. The goal of our presentation is for the client to fully understand and accept our design choices, not to overwhelm them with visuals.

The simplistic approach consists of organizing all your reference material and storyboards into either printed material or a digital format. No matter which format you choose, it should represent your thoughts in an organized manner, to the point that it can stand on its own without explanation. If you decide to combine a printed presentation with a digital one, just make sure your digital files are named in a way that's easy to understand, like "Nokia_concept1_storyboards." When you are finished with your presentation, it should contain all the information necessary to outline your inspiration, animation concepts, and the deadline.

Warning! Never include original drawings in a presentation you're handing off to a client! Everybody loses a document now and then and you don't want your drawings to become the latest statistic.

Printed Booklet

Choose a size, most likely 8½" x 11". Include a cover page with a title, and then subsequently organize images, drawings, and storyboards into an order that makes sense to the client. Print it all out and bind the pages together in a nice presentation folder.

Digital Format

For a digital presentation, try to use the most commonly used digital files like JPEG, QuickTime, PDF, Word, Excel, etc. The best solution for a digital presentation is a file that nearly everyone can open on his or her computer — an Adobe PDF. Adobe Acrobat software is used by many animation professionals to organize text, images, and graphics similar to a printed booklet. If you don't have it, at least look into it. Another approach to the digital solution would be to have your cover sheet, concept explanation, and schedule as a single Word document and your research collage and storyboards as JPEGs. The easiest way to find out how to present your digital material would be to call your client and ask their preference.

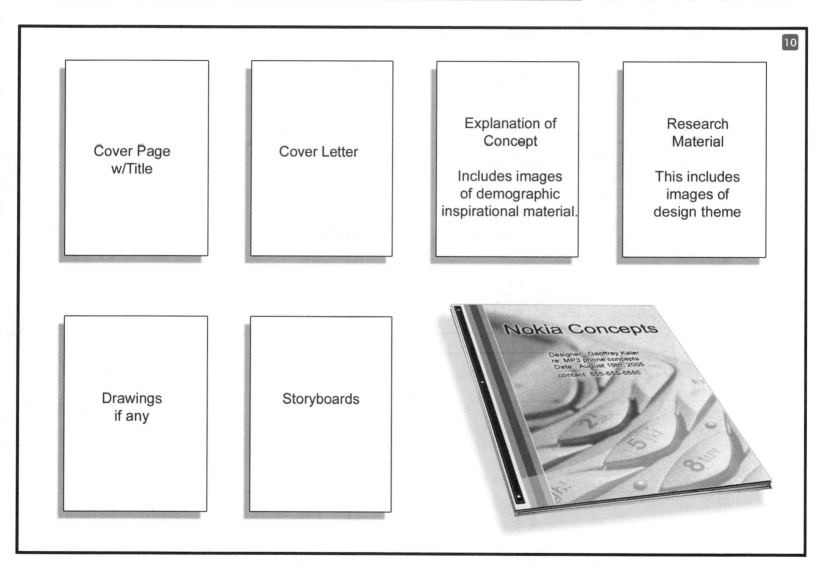

Thank You Note

This is part of servicing your client. No one likes to feel unappreciated, so always include a thank you note with anything you send to a client. It's a courtesy that you owe them for giving you this opportunity. It should read something like this: "Dear Client, I just wanted to thank you again for giving me this great opportunity. I think this project is going to look great. I feel pretty happy with my design choices and look forward to your input. I'll be available to discuss the project when you have time available. Thanks again…. signed me." Keep the note informal and friendly. Sometimes too much formality, like "fantastic opportunity," "I will await your call," or "earliest convenience," comes off a little insincere. Since client input is essential, include a little blurb about their participation in the design process so they feel you're open to critique. Sign it, seal it, and send it along with your presentation material.

Ultimately the Client Knows the Business

Now that we've gone through the steps to get our presentation material to the client, our next step is to get the client's feedback. It goes without saying that you feel your concepts are unique, well researched, and fit the client guidelines, but don't get too attached to your ideas because ultimately the client knows their business. What I mean by this is a client understands their corporate image and the core message the company is trying to project to a specific demographic. We were given the teen demographic and thus created three concepts that cater to the wants and needs of teenagers, but we could be wrong. The client is going to know whether your concepts fit within the parameters of their corporate image and won't be afraid to tell you. Our hope is that our proposal convinces the client that somewhere within our three concepts lies a golden idea, one that projects their corporate image and entertains as well.

If They Like Your Ideas

If the client likes your ideas, they'll either choose one concept and move ahead, or try to combine elements from them to create a new concept.

If They Don't Like Your Ideas

They could say that although they think your ideas are really cool, somehow they don't think they apply to this project. If they don't like your design approach, then you need to get details as to why. Perhaps they might say that '80s themes are old news and they're looking for something more glitzy and futuristic. If this is the case, then you should make it a point for them to give you another chance. If they agree, then it's time to revisit the research and presentation phase. Start your research while talking to the client for examples of commercials, fashion, or design themes they feel exemplify that design approach. Take good notes and then end the meeting with a phrase like, "I'll get going in this new direction and get some ideas to you soon." Have no fear, at least they're giving you another chance, probably because you gave them such a comprehensively researched proposal. The professionalism you display in your presentation will go a long way toward client confidence in your abilities.

Review

The Nokia situation is a real-world scenario that many professionals deal with on a daily basis. My approach is to be as professional and organized as possible to instill confidence in your client about your work. As for the aforementioned example of the client not liking your Nokia concepts, this can be resolved through a good client relationship and will give you the opportunity to develop new concepts based on a client's idea. Your goal is for the client to award you the job, so being organized, creative, flexible, and focused will give you the edge to finish what you start.

6

Your Project

Introduction

The process for executing your own project requires several stages, some of which you are familiar with and others that you're going to learn, so the key focus for this chapter will be to create a foundation of design for your own personal project. The foundation for any given project consists of phases like inspiration, story, and design focus. Without these, there would be nothing to create. You're going to need to dig deep into your creative mind to develop an idea that you really like and apply foundational design techniques to bring that idea to fruition. Since I don't want you to go it alone, I will develop my own project and teach through example in order to get you through each phase.

With careful thought, I have created a quick, fun story called "Feed the Dog." The subject matter and design content of "Feed the Dog" have been chosen to reflect the unique tone and purpose of this book, using design first. Your task will be to read through each section and start working on your own idea in conjunction with mine. This way you're experiencing the design techniques and project phases in real time.

The Assignment

Your assignment is to create a short animation no longer than three minutes. Since animation can take several weeks or even months to produce, we're going to focus on the traditional design aspects of your project without the requirement to animate the entire story. Since some of you have lots of animation experience and could animate the entire story, to you I say, "Go for it." For those of you just learning about 3D, you should focus on a simple subject and choose a simple scene to animate. Either way, if things go the way they should, by the end of this book you will have an outstanding foundation from which you can create your own animated short.

You can choose any subject matter, as long as it's designed in a simplistic manner with your focal point being no more than one main object of focus. This object can be a character, a vehicle, architecture, a favorite toy, whatever… just make it simple and easy to execute. Good examples of a main character or object of focus would be a race car taking a turn at a speedway, an alien character dancing the hula, a honeybee collecting pollen, even a telephone coming to life. ;-) Whatever you choose, it should be something you like, something you'll feel passionate about and be proud of. Whatever you choose, your focus will be to use traditional design techniques to create design concepts from which your final animation will benefit. A good animation is always properly planned, creatively designed, and well executed.

Short Animation Concepts

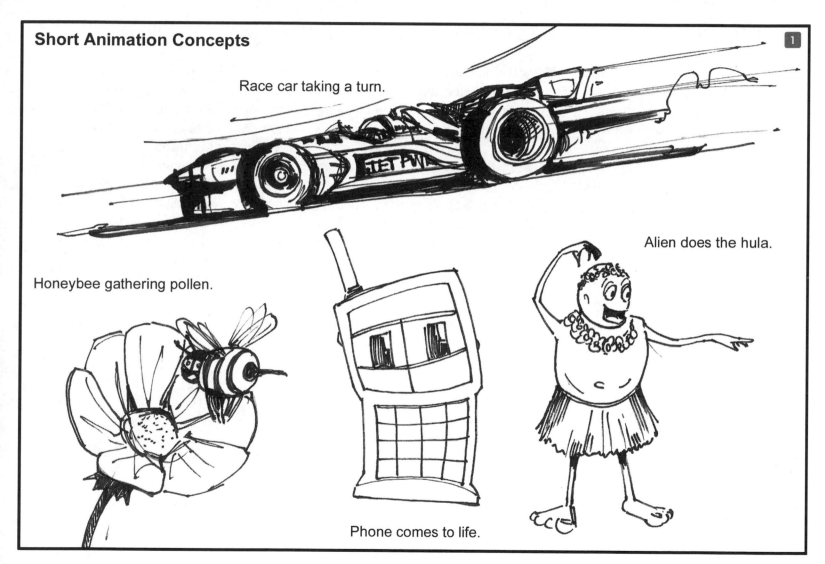

Race car taking a turn.

Alien does the hula.

Honeybee gathering pollen.

Phone comes to life.

Character

An adventure can be fiction or nonfiction, but no matter what, a good story is always based on good characters. Before we get into developing a story idea of our own, I feel it's important to spend some time understanding "character." Character is defined as "one of the attributes or features that make up and distinguish an individual." In other words, personality.

As a designer, your goal would be to make the character have an aesthetic that matches his or her personality.

Now remember, a character needn't be a living thing; it could be a talking candle, a dancing phone, or even a singing bush. Whatever it is, your main character needs to exude personality.

Since there are so many factors that go into creating that character from scratch, like attitude, gender, artistic style, physical stature, costuming, back story, etc., it takes a methodical process called character development to define the aesthetic nature and narrative of any given character. Once defined, those qualities are used to influence our character's actions during the character animation phase. Some liken character animation to acting, and I would agree. Most character animators have a mirror next to their computer, not to comb their hair but to work out facial expressions. I've even seen animators film themselves walking around like the character, just to be used for reference during the animation phase. No matter what, it all boils down to character development.

A good example would be if your character is defined as a bounty hunter who used to be in a motorcycle gang. On the visual side, you would have a lot to work with. I'm sure we all picture a bearded, burly, leather wearin', brass knuckles havin', tattooed biker dude who is as mean as can be and gets pissed when criminals make him drop his cigar. If we were to draw this guy, his character or personality would be apparent in our sketches.

Define "character" within your designs.

Creating a compelling unique character from scratch is incredibly complicated. In fact, that's a whole other book, but for us, just knowing that a character's outward appearance should match our character's personality should be enough for you to start.

To take that kind of thinking to the next level, let's examine a couple of known characters in order to further enhance our design choices. One of the best examples of great character development is that of Darth Vader. Darth Vader's role within the *Star Wars* universe was that of the villain. His character created tremendous conflict within the storyline because he was so evil and so unyielding in his commitment to bring the universe to the dark side; you almost couldn't wait to see what he was going to do next. His character was that compelling. Not only did he act evil, but he looked evil. A towering, black-helmeted, half man/half machine, with an ominous voice and an even more ominous presence, Darth Vader's aesthetics matched his evil ways and even today, the name Darth Vader will bring an instant vision of evil… he's unforgettable. It is with this goal in mind that we strive to create animated characters that leave an unforgettable impression on those who watch our stories.

The following is a good example of two characters that have had equal screen time but completely different recognition. If I bring up the name Dr. Aki Ross, I bet that less than 10% of you know that Dr. Aki Ross was the central character in a hugely anticipated big budget feature titled *Final Fantasy, The Spirits Within*. I also bet that if I use the name Mr. Incredible, nearly 98% of those reading this book know of his character without giving it a second thought. This kind of strong character recognition can only come from a combination of great design, great acting, and great story.

Final Fantasy, albeit a beautiful movie, unfortunately suffered from an unclear, complex storyline and stiff character animation. Seeing some of the production design artwork, you'd be convinced that the creators had an amazing movie in their grasp. The visuals were wonderful and groundbreaking, yet the characters weren't convincing enough in animation and story to leave our central character, Dr. Aki Ross, emblazoned into our psyche forever.

In complete contrast, *The Incredibles* created such a rich and encompassing vision that it was hard to take your eyes off the screen. The story was brilliant, the character animation was amazing, and the production design was in perfect tune with the fantastic world they inhabited. Each character was as good as the next, with a great range of emotion and movement. I bet if you were to look at the original character sketches of Mr. Incredible, you would see an awe-inspiring pose and a magnetic personality that just radiates off the page. As a superhero, his body is sleek and majestic, with a square jaw and inviting grin, his eyes are stern with conviction, and yet he looks friendly and humorous. An inspiring sketch like that embodies the spirit, soul, and story within a well-developed character.

Whether it be in the written word or from a beautiful sketch, we all have a lot to learn from those who've made a success out of the characters they've created.

Inspiration for Story

Inspiration was covered quite a bit in Chapter 4 with the "how to find it and how to apply it" scenarios and how others like Volkswagen used inspiration to create the new Beetle. In Chapter 5's Nokia project, we did a real-world scenario of taking a client's general ideas and using them as a springboard to construct a full creative vision.

As for finding inspiration in this chapter, this should be all about YOU. I want you to let your imagination run wild as you develop ideas that you think are cool pertaining to your animated project. Don't be afraid to first start with broad strokes, big ideas, and the like, because you can always whittle them down to a simple subject of focus later. For example, I see an overall World War II air battle, with thousands of fighters and bombers, slowly condense into a simple dogfight between two war-hardened air aces (image 3). As it pertains to our simple animated project, the war ace idea is a pure example of taking a big idea and then interpreting it into something real and applicable. Focus on finding an idea that you really like and then stick to it. Choose something that fits your skill level and don't overcomplicate the process by choosing a subject or story that is way out of your league. Even a simple story can be fun and applicable, like a flower blowing in the breeze, a fly-through of a living room, or a brief-case that opens and closes. The important thing is for you to apply your newly developed design skills to create a well-designed 3D animation.

At this time, put on your inspirational thinking cap by whatever means you deem necessary: walking in the park, surfing the net, reading a magazine, sketching odd shapes, or just staring at a blank page. When you come up with some cool ideas, jot them down. Even if you're not 100% happy with all your inspirational ideas, don't trash them; you never know if they will come in handy at a later time. When you eventually have that golden idea, go back to your work area and put it into words in a more formal context, like a paragraph or short outline. Whatever you do, formalizing your idea gives it purpose and helps keep things organized.

The following section gives an example of how I condensed some of my inspirational thoughts into a formal context that I later expanded into a story.

Narrow down concept to a single instance.

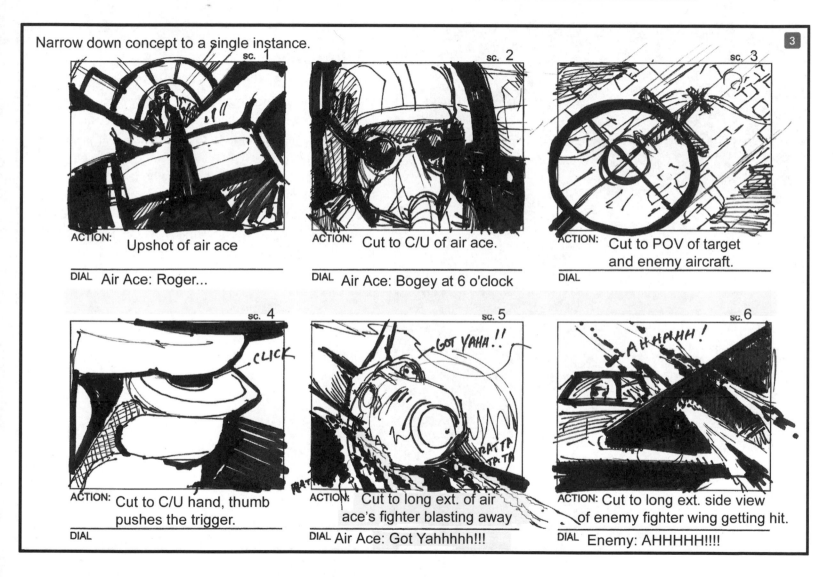

sc. 1
ACTION: Upshot of air ace
DIAL Air Ace: Roger...

sc. 2
ACTION: Cut to C/U of air ace.
DIAL Air Ace: Bogey at 6 o'clock

sc. 3
ACTION: Cut to POV of target and enemy aircraft.
DIAL

sc. 4
ACTION: Cut to C/U hand, thumb pushes the trigger.
CLICK
DIAL

sc. 5
ACTION: Cut to long ext. of air ace's fighter blasting away
GOT YAHH!! RATTA TA TA
DIAL Air Ace: Got Yahhhhh!!!

sc. 6
ACTION: Cut to long ext. side view of enemy fighter wing getting hit.
AHHHHH!
DIAL Enemy: AHHHHH!!!!

Angus

4

My Inspiration

My inspiration came from my friends' dog Angus, who happens to be a small and incredibly rambunctious terrier with unending amounts of energy and playfulness. When I walk in the door, Angus gets so excited he leaps nearly two feet into the air, hopping around as if on a pogo stick because he is sooooo happy to see me... it's his way of saying hi. It cracks me up every time I see him because he's such a character... literally. Over time Angus became a character in my head and helped to inspire my animated story.

Story, Story, Story

The goal here is to establish a story based on my inspirational thoughts, the source being Angus the overexuberant dog. As I spent time writing ideas based on Angus, I couldn't help but think of how cool it would be to create a funny dynamic between our excitable little dog and his loving master. It was at that time I remembered our good little buddy "Bleep" from Chapter 4, you know, the "cute" little robot who is secretly a master of espionage. I really loved Bleep's character because he is so serious, yet because of his cuteness, no one takes him seriously. That's a hard reality to accept if you're a master of espionage, so I figured a frustrated little robot like Bleep deserves the unconditional love of a dog like Angus.

I wrote up a story I've titled "Feed the Dog" that goes like this:

Ext. Open on a firefight in progress … blam, blam, etc.

Bleep is fighting like mad, an evil bot named "The N4CER" lunges at him and misses!!

"Ha Ha!!" Bleep exclaims and without a beat jumps on The N4CER's back. While beating him from behind and holding on for dear life, Bleep remembers (flashback to his kitchen, wife standing there polishing one of a huge collection of knickknacks hanging on the wall) his wife saying, "Now honey, I know how busy you are defeating killer robots and vicious double agents, but don't forget to feed Angus before you leave. You know how he gets when he's hungry." Back to reality, Bleep jumps off The N4CER and transforms into a mighty fighting machine as his chest opens to reveal guns a-blazin' and he opens fire. Blam, blam, ratattatattattat, blam, blam!!!! The N4CER falls to his knees and is knocked out… stars circle above his head. Bleep quickly transforms to normal and takes off.

Cut to — Bleep's kitchen. Angus is waiting patiently and then flies off the floor at the sight of his master. Angus is superexcited, buzzing around and barking…

Bleep — "I know, I know… sorry, dude… I forgot… uugh." Bleep sighs… He grabs a box of "Bowser Bolts" and starts to fill the doggie dish with nuts, screws, and other metal pieces when suddenly KABLAM!!! Over the shoulder we see The N4CER blast through the wall, smashing the wife's entire knickknack collection.

Bleep — totally surprised, "Awwww maaaaaan! My wife's gonna kill me!"

Angus, thinking The N4CER is a visitor, starts buzzing around him and jumping up and down with excitement.

The N4CER doesn't know what hit him. "What the…." He's never seen such an overly excited dog. He tries to stop Angus by saying, "Down boy, down… go away, stop… come on now… down boy… good boy…" Even The N4CER can't help but be smitten by Angus' charms.

With The N4CER distracted, Bleep picks up a nearby chocolate cake and smashes it into The N4CER's face.

"Awwwww!!!!" The N4CER screams. "Awwww, I hate chocolate!!!" The N4CER has cake all in his eyes — he can't see a thing! The N4CER stumbles around, swinging into thin air, while Bleep and Angus dodge The N4CER's attempts to capture them. Bleep picks up Angus' doggie dish and repeatedly bangs The N4CER on the head… Bong! Bong! Bong! Bong! Bong!… forcing The N4CER to stumble backward. While this is going on, Angus opens the door behind The N4CER labeled "Trash Incinerator" and The N4CER falls in. Angus shuts the door, and with a push of the "Incinerate" button, Angus, our fearless hero, saves the day.

Angus looks to Bleep for approval and Bleep says, "How could he not like chocolate cake?" Angus leaps up and licks Bleep on the face…

Bleep says, "Good boy… you did good."

— end

The next goal will be to find visual inspiration that matches the story. In a production situation you would have to

5

adhere to stricter guidelines as far as what you design and what is used as an influence, but in our case, we're not working from anybody else's script, just our own. We have the freedom to do what we want because we're the writer, designer, and animator, and if our story evolves into something better through the inspiration of our visuals, then so be it. As for "Feed the Dog," I have some initial design ideas but I really want to do my research and find something unique. Hopefully I'll find something unique and compelling that will enhance my storyline. It's really hard to judge what you might stumble upon as far as visual inspiration. In fact, some people start with visual inspiration first and work toward a story. In our case, like production, the story has already been written; we just happen to have creative license to change it. All I can say is leave yourself open to whatever you think is cool, because you can always adjust your story to meet the needs of your visuals at a later time.

Breakdown: What Is Your Design Focus?

Our design focus here is to break our story down into its essential elements, which include characters, props, and backgrounds. This process is called a *breakdown* and is done simply by listing each character, prop, and location in the order in which they appear to give us a comprehensive list of all the items we need to design. My breakdown for "Feed the Dog" is as follows:

Characters
Bleep
The N4CER
Bleep's Wife
Angus

Props
Knickknacks
Polishing cloth
Box of Bowser Bolts
Doggie dish that says "Angus" on the side
Nuts, screws, and other metal pieces
Chocolate cake
Trash incinerator button

Backgrounds or Locations
Exterior (or Ext.) Open field for firefight
Interior (or Int.) Wall of knickknacks
Int. Bleep's Kitchen
Ext. of Trash incinerator
Int. of Trash incinerator

Before we start designing anything, we have one more final step: design direction.

Design Direction

There are two key elements that make up your design direction: style and inspiration. Style is more concrete, like designing something whether it be modern or retro, organic or industrial, classic or futuristic. Inspiration is responsible for the design spin that you give an object, for instance, a plasma screen inspired by an art deco building from the '40s, a spaceship inspired by World War II tanks, or a sofa inspired by the architecture of Frank Gehry (image 6).

This added level of inspirational themes that permeates your design style combines to create your design direction. Once you choose this direction, it will influence everything you design from the overall structure to the smallest detail. This is the goal of all designers, to choose a style and instill it with something unique, whether from the past or right out of their heads. I've seen a motorcycle inspired by a cheetah, a coffeemaker inspired by a streetlight, headphones inspired by a modern bridge, even a modern character inspired by the wings of a dove. The combinations are endless and it is your job to capture those design themes and apply them in the most tasteful and simplistic way. The only thing left to do is choose.

How to choose can be very frustrating and time consuming, but use the methods taught earlier in the book for finding inspiration, and everything else will fall in line.

A good place to start would be to think about the time and location in which your story takes place. Is it a modern story or a period piece? For instance, if your story takes place in the wild west, most of your design direction is gathered from old western art, clothing, tools, architecture, etc. The design, clothing, and architecture reflect the style of that period. You can easily achieve this because there is more than enough reference to help inspire your designs, but translating it literally leaves less to the imagination. It may be fun to draw all those cowboy costumes and horsedrawn wagons, but it would be a lot more fun to put your own personal spin on the design from that era. The movie *Wild Wild West*, starring Will Smith, is a great example of western style with a retro-technology influence. The production designers

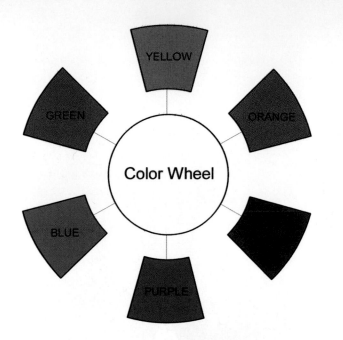

Color Wheel

YELLOW
GREEN
ORANGE
BLUE
PURPLE

WARM COLORS

COOL COLORS

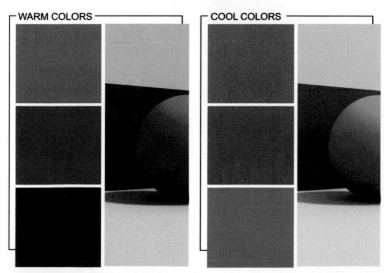

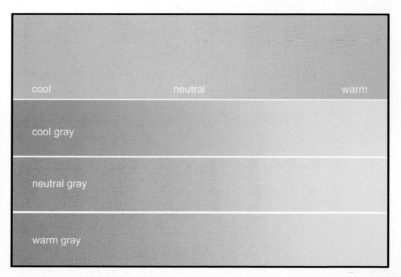

cool   neutral   warm

cool gray

neutral gray

warm gray

C-1

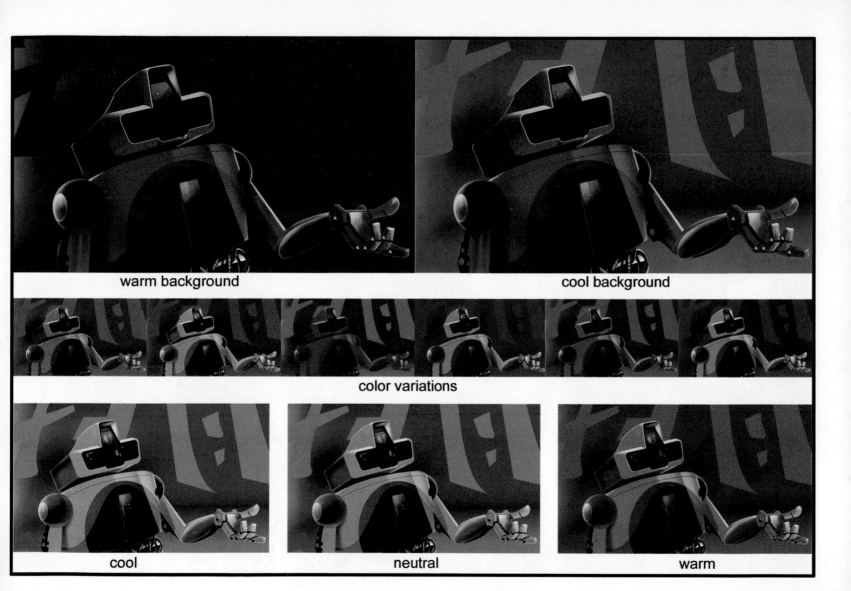

warm background

cool background

color variations

cool

neutral

warm

C-6

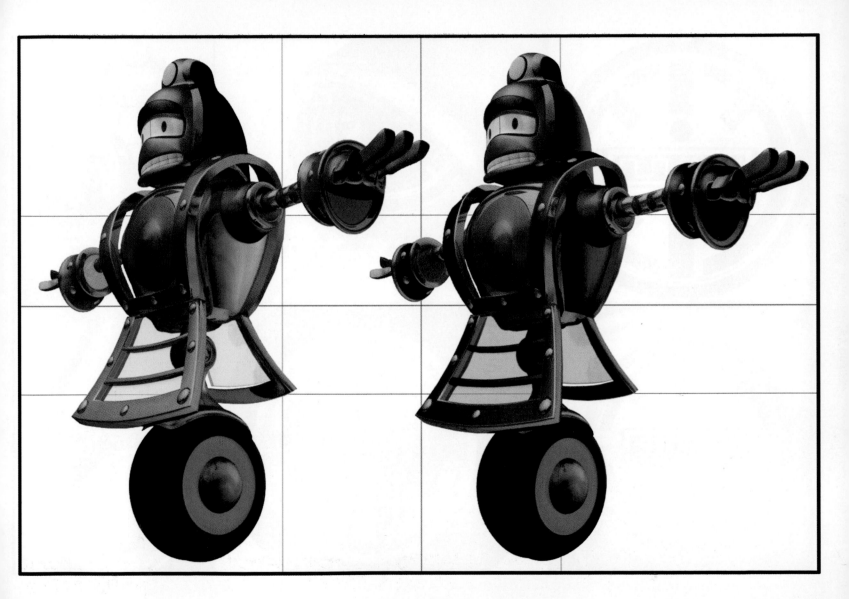

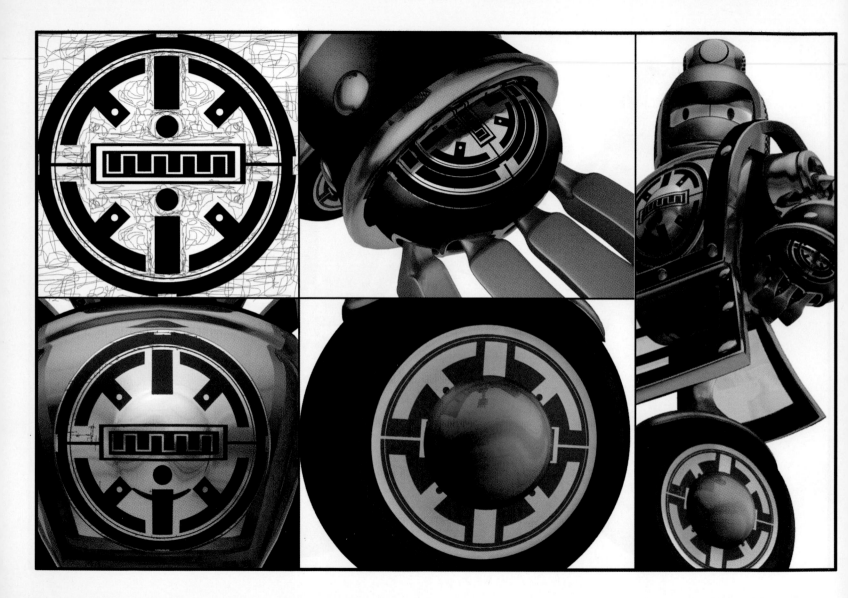

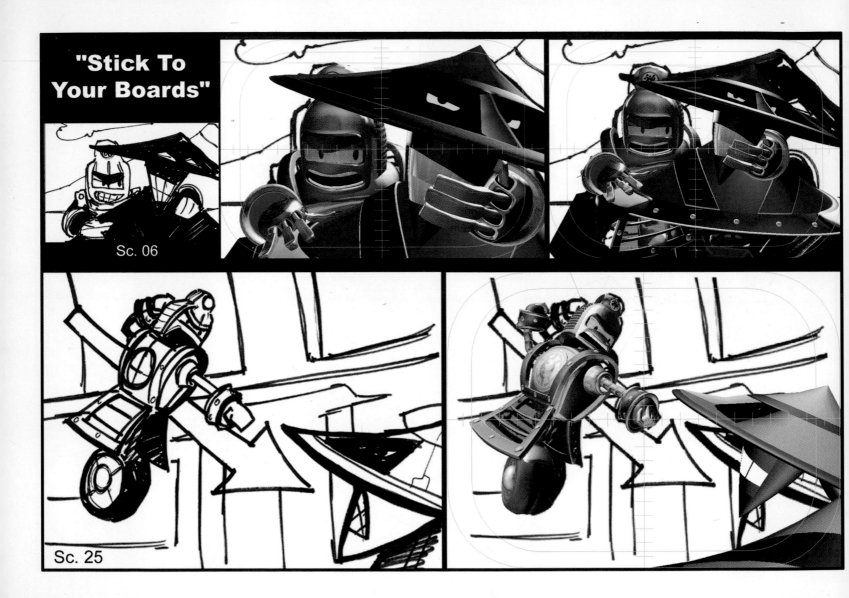

No light

Sun light only

Sun, reflected and bounced light

Sun, reflected, bounced and ambient light

Bleep 3D Orthographic

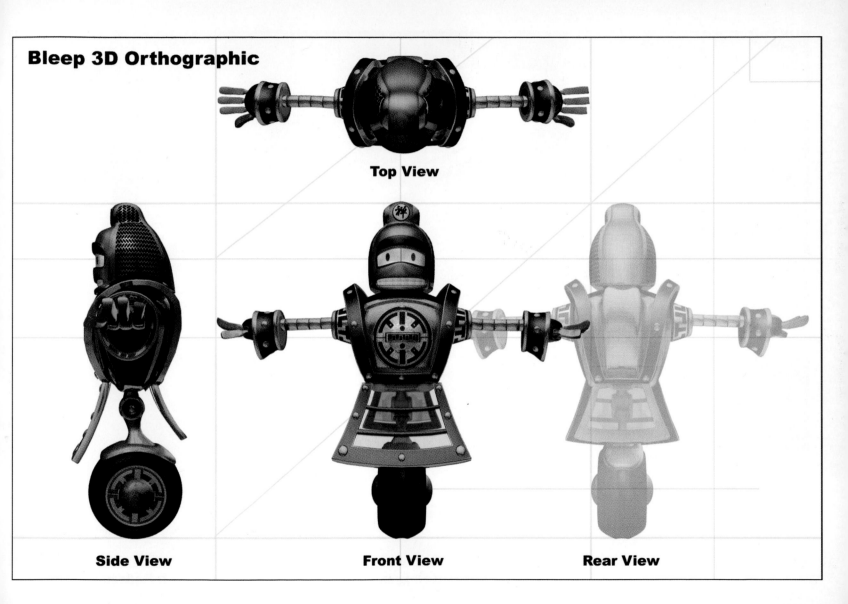

Top View

Side View

Front View

Rear View

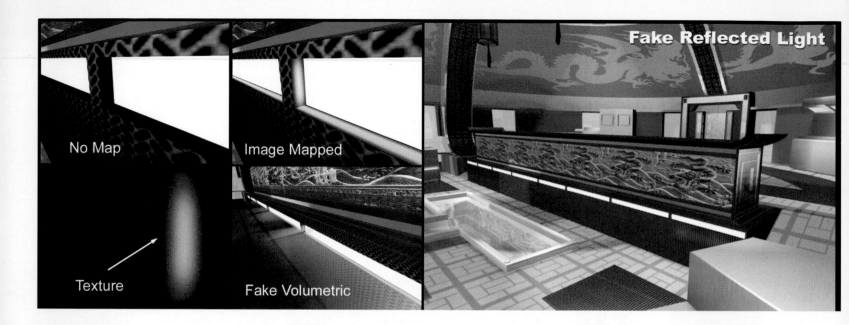

No Map

Texture

Image Mapped

Fake Volumetric

Fake Reflected Light

Hard Reflection

Blurred Reflection Map

Soft Reflection

Fake Depth of field

Edge Blur

Motion Blur

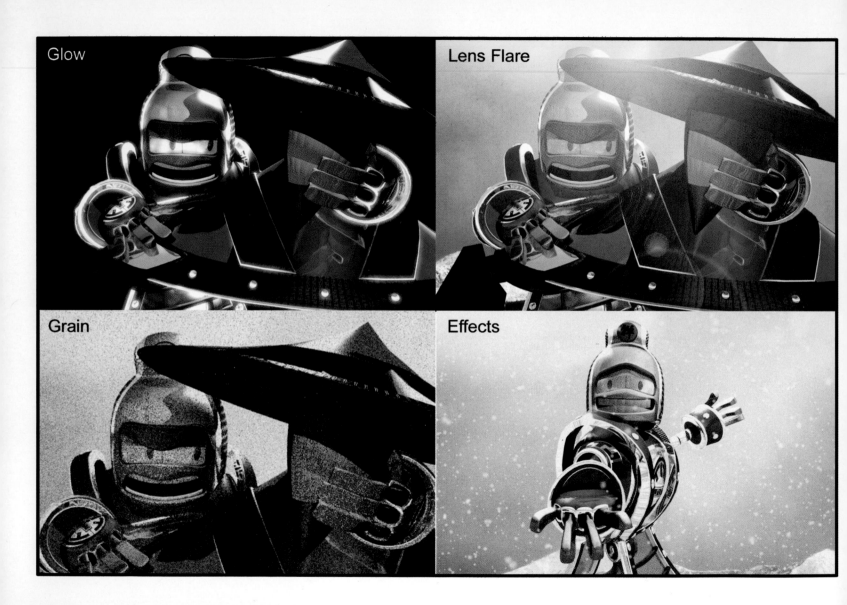

Glow

Lens Flare

Grain

Effects

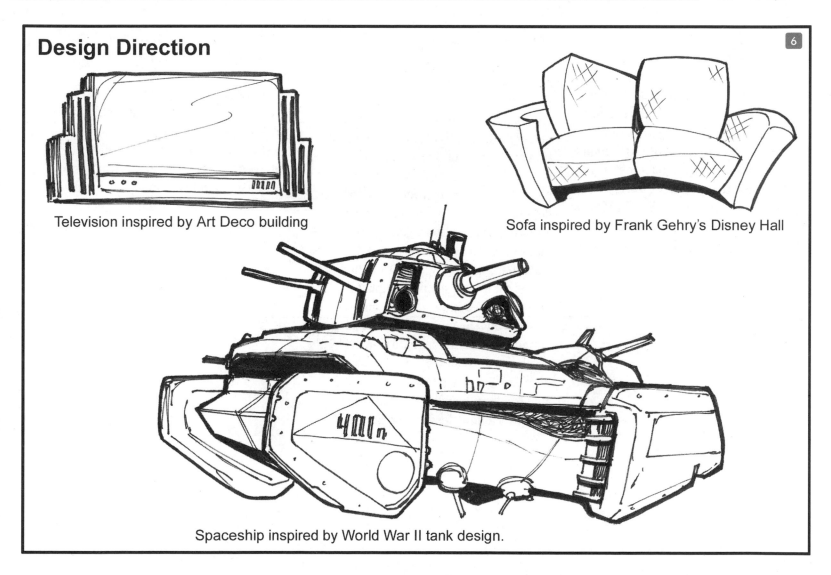

Design Direction

Television inspired by Art Deco building

Sofa inspired by Frank Gehry's Disney Hall

Spaceship inspired by World War II tank design.

created gadgets that didn't exist in those days, like a steam-powered wheelchair and a giant steam-powered spider walker, yet the wheelchair and walker exuded the exquisite detailing, craftsmanship, and western design themes of that time. My original point, that you can add a spin to almost any style, means that you have a wide-open opportunity to discover something new. As long as it makes sense, feel free to merge style and inspiration to develop a design direction that is truly unique.

My Design Direction

After a lot of research, I have chosen ancient China as the inspiration for my visuals. I felt that a strong cultural influence from the past could add a rich quality to the design, color, and execution of my project. I picked up a great book titled *Ancient China* and am completely entranced by the level of artistic detailing in the clothing, armor, art, architecture, weapons, sculpture, and tapestries. The intricate use of floral patterns, calligraphy, sculpture, and bright colors set against simplistic structures of bamboo, wood, and rice paper is awe inspiring. Awe inspiring enough that I am hooked. I figured by using ancient Chinese art as an influence for "Feed the Dog," I might be able to fuse a visually exciting story that puts a new design spin into the often used theme of *robotic machines*. With the popularity of Japanese manga and animé, there is no doubt that traditional Japanese art and design has inspired futuristic fantasy animation works, but it also goes without saying that the use of animé design will eventually become so common it won't be considered unique anymore. So if we use a different inspiration, like that of the great dynasties of ancient China, we might beat the odds by creating something distinctive and fresh. With the correct application, "Feed the Dog" may not only be a fun little story, but may offer a unique visual twist that adds to the compelling visuals of my animation. So, with all of that in mind, I've chosen the design direction of futuristic robot world meets ancient China — and with that, the fun part begins… design!

See color plate on page C-4.

Design It — Make It Fresh, Different, and Inspiring

I've laid out my breakdown, sketch pad, and a few selected images from ancient China that will serve as inspiration. The images that I found the most inspiring and applicable to my story are the more solid architectural shapes found in the armor, weapons, helmets, and sculptures. My goal is to capture some of these architectural shapes in the overall structure or silhouette of my designs, and at the same time detail the broader parts with intricate Chinese patterns and calligraphy. These broader parts would include backgrounds, flooring, armor shielding, furniture, and any other object or place that would benefit from an artistic pattern. As for color, that will come later. For right now I want to focus on capturing key shapes and subtle detail with a Chinese influence.

Now that we have a solid design direction and full breakdown, we can start designing each item on our list using what I call design exploration. Design exploration is just that, letting your pencil explore the paper with line work that finds the unique shapes and details that will become the springboard for your designs. Exploration is not just a manual process but a mindset. Some people can actually picture their ideas in their heads and, without even thinking about it, translate that to inspirational sketches, while others find themselves drawing aimlessly until a shape or line appears. Either way, your mind should be consumed with your design direction. Whether you sketch your design the first time or the tenth time, design exploration is a technique that requires focus and discipline.

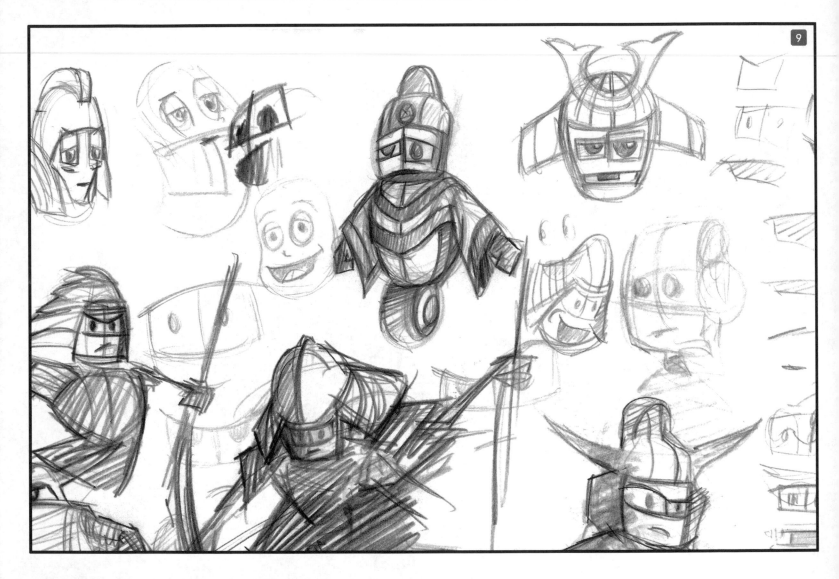

Let's begin. Choose your first design element, whether it be a character, prop, or BG, and using your inspirational material, start with an easy sketch technique like gesture drawing or thumbnail sketching (image 9). This process is a little more abstract because we're not sure what designs are going to develop, but try to think of your subject matter and put that down onto paper. Open your mind, let the pencil explore, and the more you sketch, the more options you will have. Don't settle too quickly; be sure to let your hand warm up.

Bleep

I've sketched many pages that contain my ideas for my characters and how they might look. Bleep gets his inspiration from an ancient Chinese soldier (image 10). The soldier's armor suit is incredibly intricate with woven leather sleeves, pants, and skirt. His brass helmet is embossed with detailed patterns and calligraphy. His suit also contains thick black horizontal and vertical stripes, strewn with small brass rivets. That kind of stuff is so awesome that I feel inspired just thinking of the possibilities.

Most of my sketches at this time are exploratory, meaning I'm not settled on one or another. I'm still searching for a character expression or pose that feels right to me. This is truly the development experience (image 11). Bleep's body is comprised of interpreting those large black stripes into some sort of exoskeleton that surrounds his body. Most of Bleep's shapes are organic and curved, which give him a more friendly and likeable quality, but in the interest of his tougher side, I created a "contrast" in aesthetics by using big industrial rivets to harden his appearance. Bleep's head is not only similar in shape, but contains the same kind of unique patterns and calligraphy that you would find on an ancient Chinese soldier's helmet. I have probably traced Bleep's head 15 times looking for the right contours, proportion, and shape. If you find a design you really like, do overlays until you get something that looks good (image 12).

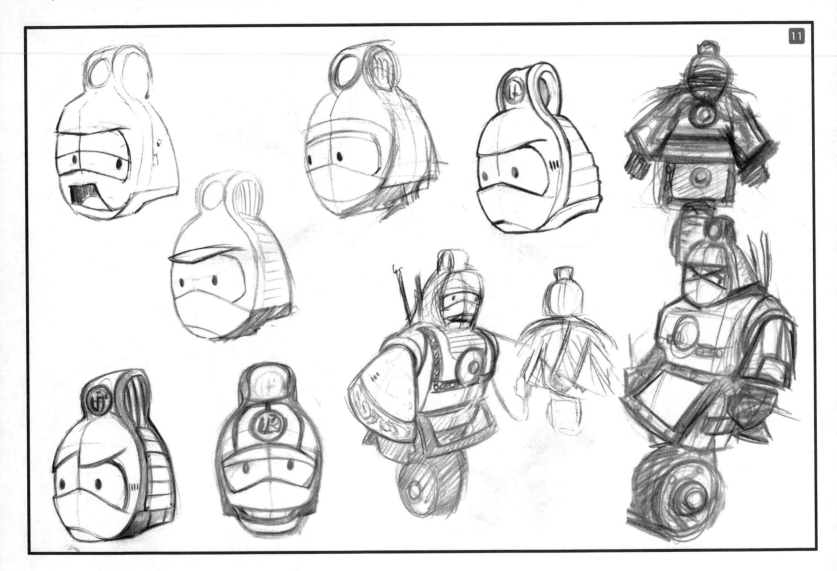

Angus

My next character is Angus. Angus gets his inspiration from a teapot (image 13). I just love the iconic shape of Chinese teapots, and in fact some of them even have legs. Those little teapots are kind of cute in a way, and since Angus' personality should personify cute, it was an instant match. However, I did go through a lot of design directions as seen in the sketches (image 14). I was also very inspired by the intricate patterns and calligraphy that seem to cover every inch of some of these teapots and actually found the calligraphy symbol for "dog" and embossed that on his side. I feel pretty good about my exploration with Angus, and with that I move on to our villain.

ANGOS "LAUGHING"

The N4CER

The N4CER gets his inspiration from a Chinese peasant hat (image 15). I thought a disc-shaped head with hidden glowing eyes would really add to The N4CER's mystery. From the standpoint of shape, the front of his head looks to be triangular, so I repeated that triangular shape throughout the rest of his body. His overall design is more angular and more aggressive than Bleep, giving us that "contrast" in their personalities. I've achieved what I feel is the most important design goal — The N4CER's exterior matches his personality... rough, tough, and aggressive (image 16).

At this point, your focus is to capture essential details and a strong silhouette; without them, moving on to 3D would defeat the design process. Perhaps you find that you don't like the direction your designs are taking, so feel free to move back to the thumbnail stage and do more exploration. Remember all the things we learned about design: odd proportions, silhouettes, gesture drawing, contrast, and line thickness. Give your designs a unique, inspired quality with fun, undulating line work and oddly proportioned shapes. I know this may be tough for some of you, but the more you draw the easier it will become.

At this point I want to work on all the items in my breakdown and bring them to a rough sketch level.

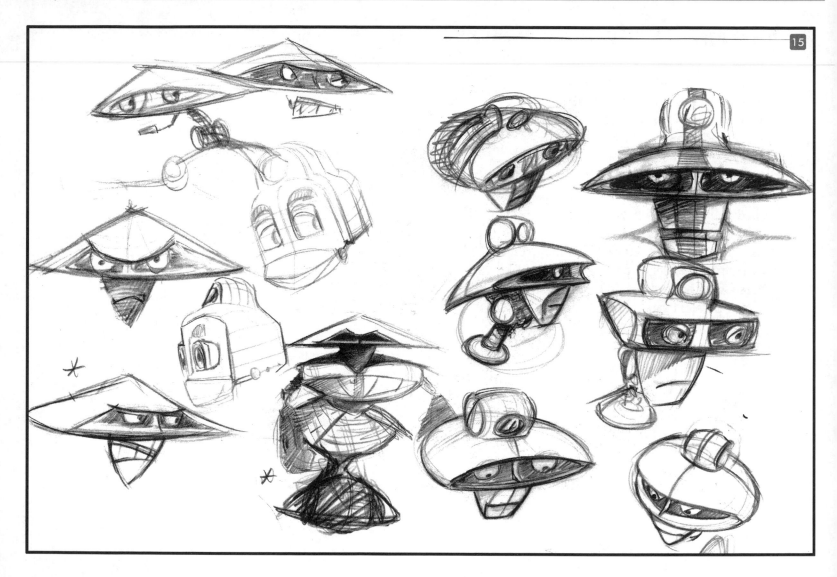

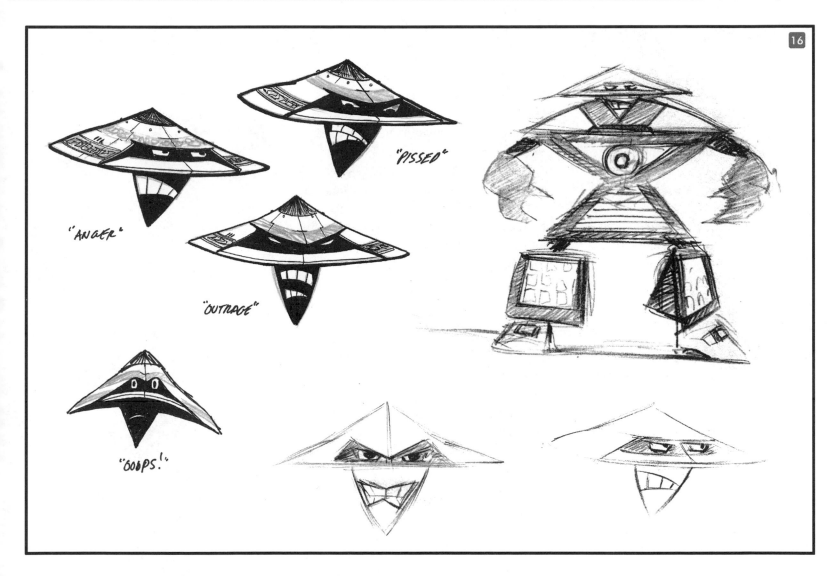

"ANGER"

"PISSED"

"OUTRAGE"

"OOOPS!"

Keep the Gesture

As covered in Chapter 4, some of your new sketches could have started with an initial gesture drawing — that real quick, get it down now and capture the inspiration in under a minute type sketch. Keeping the gesture is about keeping the loose, fun, gestural line quality of your initial sketches into the tight line work of your final designs. Adding design detail and cleaning up my roughs with tighter line work will impose a much more controlled, strict, and well-defined line quality. This tightening up of the line quality has a tendency to lose the gestural quality of your initial sketches and result in a stiffer, less interesting final design. A stiffer final design will have less character and inspirational qualities that make a character compelling to watch as well as animate. The real question is how do we translate gestural line quality into the final? As an example, I've created two versions of Angus (image 17). One version is very loose and sticks to the organic line quality of my initial sketch. This drawing has lots of character and even though it's a tighter drawing, it still feels fun and energetic. The second is a stiffer interpretation of the line work and has a lot less character.

Our next section, "Refine Your Designs," is about applying the gesture to the final design. As you start the refinement process defining contours, shapes, and details, keep the gesture by staying loose yet controlled and fulfill your design's potential with character and energetic line work that leaps off the page.

Keep the Gesture: It's the subtle things that matter.

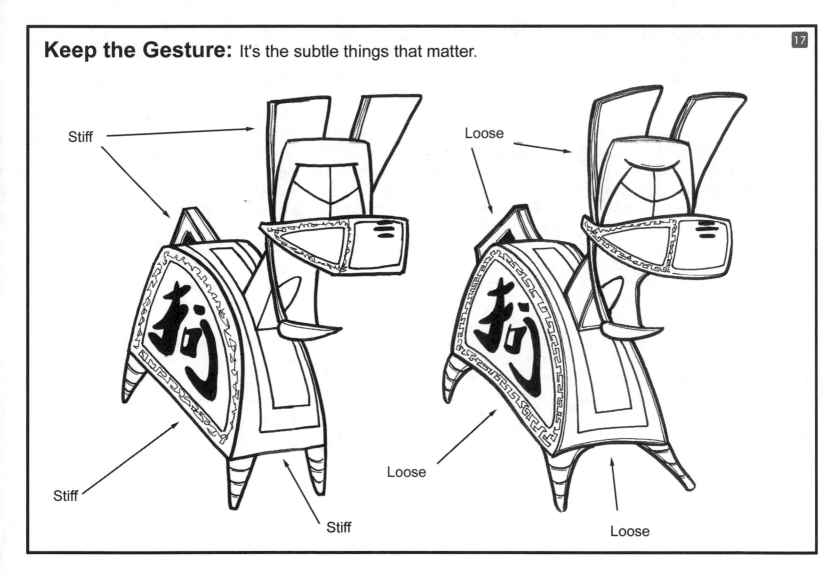

Stiff

Loose

Stiff

Loose

Stiff

Loose

Refine Your Designs

As we progress into refinement, it ultimately leads to our final design, which should encompass a strict focus on everything we want our design to exude, both visually and narratively. Visually, from the standpoint of our design looks appealing, and narratively in that you know the design's role within the story. Refinement of our sketches into a more finalized and tighter line drawing will take some time, but will give us a solid foundation from which to add color and start the 3D modeling process.

I'm going to tighten up the silhouette and details of my designs through the use of variation in line quality and line thickness. If you remember from Chapter 2, a silhouette is the outline of an object. A strict focus on silhouette in this phase will make itself very apparent in our final 3D animation. In the case of The N4CER, I focused on emphasizing his characteristic triangular shaped body parts and keeping it simple by only adding design details like rivets, patterns, and piping in specific areas (image 18). Overall, his design is simple and architectural, so in designing his body I used a thick line to define his silhouette to add a feeling of weight and strength that further refines his heavy structure. His overall look is now that of a tough and impenetrable fighting machine. Notice the use of Chinese themes within his armor plating, helmet, and weapons to give him more visual interest and style. Overall you could describe him as simple, architectural, tough, and focused. The N4CER's character is now more defined than ever and exudes brute force machine with very little empathy and even less brainpower.

As I wind my way through each of my drawings, I'm reminding myself of one of the most important rules I adhere to, the contrast rule. I've purposely designed Bleep and Angus with a focus on softer organic shapes to make them a direct contrast of the more angular aggressive shapes of The N4CER. I applied the contrast rule to Bleep's and The N4CER's aesthetic detail through organic vs. angular, more detail vs. less detail, elegant vs. crude, and so on.

For now I feel satisfied with a nice line drawing of my designs, so I can move on to the next phase — color.

Color: Choice and Application

Color is the final stage in traditional design that leaves an open door to the final look and feel of our animation. Even though I encourage you to experiment with color and texture in 3D, your designs should be fairly concrete in shape, proportion, and color before we get into the modeling process. Once we get into 3D modeling, it's going to be challenging enough to capture the unique character and proportion of our designs, so let's make all the big design decisions now and save the little tweaks in 3D for later.

At this stage, gather reference material to be used to form an approach toward color. What should you gather? Depending upon your research material, any kind of color, pattern, or texture you feel accurately represents your inspiration. In my case, I've collected color images of Chinese art, architecture, and sculpture to form an idea of what colors I think will be of best use to my project. The process of gathering and applying color for your designs varies from person to person, but I'm going to teach you my way. I think it's a fairly efficient approach and will not only help to establish a color palette for use during your project, but will keep you very organized.

I used to work on paper with markers, colored chalk, and colored pencils, but that process can take a long time and with no Undo button, if you screw up, you might spend a half hour trying to repair a mistake. So, with the advent of digital paint programs like Photoshop, Aura, and Alias Sketch, the Undo button was included along with the tools for creating layers, transparencies, soft edges, masks, and textures. With these programs the user has a powerful suite of tools that far outweigh anything you could do on paper in the same amount of time. It's always nice to break out the markers every once in a while to help refine some design issues, but all in all I choose to work digital because of its efficiency.

Note: If you don't have a digital paint program, go get one. If you still can't get one, then follow the lessons using color markers or color pencils.

Color Phase 1: Gather Color Reference Material

The first thing to do is to gather all your reference material into a digital format. Whether you scan it in from books or magazines, or it exists as a digital file already, gather it into a folder that we will call "Color Reference."

Color Phase 2: Determine a Few Colors of Interest

Sort through your files and start to determine the colors that are the most commonly used within the context of your reference material. When I mean colors, I don't mean black and white; black and white are a given. I mean look through your reference material and choose a few colors that stand out as being the most applicable to your project. I have chosen four colors: red, green, gold, and brown. These four colors were the ones most commonly used during the ancient Chinese era. Perhaps it was their love for nature and living off the land complemented by the use of highly detailed pieces of craftsmanship like golden dragons, giant green vases, red calligraphy on rice paper, and wooden sailing ships striped with red and green from bow to stern. I believe their choice of color was to complement their natural landscape, not to compete with it.

Color Phase 3: Create Your Color Palette

I've created a new document in Photoshop and, using my reference material, I can use the eyedropper to sample color or I can use my design eye to do the same job. I prefer using my design eye, because it further enhances my ability to mix and match color without the aid of a digital program. I then created four bars of color: red, green, gold, and brown. Each bar has a dark, medium, and light section to give me a good range of values to choose from. If I were to put the middle range value of gold up against my dark value of red, it would create an incredible amount of contrast. This is a good indication that I'm on the right path, because the Chinese often use high contrast to create focal points within their architecture and art.

See color plate on page C-5.

Color Phase 4: Apply Your Color Palette

The goal of this phase is to apply our color palette to our designs. This gives us an idea of how our colors will work together to create a high amount of visual interest as well as give our compositions dynamic focal points and good contrast. Not only will value play a huge role, but the correct contrast of color is crucial to keeping our focal points clear and engaging. Once we've colored a few of our designs we can examine how they look as a unit. Since we only want to create a quick color reference, or a *color key,* it's not important that we render our designs to a very high degree. I leave it up to you to choose to what level of detail you want to illustrate your designs. But don't get too caught up in illustration and spend less time thinking about overall color for the entire project. Whatever level of illustration you choose, utilize this phase to make crucial color decisions before jumping into 3D.

The first step is to scan one of my characters. Let's start with our co-hero Bleep. I pull my scanned image of Bleep into Photoshop and put him next to my color palette (image 19). Your scanned image should be clean and of high enough resolution so you can paint the drawing. It's kind of like a coloring book. You can use the eyedropper to choose a color off the palette and then fill in the open areas within your design. If you need to reduce both images so they fit side by side, do so; if you can work with two different sizes, then go for it. The next thing is to look at both Bleep and the color palette simultaneously and try to visualize what colors work best for him. He is kind of a good guy, so his colors should reflect that. Within my color palette the color that comes to me as being pleasant, peaceful, and a good guy color is gold. In contrast, the color that feels the least pleasant and is most suitable for our bad guy is red. This is great because The N4CER's red coloring will work in contrast to Bleep's gold coloring. With all of my designs ready to be scanned and colored, the only thing left to do is to complete that task. Bleep is in good shape and I think his overall appearance sets a good precedent for all the other designs.

See color plate on page C-6.

Color Phase 5: Compare and Contrast Designs

Now that I've completed coloring several of my designs, it's time to put them up against one another. The first thing I notice is that The N4CER seems a little too bright and saturated (image 20). He contrasts with the background very well, but so much so he takes too much attention away from Bleep. I think toning down The N4CER's colors helps establish a better balance between the characters. So using some cool Photoshop tools, I make the necessary adjustments (image 21). Angus looks perfect next to Bleep, and in fact they look like they belong together. This pairing off of visual styles gives our audience another clue that Bleep and Angus are two peas in a pod, and that they belong together and deserve each other. Wow… our project is really starting to take some shape. The design, color, and compositions are working together perfectly. All of our hard work and research is really paying off. As the designer, we've achieved our ultimate goal. It almost doesn't matter what story lies within this composition because it's so cool to look at. It speaks volumes about the amount of research and planning that went into this visually exciting project. So far so good, but now I have a question… how does all this ancient Chinese design affect my story?

Rewrite: How Visuals Influence Story

The only question I might have at this stage in the game is do our Chinese art-inspired characters fit within the context of their story? Doesn't it seem like our story should be more like a Chinese folk tale or martial arts adventure? Well, I would say yes and no.

What we are talking about is a classic case of how design can affect story. As a designer, your greatest influence is when your visuals inspire the writing to evolve in a way that elevates the story. How this relates to "Feed the Dog" is perfectly simple. Our story is a light-hearted action comedy about a character named Bleep and his loving dog Angus, who by circumstance is called to defend his heroic master from an evil villain named The N4CER. When you read that log line, a vision of ancient China is the last thing to cross

your mind. So perhaps I overstepped my bounds by bringing the design into a theme so foreign and outside of what our initial story had in mind that neither story nor design work together. The reality is, being the writer, designer, and animator gives me the license to change anything I want. In a production environment, sometimes the development phase will allow for the writers and designers to work together to influence each others' contribution to the project. I've seen an entire story change based on an artist's sketch and likewise a character change based on a writer's story. With that, we can get back to my original question about whether or not "Feed the Dog" should be more like a Chinese folk tale with lots of martial arts. The yes and no answer to that question would be, yes

our story can contain some folk tale-like moments, and our action can contain some martial arts moments, but all in all, tone, characters, and storyline will remain the same.

Rewrite Changes

I wanted to create a mood of Chinese folklore, filled with Zen-like moments, underscored by dynamic martial arts action, and perhaps accompanied by a traditional Chinese tune with a flute or something. I've created a final script that I feel encompasses both my initial story and my new Zen-like changes. With a simple change to the opening and the overall choreography, I've been able to pull my story into line with my ancient Chinese designs. Story and design are now in harmony.

"FEED THE DOG"

A script for a short animated film by
Geoffrey Kater

1st Draft
June 30, 2005
© 2005. Geoffrey Kater. All rights reserved.

FADE IN

EXTERIOR - HUGE WHEAT FIELD WITH BEAUTIFUL MOUNTAIN VISTA AND FOREST IN
THE DISTANCE - DAY

We open wide and our camera slowly pans right to reveal our lone
warrior sitting in the distance. Suddenly, like a rocket, our camera
zooms across the field to a close-up of our hero meditating in a
Zen-like state. There is a moment of pause, as if our warrior waits
for something to happen.

Suddenly, out of nowhere The N4CER jumps into the scene and lunges at
Bleep...

The N4CER

Yaaaaahhhhhhhhhh!!!

With lightning-like reflexes Bleep leaps over the head of The N4CER and lands on The N4CER's back.

BLEEP

Ha-ha! Nice try, metal head!

While beating him from behind and holding on for dear life, Bleep suddenly has a strange flashback to something earlier in the day in his home kitchen:

CUT TO:

INTERIOR — BLEEP'S KITCHEN

We see his wife PINGETTE standing there polishing an item in a huge collection of knickknacks hanging on the wall. She's cute, too, but really annoying to Bleep. He sits at the kitchen table, reading the morning newspaper, drinking his coffee, and trying to ignore her.

PINGETTE

Now Bleep, this delicious chocolate cake
is for my sister's birthday party tonight.
So I don't want to see any finger marks
on it just because you thought you'd just
"try a little taste."

BLEEP (teeth gritted)

Yes, dear.

                    PINGETTE
Now honey, I know how busy you are
defeating killer robots and vicious
double agents, but don't forget to feed
Angus before you leave. You know how
he gets when he's hungry.

                    BLEEP (teeth gritted)

Yes, dear.

Bleep glances over to see:

CLOSE-UP of one of the cutest, most wonderful dogs you've ever seen in
your life---ANGUS.

CUT BACK TO:

EXTERIOR - DESOLATE, RUINED CITYSCAPE - NIGHT

Bleep is thrown off The N4CER. The horrible robot laughs maniacally and
lunges toward Bleep. But in an instant, Bleep transforms into a mighty
fighting machine. His chest opens up to reveal giant photon cannons,
death lasers, you name it. He opens fire, guns a-blazin'. Through the
blasts of energy, we see The N4CER fall to his knees, knocked out.
Stars circle above his head. Bleep quickly transforms back to normal.

                    BLEEP
        Darn it! I forgot about Angus.

Without any hesitation, he takes off.

CUT TO:

INTERIOR - BLEEP'S KITCHEN

We see Angus waiting patiently. Bleep enters and Angus goes nuts, leaping off the floor at the sight of his master. Angus is superexcited, buzzing around and barking.

> BLEEP
>
> I know, I know. Sorry, dude. I
> totally forgot to feed ya.

Sighing, Bleep grabs a box of "Bowser Bolts" from the counter and starts to fill the doggie dish with nuts, screws, and other metal pieces.

Suddenly, KABLAM! AN EXPLOSION! Over Bleep's shoulder we see The N4CER blasting through the wall, smashing the wife's entire knickknack collection to bits.

> BLEEP (surprised, not scared)
>
> Awwww maaaaaan! My wife's gonna
> kill me!

ON ANGUS:

Angus pulls his snout out of his feeding bowl. He becomes excited. He thinks The N4CER is a visitor. Oh boy!
Angus starts buzzing around him and jumping up and down with excitement.

The N4CER doesn't know how to respond to Angus. He's never seen such an overly excited dog, or anything like Angus before.

                    N4CER
          What the...! Down boy, down! Go away!
          Stop! Oh come on now! Good boy, yes?

Even The N4CER can't help but be smitten by Angus' charms. With The N4CER distracted, Bleep launches an attack.

                    BLEEP (War face on)
          YAAAAAAAAAAAAAAAAHHHHHHHH!

He kicks The N4CER right in his chest... BLAM! The N4CER smashes into a nearby table and goes head first into Bleep's sister-in-law's birthday cake.

                    N4CER

          Arggghh! Chocolate, I HATE
          chocolate cake!

                    BLEEP
          Ohhh crap!

The N4CER has cake all in his eyes - he can't see a thing! The N4CER stumbles around, swinging into thin air, yet Bleep and Angus dodge The N4CER's attempts to capture them. Bleep picks up Angus' doggie dish and repeatedly bangs The N4CER on the head. The N4CER stumbles backward.

While this is going on, Angus opens the door behind The N4CER labeled "Trash Incinerator" and The N4CER falls in. Angus shuts the door and with a push of the "Incinerate" button and the SOUND of a WHOOSH, Angus, our fearless hero, saves the day. Angus looks to Bleep for approval. Bleep looks at him with love and says:

                    BLEEP

        How could he not like chocolate cake?

Angus leaps up and licks Bleep on the face, his tail furiously wagging.

                    BLEEP

        Good boy! You did good! Who's my good
        boy?

FADE OUT

Chapter Seven

Thinking Your Project Through

Introduction to Storyboarding

It goes without saying that any of the concepts that are taught in this book, like design, modeling, animation, storyboarding, and the like, can become lifelong pursuits both artistically and professionally. I'm just trying to give you a broad-brush overview and an applicable method of these concepts in order to help you improve your work. As for this chapter, storyboarding and animation planning can be a huge undertaking, requiring dozens of people and even hundreds to help complete. In order to teach basic storyboarding and animation planning, I'm going to pick a few choice scenes from my story "Feed the Dog" to break down, storyboard, and plan. Assuming that you grasp these basic concepts and with a little more experience, you'll be able to extrapolate this method into a longer project, let's say something with 350 scenes, which by the way is the average 22-minute Saturday morning 3D cartoon. At any rate, just focus on the lessons and then apply them to a few of the scenes from your own story. Feel free to copy my camera notes, action, and even my cinematography; there's no better way to learn than through example.

Words into Pictures

Storyboarding is quite possibly one of the most crucial phases in animation. It is the first glimpse of a story that goes from the written word to a visual context. A great storyboard artist influences storytelling, cinematography, and pacing of any animated script he or she chooses to interpret. With that said, the storyboard artist becomes one of the most crucial artists on the team and should be respected for both his narrative vision and artistic talent. Some believe that the storyboard artist is akin to an animation director, interpreting each script into cut scenes that tell a visual story. This couldn't be more true for any other storytelling medium than animation. Each frame in animation must be planned, anticipating every scene's contents, action, dialogue, and flow, because what you see is what you get... literally.

On the other end of the spectrum, live action has the luxury of shooting what's called *coverage*. Coverage is the method of shooting the same scene, with the same line, from the same actor over and over again, but each take is from a different camera angle, like close-ups, wide shots, top-down shots, etc. This gives the editor and director the most choices when it comes to constructing a scene. For example, say you shoot a scene with an actor delivering the line, "How do you like your new digs?" The editor or director can choose between starting with a wide shot at "How do you like" and then cutting to a close-up of "your new digs?" Get it? The director isn't locked down to just one choice; she can cut from one angle to another in order to maximize the narrative. For the live-action process, it's a necessity.

With storyboarding as our only method of translating words into pictures, it makes sense that this phase of the process be treated with careful consideration, planning, and execution, because in animation what you see is what you get.

Shot Breakdown

The process of breaking down a script into a written form with scene-specific details like contents, dialogue, camera angles, and action is referred to as a *shot breakdown*. This process happens just before the storyboard phase to get an idea of how the script will translate to a visual medium. Every storyboard artist has his or her own method for breaking down the action of the script and then drawing each panel as it relates to the story. Some artists are more vague in their breakdown, just circling entire paragraphs, giving a scene number, and then working out the action visually. Others, like myself, tend to be a little more detailed by working out some of the action, cuts, close-ups, etc., on the actual script first, then working on the board to resolve action and composition.

For example, if you look at my script page for "Feed the Dog" you'll notice that **scene 6** has a notation, **Cut to C/U of Bleep**, with a line leading to the words **Push-in slowly**.

This is a direction note in which I establish a cut from the previous scene (**scene 5a**) to this scene, and then using the acronym C/U (close-up), I go on to describe the character that is the focus of that shot.

The next notation says **Push-in slowly**. A push-in is a move that pushes the camera slowly toward our subject, in this case to maximize the effect of Bleep having his flashback.

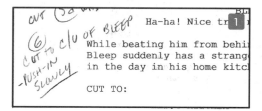

I've provided all three panels from **scene 6** of the storyboard so you can see how it works visually.

I have also transferred my notations to the actual storyboard. As you can see, each action, scene number, line of dialogue, and camera note has its own place.

Now that you understand a little about the shot breakdown and how to apply it, moving forward into more complex methods will be a snap to understand.

SLUG   sc. 6

ACTION:

NYCEMS BACK

DIAL

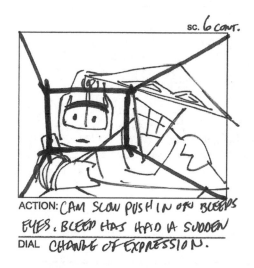

sc. 6 cont.

ACTION: CAM SLOW PUSH IN ON BLEEPS EYES. BLEEP HAS HAD A SUDDEN

DIAL CHANGE OF EXPRESSION.

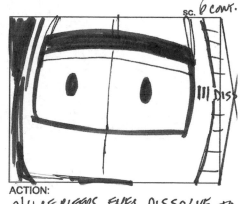

sc. 6 cont.

ACTION:

C/U OF BLEEPS EYES DISSOLVE TO

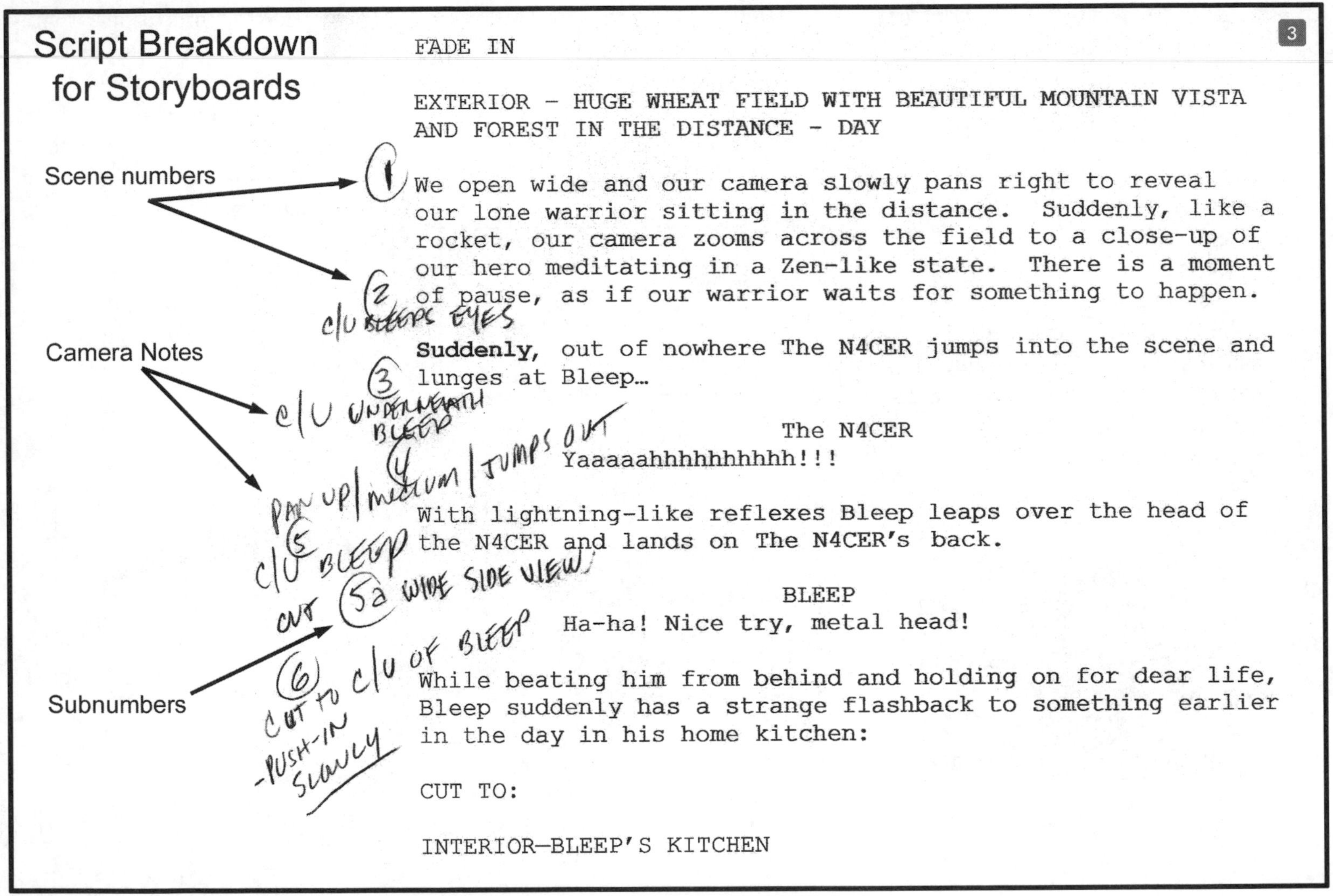

Script Breakdown for Storyboards

FADE IN

EXTERIOR – HUGE WHEAT FIELD WITH BEAUTIFUL MOUNTAIN VISTA AND FOREST IN THE DISTANCE – DAY

Scene numbers

(1) We open wide and our camera slowly pans right to reveal our lone warrior sitting in the distance. Suddenly, like a rocket, our camera zooms across the field to a close-up of our hero meditating in a Zen-like state. There is a moment of pause, as if our warrior waits for something to happen.

(2) C/U BLEEPS EYES

Suddenly, out of nowhere The N4CER jumps into the scene and **(3)** lunges at Bleep…

C/U UNDERNEATH BLEEP

Camera Notes

                    The N4CER
(4) PAN UP/MEDIUM/JUMPS OUT   Yaaaaahhhhhhhhhh!!!

With lightning-like reflexes Bleep leaps over the head of the N4CER and lands on The N4CER's back.

(5) C/U BLEEP OUT   *(5a) WIDE SIDE VIEW;*

                    BLEEP
          Ha-ha! Nice try, metal head!

(6) CUT TO C/U OF BLEEP -PUSH-IN SLOWLY

Subnumbers

While beating him from behind and holding on for dear life, Bleep suddenly has a strange flashback to something earlier in the day in his home kitchen:

CUT TO:

INTERIOR—BLEEP'S KITCHEN

sc. 5A

ACTION: *CUT TO WIDE SHOT*

BLEEP LEAPS OFF OF GROUND AND DIAL *DOES TWISTING FLIP, LANDING ON . . .*

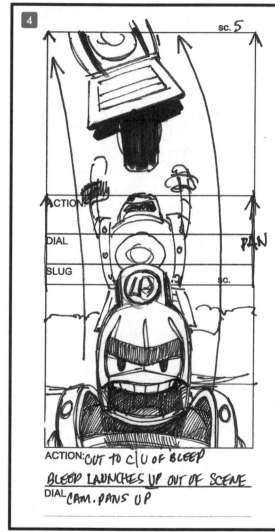

4

sc. 5

ACTION:

PAN

DIAL

SLUG

sc.

ACTION: *CUT TO C|U OF BLEEP*

BLEEP LAUNCHES UP OUT OF SCENE DIAL *CAM. PANS UP*

Exercise 1: Break down your boards into what you feel are key scenes. Then make simple notations to indicate scene numbers.

Subnumbering

I've taken the liberty of breaking down my entire script and in doing so, I've found some serious revisions in the numbering of those scenes. Sometimes you don't expect to break down a scene into multiple angles, etc., but if you have to insert a scene between scenes, the solution is subnumbering. *Subnumbering* is the adding of a letter to an existing scene number, like scenes 5a, 5b, 5c, etc. In scene 5 I did just that. At first, I had the scene as a single wide side shot, but then felt a close-up was needed to emphasize Bleep's exclamation, "HA, HA!" I labeled the close-up as scene 5 and the wide shot as scene 5a. In this scene, by moving my camera to a close-up of Bleep's face, I've created a more intimate moment between Bleep and the audience. When the camera is close to someone's face, you can really feel his or her intensity, which has a way of engaging the audience in a very effective manner. It's hard to feel this intensity if the camera is far away, so it goes without saying that an intense moment may require a little intimacy.

Storyboarding: Your Road Map to Success

I can't stress enough how important storyboarding is to animation. It is the foundation of how your story is told in a visual context. Since storyboarding is merely a *guide* for the visual story, don't stress out on how well you draw. Even if you have to draw stick figures to get your story across, the point is to get an idea of how your story sews together visually. This is one of the most important sections of the book because of its profound impact on your animations. That impact is in direct correlation to how much you practice and how much you apply. Start slow and I guarantee

that you'll approach your 3D projects with a new design eye and sense of story that will dramatically improve your animations.

I'm going to take you through some simple translation techniques. By translation I mean from words into pictures. Our key focus will be on three distinct areas: flow, composition, and transitions. These three techniques will be our basic approach to the storyboard, so get your pencil and paper and sketch as we go in order to learn these techniques and their application.

Technique

At this point I don't expect you to be drawing full-fledged inked storyboards like the ones used in animation. What I expect is that you'll do your best to focus on composition, story, content, action, and dialogue. Your drawing skill is the last thing that should get in the way. The value of storyboarding is immeasurable and should be a foundation of your animations even at the most simplistic level. Image 5 shows a few examples of the same scene drawn with different skill levels.

Panels 1, 2, and 3 tell the same story; the only difference is how good the visuals are. As a 3D animator, you just want to get enough information to set up your compositions and story flow. Your 3D animation will more than make up for any lack of visuals in your story-board. So don't worry too much about how good your drawings are; focus on basic composition, camera moves, and story.

5

sc. 1

ACTION: Up shot of city

sc. 2

ACTION: Cut to down shot
Perry is driving Mr. Smith
in his Mach 1.

sc. 3

ACTION: Cut to inside of car
Mr. Smith: So...Perry, how
long you been out.

sc.

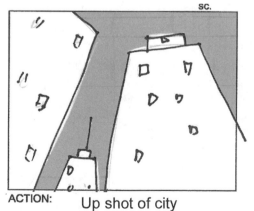

ACTION: Up shot of city

sc.

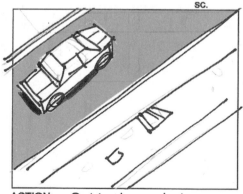

ACTION: Cut to down shot
Perry is driving Mr. Smith
in his Mach 1.

sc.

ACTION: Cut to inside of car
Mr. Smith: So...Perry, how
long you been out.

Flow

The camera is our eye into the animated world and moves around that world in order to tell the story. An important aspect of telling the story is establishing a flow. What I mean is the flow of dialogue, the flow of the visuals, one into the next, the flow of one scene into the next. We discussed flow in Chapter 3 by saying, "the flow is kind of like an arrow that points to our subject matter saying, 'Look here!'" This theory applies to action as well as composition, and using your camera to lead the viewer's eye to a specific area within the frame is part of establishing a good flow. In scene 14 of "Feed the Dog," we start our camera behind Angus. The camera slowly pushes in toward the door, which soon opens and Bleep walks in.

This technique uses a push-in toward the door and Angus to guide the viewer's eye to our new focal point, Bleep. Consequently, the next scene, scene 15 is a POV, or point of view, shot. See image 6. Point of view shots are often used to get the viewer inside the character's head... to see what they're seeing.

This is a very valuable concept called *screen direction*. The screen direction is the direction — left or right — in which our eyes are looking. It's important that our characters or focal point follow the same law of screen direction when they look at each other or motion a certain way. I'll show you what I mean.

Scene 14 starts off leading our eyes screen right toward Angus, then our eyes travel to what Angus is looking at: the door, which is at screen left. Scene 15 is a POV shot with our eyes looking screen left to Angus. When Bleep walks in the room, his point of view is to look down and to screen right toward Angus. When we cut to the POV shot, Angus looks as if he's looking up to screen left, the opposite of Bleep. When two characters look at each other, one must look left and the other right... get it?

Our camera must emulate this natural occurrence by structuring the shots to include proper screen direction. If I were to flip scene 15 around and have Angus looking to screen right, there would be a disconnect in the flow.

6

sc. 14

ACTION: C/U Over the shoulder of Angus Bleep enters the house.

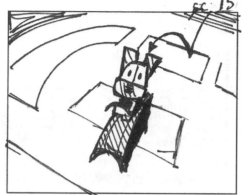

sc. 15

ACTION: POV of Angus looking up at Bleep

Good screen direction, they're both staring at each other.

sc. 14

ACTION: C/U Over the shoulder of Angus Bleep enters the house.

sc. 15

ACTION: POV of Angus looking up at Bleep

Bad screen direction, they're both staring in the same direction.

This kind of mistake can be avoided by thinking about what direction the camera is pointing and to what direction the action is happening. This kind of simple staging stuff can be worked out on paper before you get into any animation.

Another good example of using screen direction to control flow is that of something moving or leaving the scene. If an object leaves the scene, then the next scene should contain that object coming into the scene from the same direction that it did upon exit. See image 7.

In scene 1, I've drawn a ball rolling from screen left to screen right and then out of the scene. I then draw scene 2 with the ball rolling in from screen left and stopping. It wouldn't make any sense to your eyes if the ball came rolling in from screen right (image 8).

This goes for camera moves as well. Focus on screen direction and using focal points to lead the viewer's eye to what makes sense visually and you'll obtain good staging habits for the visual flow of your story.

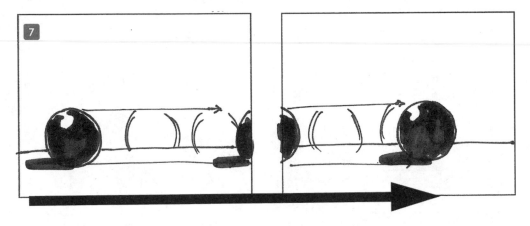

Good screen direction

Bad screen direction

Composition

In the case of storyboarding, composition is king. If you need a refresher, review Chapter 3. It covers all the composition basics that make for a good shot, including hints on using negative space and tension to create good focal points. See example (image 9).

In scene 3 of "Feed the Dog" I've figured a way to force the viewer's eyes to look into the distance, from which our villain, The N4CER, appears. I've first used the natural tension of Bleep hovering above our heads. I also increased the dark value of his bottom side and his shadow to create a contrasting horizontal stripe of white from which The N4CER emerges. The N4CER is also dark and becomes the focal point because of his extreme contrast with the white background. Again, this is just one example of how to stage a shot, so look at other finished work to gain more knowledge of compositional technique and soon it will come to you naturally.

SC. 3

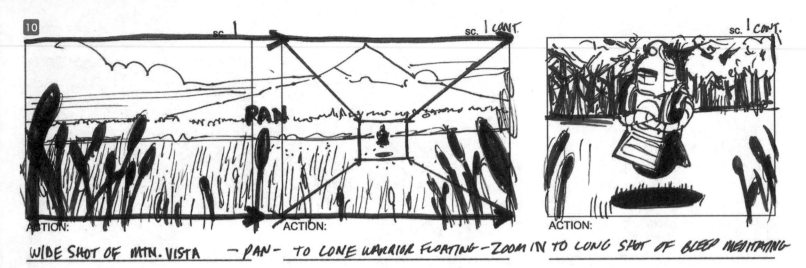

10

sc. 1   sc. 1 CONT   sc. 1 CONT.

PAN

ACTION: ACTION: ACTION:

WIDE SHOT OF MTN. VISTA   — PAN —   TO LONE WARRIOR FLOATING — ZOOM IN TO LONG SHOT OF BLEEP MEDITATING

Transitions

The next concept I'd like to talk about is transitions. A *transition* is either a camera move from one place to the next or a function of editing from one scene to the next. A camera transition example would be: Camera is focused on person 1. You hear a voice off-screen as if from behind, then the camera swivels around 180 degrees to focus on person 2.

This was an in-camera transition because we never cut to a new shot; we stayed in-camera and transitioned to our next destination. To further explain, I've provided an example of scene 1 from "Feed the Dog" (image 10).

We open on a wide shot of a field with a beautiful vista. Forest and mountains recede in the background. We can barely make out our hero Bleep in the distance. Just as our audience is starting to take in the beauty of the scene, the camera zooms in like a rocket across the field to land upon a medium shot of our hero hovering in mid-air. Rather than using a cut from the wide vista shot to the medium shot of Bleep, I preferred to use an extreme zoom as an in-camera transition to go from scene 1 to scene 2. To indicate this on the board, I drew a box around Bleep in the distance. This box represents the size and framing of the next panel. I included arrows indicating direction and the word zoom as an animation note. In-camera transitions can add a touch of dynamic movement and unexpected transitions from one thing to the next,

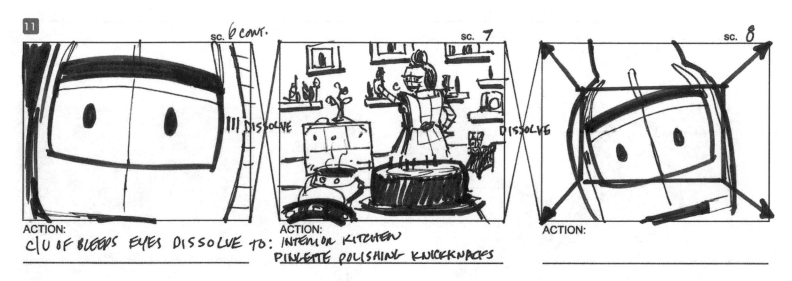

11

sc. 6 CONT. |||DISSOLVE sc. 7 DISSOLVE sc. 8

ACTION:
C/U OF BLEEPS EYES DISSOLVE TO:

ACTION: INTERIOR KITCHEN
PINLETTE POLISHING KNICKKNACKS

ACTION:

a real treat for an audience. *The Matrix*, *House of Flying Daggers*, and *Moulin Rouge* include great examples of in-camera transitions. Transitions used in editing are simple. The most common technique is to cut from one scene to the next, meaning scene 1 ends and then scene 2 starts. Cutting has an abrupt feel. It's good for when characters are exchanging dialogue and it also does well for ending a scene quickly. The next most common editorial transition would be the dissolve. This technique involves a blending or

dissolving of one scene into the next. There is a point in the middle of the dissolve when you see both scenes. The result is a sort of scene overlap that helps you transition out of a scene with a softer feel; it's often used to give the feeling that time has passed. Dissolve is also used at the end of a scene to transition from one location to the next, like from out in the forest to inside an office. As an example, I've provided scenes 7 and 8 of "Feed the Dog" (image 11). In scene 7, Bleep is in the middle of a flashback about his wife and then

realizes he needs to beat The N4CER and get home. I use a dissolve from the flashback to Bleep's reality. In this case I chose a dissolve as my transition in order to get from one location to the next, from inside Bleep's head back to reality. As a notation on the board, I use a giant X and the word "dissolve" between scenes 7 and 8 to indicate that to the editor.

Fade Out

12

SC. 38

SC.

FADE TO BLACK

ACTION: MED SHOT OF BLEEP AND ANGUS.

ACTION:

DIAL
BLEEP: GOOD BOY! YOU DID GOOD! WHOS MY GOOD BOY?

DIAL

The effect of a dissolve can also be applied to what is called a *fade*. A fade is most commonly used at the beginning or end of an entire sequence; that sequence being an entire movie or a long scene.

We can also use fade to add a feeling that time has passed. Using a black background as our example, to fade-in is to dissolve from black into picture, whereas to fade-out is to dissolve from picture to black. A good example is at the end of "Feed the Dog," where I fade out, or dissolve from picture to black, to let the audience know we're at the end of my short (image 12).

"Use editorial transitions like fades and dissolves to add depth and mood to your animation."

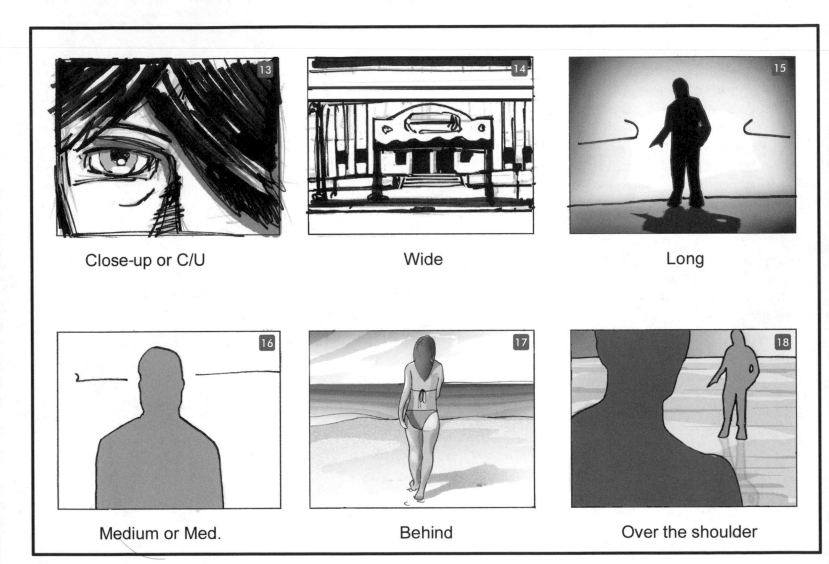

Close-up or C/U

Wide

Long

Medium or Med.

Behind

Over the shoulder

Getting a Response

In order to be effective at storyboarding, you need to understand the language of camera position. The camera is our only eye into our animated world and, with its vast power, should be the most understood tool in your arsenal. Your goal as an animator is to elicit a reaction from the audience, like laughter, sadness, fear, and so on. It's all about creating those moments. There are certain camera angles and transitions that will consistently produce a specific feeling or response from the audience, so I've included a short list of those items and how they can be used effectively. I've also included examples of the storyboard notations as they relate to each technique.

Close-up

(image 13) Close-up shots are very in your face and, depending on how they're used, can make the audience feel intimate or uncomfortable. Close-ups of body parts, mechanical items, etc., give the feeling of detail, like you are studying something closely.

Wide Shot

(image 14) Good for establishing a location, like a building, park, crowds, or city. It gives the audience a chance to soak up the whole picture and is commonly used at the beginning of a scene. Since it's more big-picture oriented, it has less detailed information and makes a viewer feel like an outsider.

Long Shot

(image 15) A long shot can contain an entire person from head to toe, but not much closer. The audience may feel like they want to get closer to this person or focus of interest, and a close-up or medium shot usually follows. It's as if the camera is surveying the scene at first and then moving close to the objects of interest.

Medium Shot

(image 16) These shots are usually of the waist up or at a talking distance, which provides a closer, personal feel. Medium shots are the most common during long sequences of dialogue, since they make the audience feel like they are there, having the conversation at a normal distance.

Behind

(image 17) The feeling of being behind someone leaves a little to the imagination, because you can't see the person's face. It can make the audience feel curious or fearful of what this person may look like. This shot can be used to follow someone walking in a certain direction or to give the feeling we are going somewhere.

Over the Shoulder

(image 18) This is a shot from behind a character and it is mostly a medium to close-up shot. It's used often when two people are talking; you can't see one person who may be talking, but over his shoulder you can catch the other person's reaction. This is also good when you want the audience to feel that they are following the character to a point of discovery. They are discovering in real time, over the shoulder, what the character is discovering.

Extreme close-up

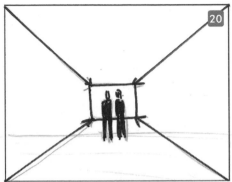

Zoom

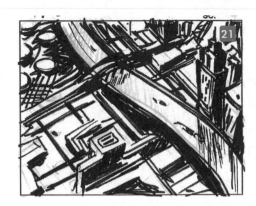

Aerial

Start of Dissolve

Dissolve @ 50%

Dissolve Complete

Extreme Close-up

(image 19) Talk about uncomfortable or unbelievable. Extreme close-ups are for shots requiring extreme detail, like eyes, mouths, mechanical parts, etc. It's almost a microscope of sorts that makes the audience feel they are looking at detail they've never seen this close before.

Zoom

(image 20) This shot is great for going from one end of the extreme to the next and gives the audience a dynamic feeling of movement.

Aerial

(image 21) Bird's-eye view. This is also used to establish locations, etc., but gives that unique God's eye view on the situation.

Cut

Abrupt and to the point. A cut is the most commonly used editorial transition. It's great for dialogue and quick transitions from one scene to the next. During a conversation, cutting from one person to the next feels fairly natural and is used often for comedic timing purposes. By nature, the cut has an abrupt feeling, so at the end of a scene a cut might make the audience feel cut off before they were ready to leave the scene. It can also work the other way by getting the audience out of a scene quickly because of a feeling of danger or discomfort.

Dissolve

(images 22-24) A dissolve gives a softer transition between two scenes. It's usually used to take the audience from one location or scene to the next, or to indicate the passage of time.

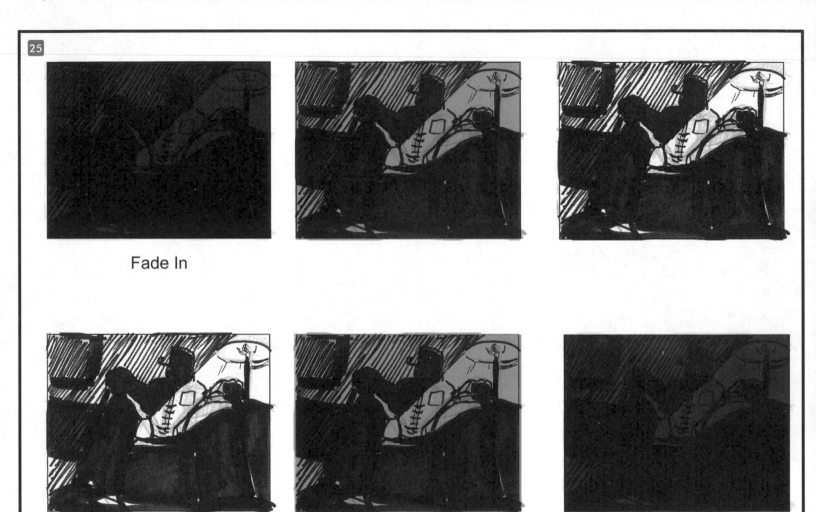

Fade In

Fade Out

Fade

(image 25) Usually used at the beginning of a story or after long sequences. A fade-in gives the audience the feeling that they're encountering a new situation that takes a little time to absorb, kind of like opening your eyes first thing in the morning. A fade-out feels kind of like you're putting the story to rest in a slow and comfortable manner, like closing your eyes for sleep at the end of a long day.

Remember, storyboarding is merely a guide for the visual story that you're trying to tell, so don't get caught up into details like having the perfect drawing or perfect composition. You can always refine those details in 3D at a later time. Make an easy go of it by using simplistic sketches to represent design, action, and flow; don't get bogged down by overthinking the situation. Your best bet is to envision the story in your head and immediately put pencil to paper. Don't hesitate, because no matter how simple your sketches, your 3D projects will improve dramatically by using the ultimate animation tool… the storyboard.

Storyboard Timing

We've done a shot breakdown and a storyboard to tell us what shots need to be animated. But how long is each shot supposed to be? That's a good question, because without figuring out whether a shot takes 1 second or 5 seconds, we could be left with a lot of guesswork during 3D animation. Timing your storyboard is the process of figuring out the duration of each shot. In more advanced timing situations, the length of the shot, movement, dialogue, and camera are all notated. For instance, movement would be indicated like so: A 3-second long shot of a man walking into the scene, waving his hand in the air and saying, "Hi, Bob." An initial timing breakdown would tell us each movement is going to take some time:

Man walking in — 1 second long. Man waving his hand in the air — 1 second long. Man saying, "Hi, Bob" — 1 second long. This can get a little tricky, because maybe the man says, "Hi, Bob" while he's waving his hand, or maybe he waves first and then says, "Hi, Bob." Does the man walk in, pause for a second, and then say, "Hi, Bob"? Or does he say, "Hi, Bob" on his way in, waves, and then stands there?

The point is, there are actually people called timing directors who do nothing but figure this stuff out. It would be impossible to create an animated cartoon without figuring out the timing of all details because of the number of variables that are contained in each shot. Fortunately for us, this book is about design, so I'm not even going to attempt to teach that stuff. Timing for us will be the most basic task; all we want to establish is "How long is each shot?" As for more advanced timing issues, you can work that out during the 3D animation process.

Each second of film contains 24 frames, and each second of video contains 30 frames. Before you start timing, you need to determine whether you're working at 24 frames per second, or 24fps (film rate), or 30 frames per second, or 30fps (video rate). A lot of this choice depends upon what your final destination will be — projected as a film or made for television. Both standards have their strengths and weaknesses. Either way, if you're doing a film, choose 24, and if you're doing television, choose 30.

I'll be using 24fps for my short "Feed the Dog." See my timing examples (image 26).

Scenes 2, 3, and 4 all indicate action and timing. The timing notes are the little numbers next to the words "timing" on the board. When visualizing the timing for each shot, I closed my eyes and tried to envision the action in my head. Using a stopwatch, I started with scene 2. Scene 2 is a calm shot, with the camera close to our meditating hero. I

26   SC. 2

ACTION: CUT TO C/U BLEEPS EYES
OUR HERO MEDITATES...HE
DIAL   WAITS FOR...

TIMING   2.¹²

SC. 3

ACTION: CUT TO C/U UNDERNEATH BLEEP
SUDDENLY NYCER LEAPS INTO SC.
DIAL

TIMING   3.⁰⁰

SC. 4

ACTION: CUT TO MED. NYCER

DIAL NYCER LEAPS AT CAMERA
NYCER: YAHHHHHHH!!!
TIMING   24 X

wanted the shot to feel peaceful and serene, kind of Zen-like. I wanted to allow ample time for the audience to feel his inner peace, so using my stopwatch I timed the shot in my head to be 2½ seconds long. In the timing area of my storyboard I wrote a big number 2 and then put 12 with an underscore. The number 12 represents the ½ second of my shot at 24fps, so ½ second equals 12 frames. To further illustrate my point, look at scenes 3 and 4. The timing indicates scene 3 at 3 seconds

even, and scene 4 at 24 frames.

If you're working at 30fps, how is that indicated? Well, timing notation for scene 2 would be a big 2 for 2 seconds and then an underscored 15, which is half a second, or 15 frames of animation at 30fps. This is easy stuff.

Okay, one more thing to learn. What if your animated shot is only a fraction of a second long? Like only ½ of a second. How is that indicated? You could put an underscore under the 12 for ½ second, but if someone else tries to

read your timing, they might mistake that 12 for 12 seconds. The correct animation notation is 12x, for 12 frames. The x represents frames.

$$12x = 12 \text{ frames}$$
$$x = \text{frames}$$

As it goes, my entire sequence of scenes 2, 3, and 4 add up to 6½ seconds. That's 6½ seconds of animation already figured out. All I have to do now is time the rest of my storyboard and that will give me a good idea of how long my final animation will be. Once I get into 3D, my scenes will be a snap to set up because my storyboard indicates composition, camera notes, and timing for each scene. Okay, your turn.

Exercise 2: Your next exercise will be to go through your storyboard and indicate timing. Perhaps it's easiest to time out an entire sequence at first to get a feel for how long it should be, then break down individual shots from there.

3D Model or 2D Replacement?

As it goes, our mediums are paper and 3D. We've figured out quite a bit on paper and, in fact, have laid out a game plan fairly well based on our designs and storyboard. The only thing left to do is to translate this information on paper into a proper format for 3D. Part of this translation will be to figure out what part of our animated shots will be 3D and what parts will be non-3D. For instance, the sky. Most 3D animations contain an image map of the sky in place of actually building little 3D models of clouds and haze and such. Most 3D packages have an approach to deal with this situation through the use of 2D backdrops seen by camera, or polygons mapped with a 2D sky image. The bottom line is that no matter what purpose your sky serves, it is usually a 2D flat image based on a painting or photo. So, with that in mind, the goal of this section is to indicate on your storyboards what is to be a 3D model and what is to be a 2D replacement. It goes without saying that every animation contains image maps, but to what benefit can we get simple image maps to take the place of literally hours of 3D work?

Breaking down your story into necessary 3D and 2D elements will give you a comprehensive list of what you need to create for each scene. Scene 1 of "Feed the Dog" is a good example of how the full combination of 3D and 2D elements work together to create the final shot.

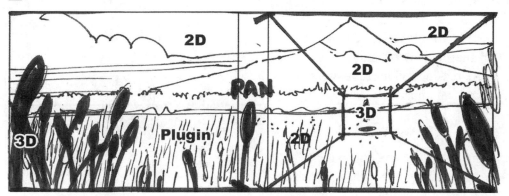

2D: Sky, mountains, and forest   3D: Bleep and tall grass   Plug-in: Grass texture

I've indicated different areas of the scene with notations like 2D, 3D, and plug-in. A listing of the elements needed for this scene looks like this:

2D elements: Sky, mountains, and forest
3D elements: Bleep and grass

My 2D elements can be a combination of basic 3D geometry and an image map. I don't need to spend hours building a 3D model of a forest when I'm not actually going into it. Through the use of a painted image map or photo, I can give the illusion that a huge forest is off in the distance. In the case of "Feed the Dog," I used painted image maps on single polygons for the forest and mountain. The sky is more of a

spherical image map projected onto a hemispherical shaped 3D model. The goal of the section called "Use Traditional Design to Save on Render Time" in Chapter 10 is learning to create these 2D assets, so for now, just do the breakdown. Make a comprehensive list of the elements you think should be image mapped and those that are 3D. It will save time during modeling, animation, and rendering.

Render Time... Recognize the Enemy!

Render time is probably the least understood phase of the animation process and, depending upon your experience, means the difference between 10 minutes or 2 hours per frame for render. How does this relate to design? Well, design has a huge impact on render time because it is the foundation of all things in your animation: models, lighting, image maps, and plug-in use. If your design foundation is well thought out and streamlined, then your final animation will reflect those choices. Those choices being good composition, proper image quality, modeling only what you need, simple lighting rigs, using 2D to replace 3D, and compositing layers of renders. You may be asking yourself, why now? Why in the middle of storyboards and animation? Right now is the best time, because moving forward into 3D is going to take some serious asset management as well as a trained design

eye. For your benefit, I'll make this lesson short and sweet and give you tips on decreasing render time without decreasing impact.

Composition

3D models are made of polygons, and the more polygons you have on screen, the longer the render. With proper composition you can decrease the number of polygons on screen. When composing shots in the storyboard, ask yourself, "What am I trying to achieve with this scene?" In this example, I have two panels, each with a bee as the focal point and legions of bees behind it. Panel 1 indicates a long shot and panel 2 indicates a medium shot. Am I getting the same point across in both panels? Yes. Move your camera around to the benefit of your render and remember that less is (usually) more.

Long shot has more bees... this means more render time.

Go to C/U and reduce render time by having fewer bees in the scene.

Image Quality

When 3D software renders a scene, one of its tasks is to load images into RAM during rendering. If you have gigantic image maps, the computer is going to not only take longer to pull those images into RAM, but it's going to take longer to recreate those images in the final rendered frame. Optimize your images for their use. For example, a simple grainy texture on a wooden floor doesn't need to be an uncompressed bitmap. Instead use a JPEG. JPEGs and PIC files are the most underrated file formats, especially for use in 3D. Yes, a JPEG has some compression, but even on the highest setting, it looks great on screen, so if it means the difference between a woodgrain image that's 1 meg instead of 20, I'll take the JPEG. Another trick is to use lots of procedural maps. A procedural of fractal noise can take the place of an image map when you need a bumpy surface.

Model Only What You Need

If you're only going to see a character from the waist up, then don't spend time modeling legs. If you're only going to see a car from the front, then don't model the back. It's not about how complete your model is, it's about what the audience is seeing. Putting a character behind something like a desk or chair so you don't have to model the legs is another good trick.

Lighting

The more lights you have, the more shadows you have, and shadows take a long time to render. Each project is so different that it's impossible to come up with a lighting standard, but perhaps using lights as a design element might alter your approach. One scenario would be that of using a very contrasty lighting scheme as a design element. The movie *Sin City* is a great example of dark, contrasted, comic book lighting. In 3D, you wouldn't need more than four lights to accomplish this look. So just remember the rule and do your best to minimize the number of lights and maximize their effect.

2D Replacing 3D

Not to repeat myself, but the obvious is apparent.

Compositing

There are certain things you can achieve within a 2D animation program like After Effects that would take more time and skill in a 3D program. Some of these are blurs, flares, 2D particle effects, faked shadows and reflections, lightning, dissolves, film grain, light bursts, and opacity changes. These 2D effects are a breeze to create in After Effects, but trying to create these in 3D might not only be difficult but will also add tons of render time to your animation. Think about using a 2D program to achieve these effects and you'll be better off at render time.

Let's move on to the next chapter with a few more tricks up your sleeve and less render time on your hands.

8

2D Translation into a 3D World

A Translation Solution

Before I get into translating 2D to 3D, let me first divulge a truth about a 2D hurdle that seems to work against the very nature of 3D: "2D drawings are cheats." When I mean cheats, I mean on literally everything, including proportion, staging, detail, extremes, etc., the list goes on and on.

Take any character in a comic book — their proportions, expressions, and uniformity totally change from panel to panel. The comic book artist is only interested in giving you the most dynamic composition, not making sure the character is in proper proportion from one angle to the next. That's sort of the beauty of traditional drawing — there are no rules. As for 3D, there are lot of rules, and the first rule states that in order for your design to work as a 3D model, you need to know what your model looks like from every angle. The top, sides, front, and back must all work together to create one whole 3D object. We can create all of those angles using a drawing known as the three-view orthographic drawing (image 1).

The three-view orthographic drawing is a very detailed blueprint of your design from three specific angles: front view (Z axis), side view (X axis), and top view (Y axis). Architects, industrial designers, production designers, 3D artists, and many others use this detailed technique on a daily basis. Its main goal is to represent proper proportion, detail, and uniformity from one angle to the next. In fact, most 3D modeling environments purposely emulate a three-view orthographic drawing because of its straightforward, no-nonsense layout. As 3D animators, how could we go wrong with a process that we already know so well (image 2)?

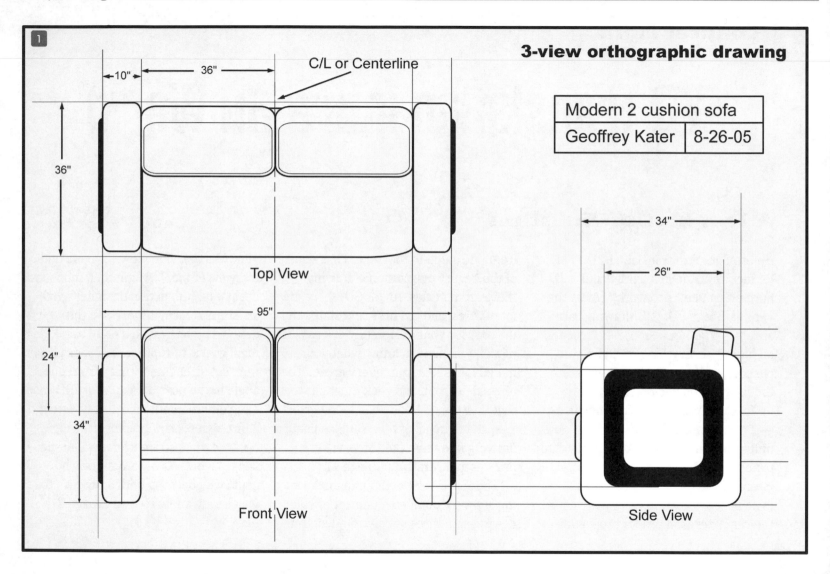

3-view orthographic drawing

10" 36" C/L or Centerline

| Modern 2 cushion sofa | |
| Geoffrey Kater | 8-26-05 |

36"

Top View

34"

26"

95"

24"

34"

Front View

Side View

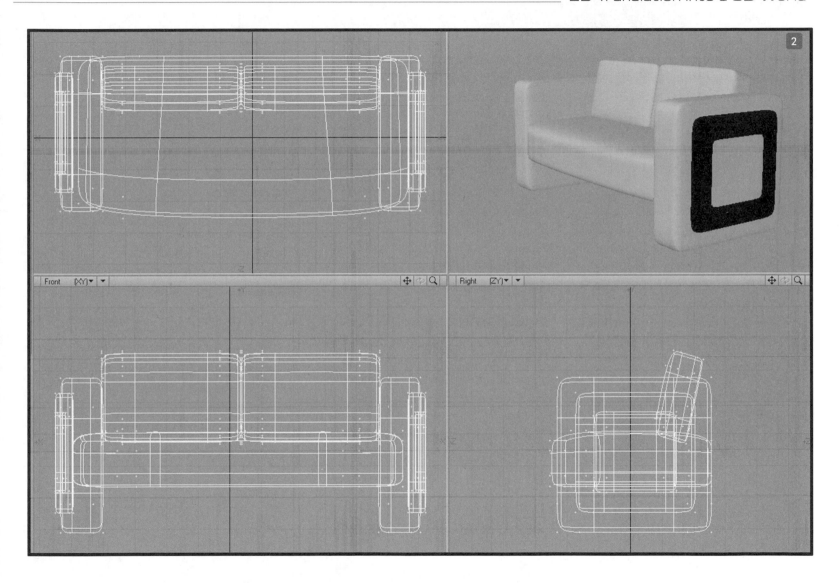

Front [XY]▼ ▼

Right [ZY]▼ ▼

My goal for this chapter is to educate you on the proper procedure for creating a three-view orthographic drawing and then encourage you to apply this new knowledge to your own designs. As it relates to this book, you should design first. Creating your own three-view orthographic drawing will give you another tool with which to refine your design and ensure a proper translation into 3D.

Three-View Basic Shape Drawing

Now that I've completed my rough sketches for "Feed the Dog," I have a good sense of my characters' personalities, as well as their physical makeup. It sure is going to be fun seeing these guys in 3D, but before we start modeling, we're going to use *construction* to aid in the breakdown of our design. We discussed construction back in Chapter 2, where I gave an example of how Mickey Mouse's head is constructed of very basic shapes at first and then detail and contour is added later. Well, we're going to do the same thing with our designs. Remembering that our goal is to have proper front, side, and top views, we're going to use basic shapes at first to establish good proportions, alignment, and layout. The next stage will be to create a final three-view orthographic drawing from our basic shape drawing. It should be an easy job considering most of our issues with improper proportion and alignment will be solved during this initial stage.

Front View

Let's get started. Using an overlay technique, I've done a construction drawing of Bleep's body (image 3). This initial drawing will give me all the shapes I need in order to transpose them to our three-view basic shape drawing. Bleep's design initially looks to contain spheres for the head and hands, a cube for the body and skirt, and cylinders for his arms and wheel.

Bleep Construction
Drawing

3

The next step is to draw those same shapes, but in what would be a front view of Bleep. This is pretty easy because I'm just using my basic shapes in a different view (image 4).

The first thing I did was to establish a ground plane and then a centerline. Like 3D modeling, we're using known reference points like a ground plane and centerline to control symmetry and size. They don't have to be very dark lines, just enough to use as a guide. In looking at my initial construction drawing, I'm paying special attention to the placement of those objects, their proportions, and their relative position to each other. Looking pretty good; let's move on.

Side View

The next view is the side view. In creating my side view drawing, I used lighter lines that extend in a horizontal fashion from my front view to serve as guides. Notice Bleep's head and how putting horizontal lines extending from the top, bottom and center of the sphere are perfect guides for his head in the side view. Using good guidelines is essential for complete accuracy.

Top View

Drawing an accurate top view can be a little tedious if you want to do it the correct way. The process requires you to accurately plot lines from your front and side views using a 45 degree angle and guidelines. The way I look at it is, if you can use a shortcut to get you there, then why bother. Over the years I've spent a lot of time drawing top views that pretty much did the job without ever having to accurately plot an orthographic top view. I know this sounds a little crazy based on how much I harped on the fact that a three-view orthographic drawing is the greatest tool on Earth... yada, yada, yada... but I had to stress its importance from an educational perspective before teaching you the shortcut.

In our case, the top view should be looked at as a reference drawing only... not a final, accurate interpretation of our design. I usually draw a top view based on the proportions, detail, and placement of objects within my initial design sketches. I usually overlay the top view onto my other views as a guide for spacing and proportion. The rest I just fake. As for accuracy, there will be plenty of time to make slight adjustments during the 3D modeling process; just do your best to create an accurate top view and everything else will fall into place.

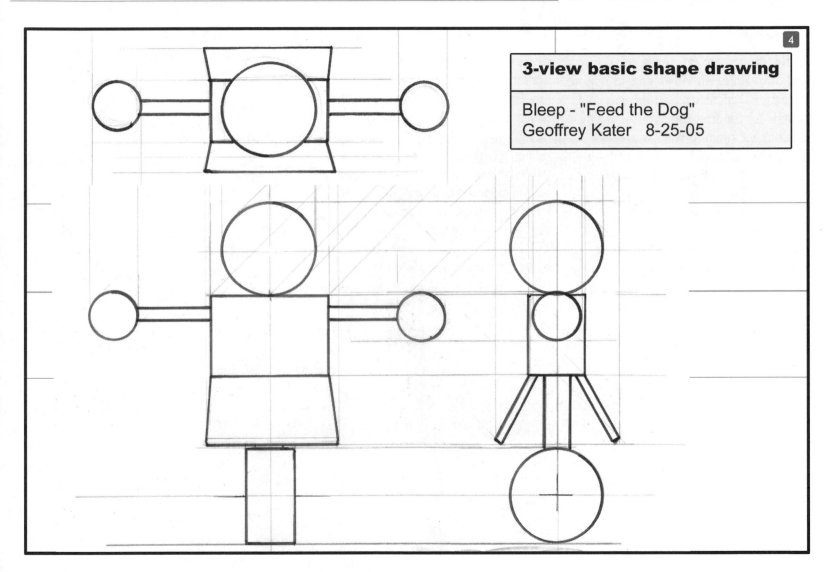

3-view basic shape drawing

Bleep - "Feed the Dog"
Geoffrey Kater   8-25-05

Analysis

At this stage, you can really see how our three different views give us a more realistic 3D picture of our design. Maybe for the first time you're seeing details that seem to work in a cool sketch but look odd or misplaced in the context of a three-view drawing. Perhaps the head of your character seems to be intersecting its own chest or maybe the wheels on your race car intersect the rear wing. The solution to these problems is to add a neck to your character and raise the wing on your race car, then revise your basic shape drawing. This type of observation is key, because it enhances your ability to problem solve and strengthens your design eye to the point that you won't make the same mistake again. In fact, you'll be able to troubleshoot these issues during the design phase, which leads to a well-conceived design and successful 3D model.

OK… moving on… now that we have our three-view basic shape drawing, it's time for the real thing.

Exercise 1: Create a three-view basic shape drawing of at least one of your designs.

Three-View Orthographic Drawing

The three-view orthographic drawing process is identical to the three-view basic shape drawing process. During the initial exercise we've identified the foundational guidelines for creating an almost accurate three-view drawing. Attention to proportion, proper symmetry, good alignment, and precise object placement are the key observations that make this drawing work. In the case of orthographic drawing, we're going to use all of these foundational processes, but to the extreme.

Exercise 2: Use a three-view basic shape drawing to create a detailed three-view orthographic drawing of your design.

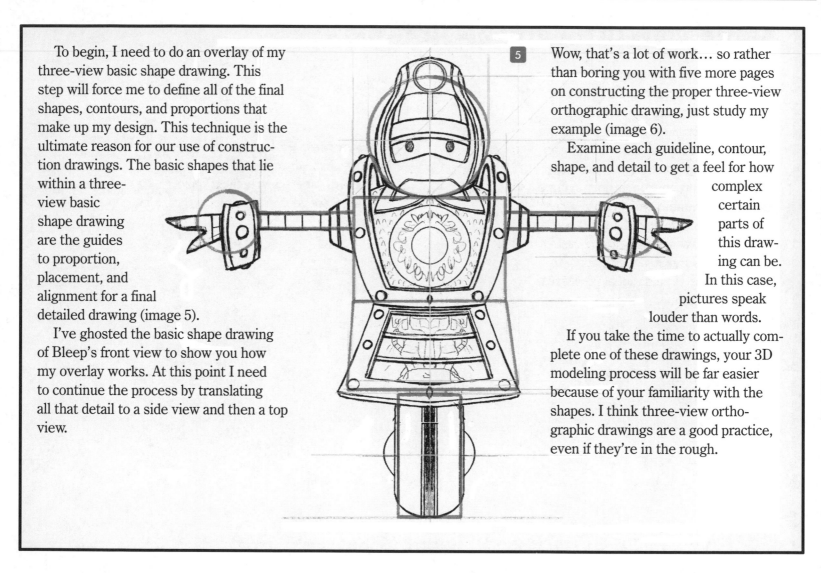

To begin, I need to do an overlay of my three-view basic shape drawing. This step will force me to define all of the final shapes, contours, and proportions that make up my design. This technique is the ultimate reason for our use of construction drawings. The basic shapes that lie within a three-view basic shape drawing are the guides to proportion, placement, and alignment for a final detailed drawing (image 5).

I've ghosted the basic shape drawing of Bleep's front view to show you how my overlay works. At this point I need to continue the process by translating all that detail to a side view and then a top view.

Wow, that's a lot of work... so rather than boring you with five more pages on constructing the proper three-view orthographic drawing, just study my example (image 6).

Examine each guideline, contour, shape, and detail to get a feel for how complex certain parts of this drawing can be. In this case, pictures speak louder than words.

If you take the time to actually complete one of these drawings, your 3D modeling process will be far easier because of your familiarity with the shapes. I think three-view orthographic drawings are a good practice, even if they're in the rough.

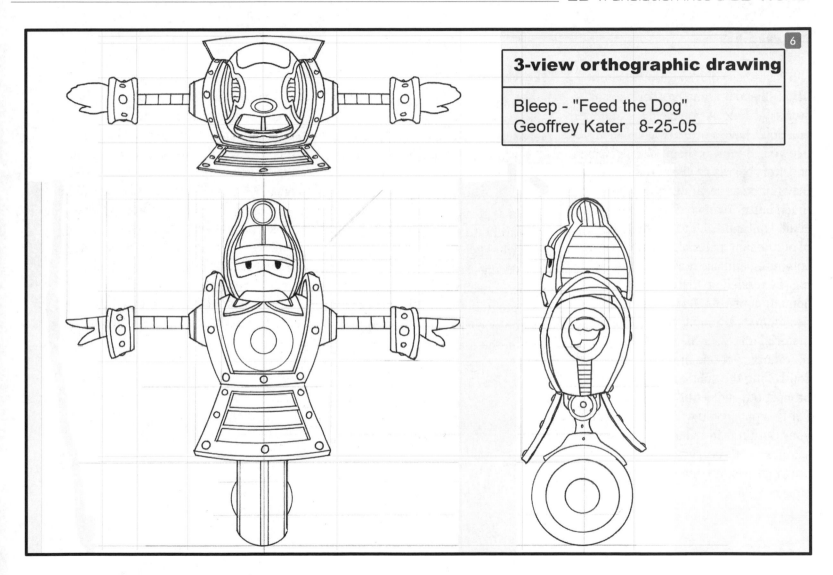

3-view orthographic drawing

Bleep - "Feed the Dog"
Geoffrey Kater   8-25-05

Scan It

Our last phase of translating 2D into 3D is all about scanning. This is easy stuff... as long as you have a scanner. If you don't have a scanner, you can still use your 3-view orthographic drawing and storyboards as visual reference. It may not be as accurate, but it's still much better than no design reference at all. Our approach will be to gather all of our design material, scan it into the computer, and use it as reference during the modeling, texturing, and animation phases. As it relates to design first, scanning your reference material into your 3D animation environment is yet one more way of controlling the subtle nuances in size, proportion, and detail of your designs. For this phase you will need to organize your design material into three separate categories: three-view orthographic drawings, texture maps, and storyboards.

3D Models

In order to get the most accurate 3D model of our designs, our three-view orthographic drawing will be used in the background. I start by scanning in each image — front, side, and top views. Do your best to scan your images as straight as possible. The more accurate you are during scanning, the fewer alignment issues you will have during assembly.

Import each view into your 3D modeling program (image 7). I've arranged the front view on the Z axis, the side view on the X axis, and the top view on the Y axis. The truth is, sometimes all you need is the Z and X axis views because 98% of your information about proportion and size are contained in those views. In that case, just use the top view or Y axis view as visual reference. Also, make sure all the views line up. Alignment is very important, and most programs have a way of adjusting each viewport to ensure proper image placement. At this point you can start your 3D model, but there are a few more scans I'd like to complete before we get into that.

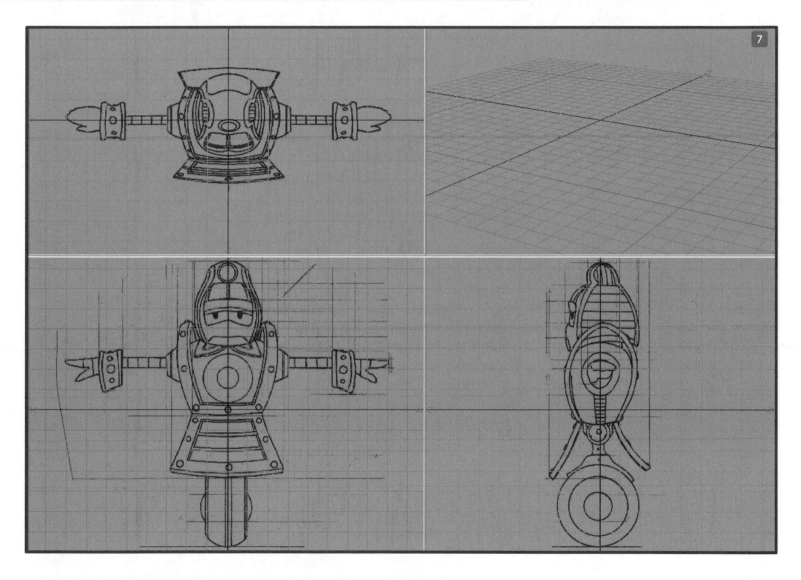

Image Maps

Having done a ton of research, we've collected more reference material of textures, backgrounds, shapes, and colors than we can even remember. The key goal of this phase is to isolate those images that you feel might be of some use during the texturing, animation, and lighting phases. For instance, maybe you came across a really cool metallic texture that you want to use to texture an object. I'm all for it — in fact there's been many an occasion that I've scanned brushed aluminum, fabric, rough plastic, dirt, stone, hair, paper, copper, and even my hand in order to create a good texture. There's nothing like creating a texture from something that already exists — it will always look more natural and give your 3D models a real leg up. As for any images that you've found, perhaps you want to scan them into your computer and make some adjustments in a paint program like Photoshop before using them as a texture map. The texture that I found for "Feed the Dog" comes from a Chinese clay teapot (image 8). I love the rich brown texture and the beautiful hand-carved calligraphy. This texture will be applied to Angus. Angus' design is inspired by this exact Chinese teapot, so I can't think of a better texture map than straight off the original. I'm going to have to make some adjustments in Photoshop in order to create an accurate texture map for Angus, but it's worth it. At this point, I have all I need as far as scanning textures goes, so it's time to move on.

Storyboards

As you know, nothing impacts the animation phase more than a storyboard, for reasons like composition, camera movement, and shot length. In this case, I want to scan in my entire storyboard and save each image with its corresponding scene number. Then, during the animation phase, I'll import my storyboard panel as a background image and use it as a guide for my scene compositions. We spent a lot of time getting each composition to look good on paper and we want our 3D animation to reflect that effort. This way you can put your models, backgrounds, and camera into each scene with the care and accuracy represented in your storyboards. You'd be surprised how inaccurate your scene compositions can be when you don't use a storyboard panel for reference. I'll get into how to apply the storyboard to our scene in the next chapter, "Animation Production"; for now, get it scanned and move on.

Chapter Nine

Animation Production

Introduction

Animation production is a phase that some of you are very familiar with and others are just learning. Either way, our goal in this chapter is to use all of our design material for 3D model creation and animation direction.

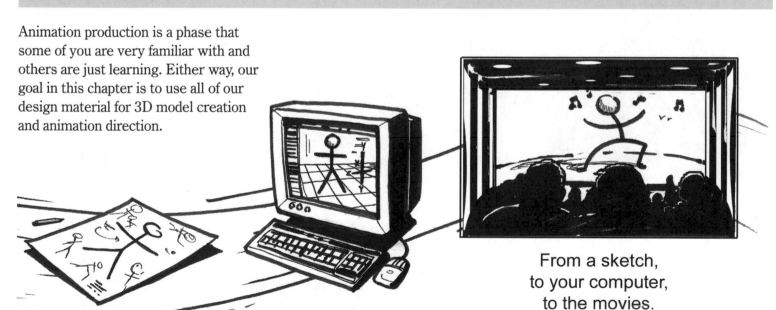

From a sketch,
to your computer,
to the movies.

3D Modeling

3D modeling is where all of our designs will spring to life into a solid 3D world. It's the most exciting part of animation because all of our design work on paper has led to this moment… the moment of truth. Remembering that 2D drawings can be cheated, truth is what you will find as you start modeling your objects because a 3D model will not allow for the loose placement of shape, proportion, or contour. Each part of your 3D model needs to work together as if it were a real-life object, and for that we have created our three-view orthographic drawing.

My first 3D model is going to be our main character, Bleep. I'm simply going to load my three-view orthographic drawing into my modeling program and get started. As you can see, I've only loaded his front and side views because I feel they give me enough information to start my 3D model (image 1).

I zero in on his head and start modeling the front half of his face. I'm going to build only one side of his face and then mirror that side at a later time.

For now I want to concentrate on proportion, contour, and shape. My goal is to build the overall silhouette of his head first, then I'll add detail like eyes, mouth, eyebrows, and design detail later. This is a good start if you have the modeling experience to just dive right in; however, if you're not quite ready to start modeling the final version and want to do a quick check on proportions, I have a good solution.

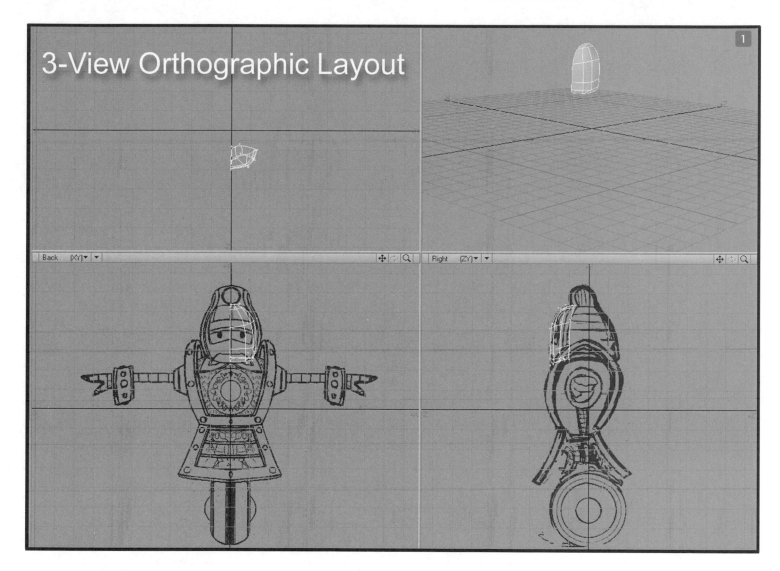

3-View Orthographic Layout

Back (XY)▼ ▼

Right (ZY)▼ ▼

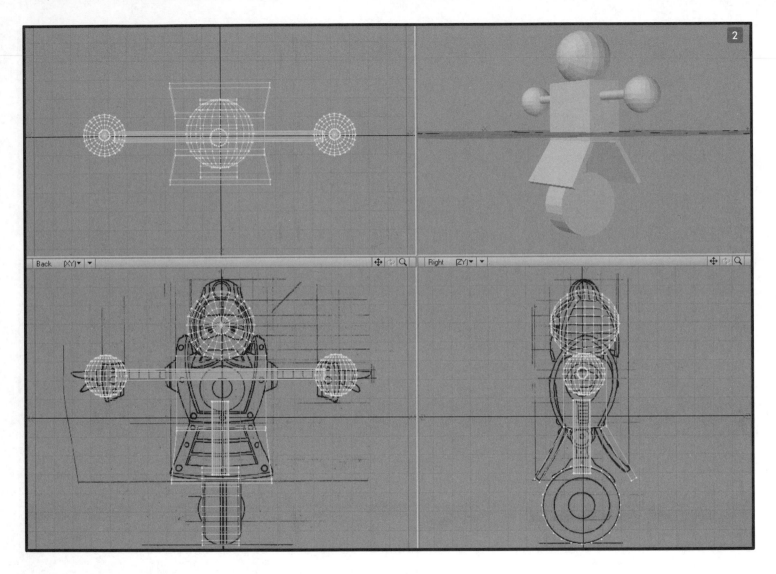

Use a Three-View Basic Shape Drawing as Reference

Sometimes it's easier to construct your 3D model with simple shapes first before starting any kind of complex modeling (image 2).

Using my three-view basic shape drawing as reference, I've blocked out a 3D construction model of Bleep and matched it up against his three-view orthographic drawing. Fortunately I planned for this stage, knowing that in certain areas my simple shapes might show me something that doesn't look right, such as odd proportions or misplaced shapes. In this case, I feel that Bleep's head might look a little too large, so I'll make a mental note of this and then make a change later. I will model his head according to my three-view orthographic reference and then make any size and proportion adjustments later when Bleep's model is more complete. This way I'm not getting caught up in details that can be worked out later; I'm just concentrating on accuracy at this point.

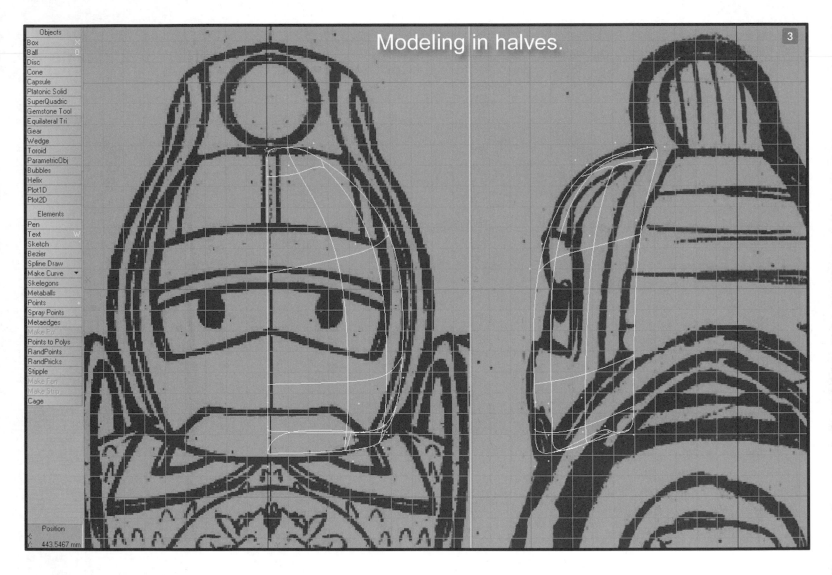

Modeling in halves.

Model in Halves

To start my 3D model of Bleep, I'll choose his head first. It's the most complicated part of his design and I want to get the hardest things out of the way first. The challenge is to build a perfectly symmetrical 3D model; that is, both the left and right side being symmetrical. The easiest approach to this challenge is to build only half of your 3D model to start. Building only half your model will give you the opportunity to focus on smoothing out contours, adjusting proportion, and delineating shape to its finest detail without doing double the work on the opposite half. In Bleep's case, I'm going to model the left half of his head first and then mirror that object to create the right half. I will then join the two halves together by welding each corresponding point until I've created a complete head (image 3).

Not only is the modeling in halves technique good for objects like Bleep's head and chest, it's also really great for cloning whole parts like hands, arms, eyes, and shoulders as well as accoutrements like rivets, fittings, and design detail. The tire portion of his wheel is built as a whole, but the two rims on either side have been mirrored to match (image 4). As for your project, think of ways to model in halves and clone objects to save you time during the 3D modeling process.

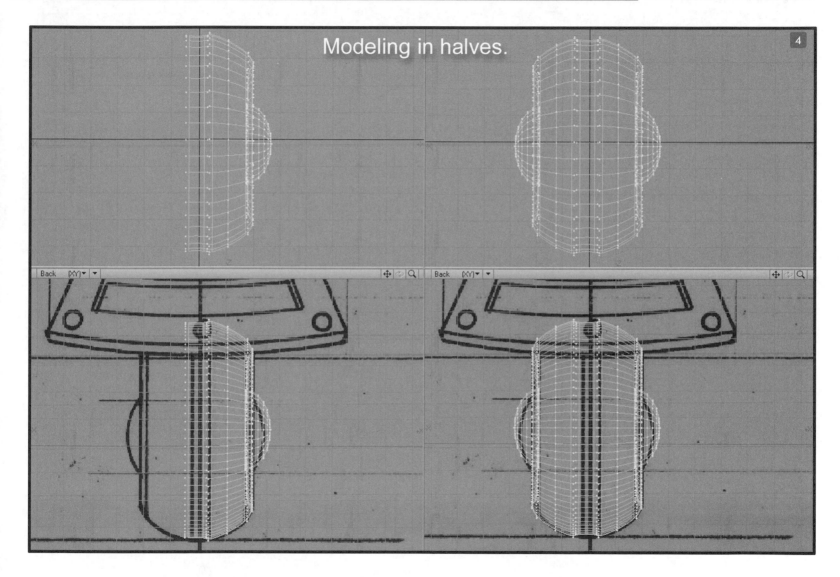

Modeling in halves.

Check Your Proportions

As stated in earlier sections, manipulating and adjusting proportion is a good way to add visual interest to your designs. When you finally translate your 2D drawings into 3D, you might find out, however, that what looks good on paper looks awkward or unfinished in 3D. This is perhaps the result of two things: poor planning or unforeseen modeling issues. The poor planning side of things is self explanatory, but the unforeseen side of things is a very likely occurrence. Sometimes it's nearly impossible to foresee the problems with proportion associated with a 2D drawing until it's actually transformed into a 3D object. For example, ask yourself these simple questions: How do the sizes of my shapes relate to each other? Are my shapes too even? Should there be more contrast in size? Does one shape feel awkwardly large? Can I reduce the size of specific shapes and still retain my overall design appeal? If you find yourself answering these questions with a yes, then maybe it's time to whip out the old pencil and do some quick sketches on improvements. Sometimes I'll just print out an image of my 3D model and use an overlay to sketch out my fixes. Whether it's in the modeling stage or on a piece of paper, proper proportions and their relationship should be applied with the utmost scrutiny.

Proportion is not just about one shape versus another; proportion is also the size relationship between details. I've intentionally designed Bleep's head with a fair amount of proportion changes. This effectively makes Bleep's head more visually appealing and functionally viable. He has to have a forehead, eyes, mouth, etc., but size and placement of those details is what gives Bleep his unique look (image 5).

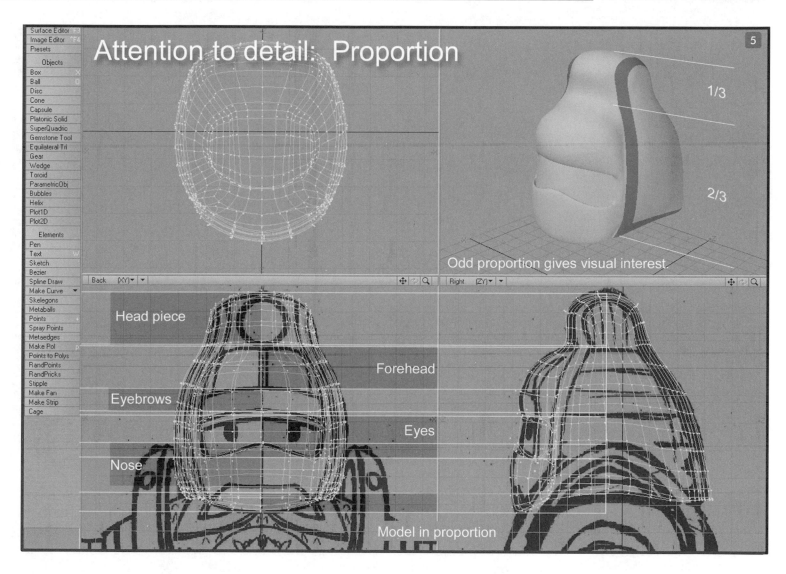

Attention to detail: Proportion

1/3

2/3

Odd proportion gives visual interest.

Head piece

Forehead

Eyebrows

Eyes

Nose

Model in proportion

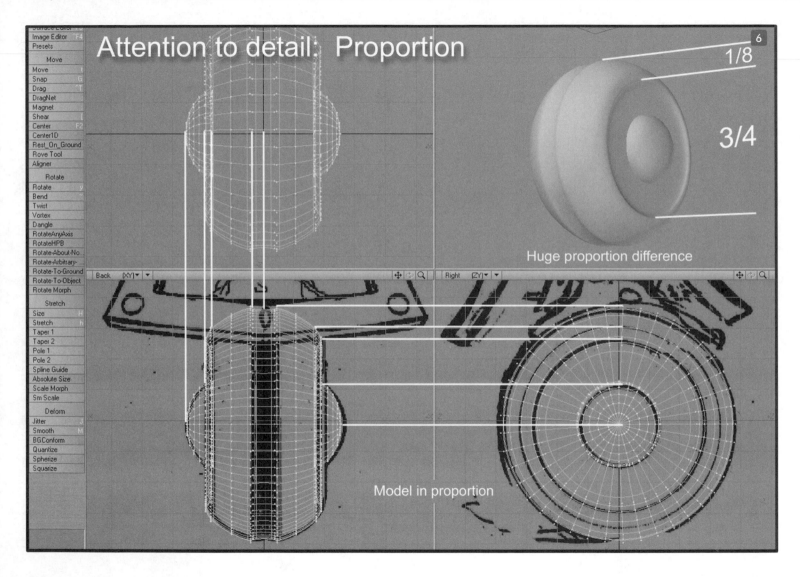

Attention to detail: Proportion

1/8

3/4

Huge proportion difference

Model in proportion

My example clearly illustrates the variation in proportion from one head detail to the next. It's not so much that I'm doing anything really radical with his proportions, I'm just strictly focused on modeling those proportions as accurately and controlled as possible. Bleep's wheel is another good example of proportion within a model detail. His tire is very low profile and must be modeled accurately in order to give the entire wheel visual interest (image 6).

It's the contrast in size between the huge metal rim and the short low-profile tire that gives his wheel a sporty look. At this stage, model your object's proportions as accurately as you possibly can. If you feel that your 3D object does not properly represent the design you have on paper or the vision you have in your head, feel free to make subtle adjustments to the proportions as long as it increases the visual appeal of your design.

Contour

Contour is another design element that plays a large role in adding visual interest to your 3D model. Much like a silhouette defines an overall shape, contour is what defines the curved or irregular surfaces in our design. For example, Bleep has many areas in which contour plays a role. My example shows a close-up side view of the top of Bleep's head (image 7).

I've done my best to make the transition from his forehead shape into his headpiece shape as smooth as possible. That smooth quality will really show in Bleep's final rendered model. I've included a front view example of Bleep's head and how I controlled each contour to work in harmony as they

move toward the center of his head (image 8). Again, all this control and attention to detail is going to make your final 3D model that much more appealing. Contour is simply one shape transitioning into the next, so if you have a rough surface, than those transitions are going to be sharper and more abrupt. If you have a smooth surface, than those transitions are going to be smooth and controlled. As a designer, my job is to make those decisions about contour and apply them to my design. In the case of Bleep, the contours of his head are smooth and refined, so my job is to model each contour with attention to subtle transition in shape and overall fluid line quality.

247

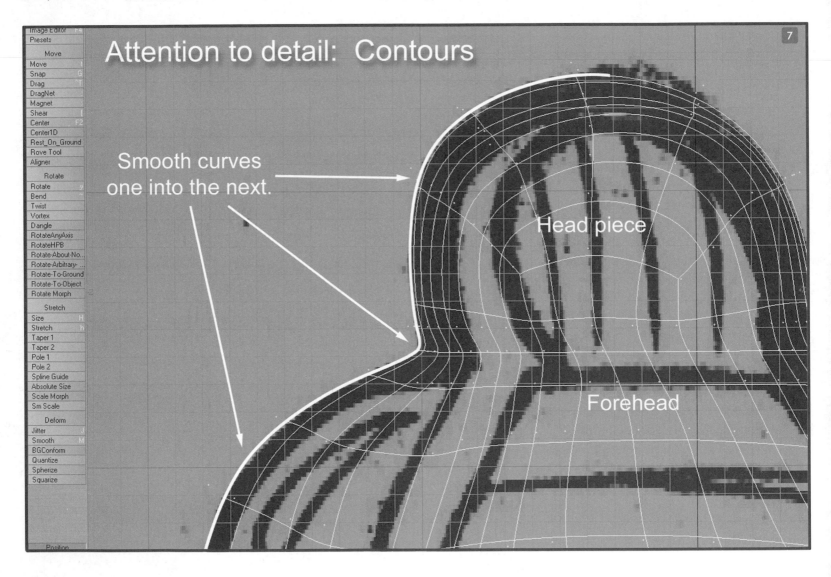

Attention to detail: Contours

Smooth curves one into the next.

Head piece

Forehead

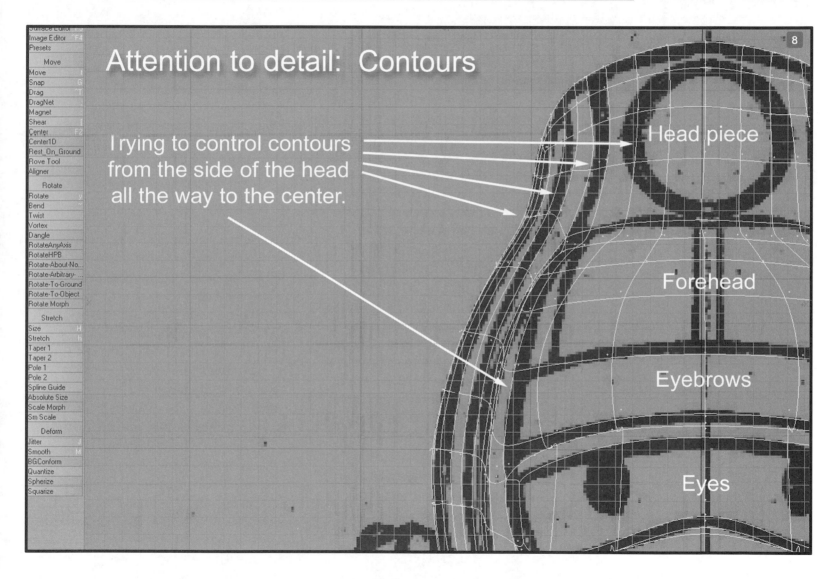

Attention to detail: Contours

Trying to control contours from the side of the head all the way to the center.

Head piece

Forehead

Eyebrows

Eyes

Observation and Final Adjustments

As stated in Chapter 3, observation is one of the most powerful educational tools available to the designer. It is from observation that you tap into the wisdom and experience of other designers and that of your own and apply it to your work. In this section I will not only teach you how to recognize design flaws but also how to cure them.

There are certain subtle details in contour and shape that are nearly impossible to sort out on paper until you've actually built the 3D model. As a good designer, you owe it to yourself to constantly scan your model for design details that can be improved upon and adjusted. Observe each shape and contour, making sure they are accurately portrayed in your 3D model. Are all the contours perfectly worked out with good transitions? Do some of the details get lost in the overall design? Is there a shape that feels awkwardly large or small? Does the silhouette of my object feel iconic and recognizable? Is there anything that I like or dislike about my 3D model that I can improve? Does my 3D model embody the spirit of my original design? All of these are questions you can ask yourself to improve your 3D work. Once you've answered your questions, ask yourself what your solutions are. Make a list or mental note of your solutions and then apply them to your model. Spending the extra time to observe and apply your solutions is what makes you a designer.

As for my observations, I've found a few things about Bleep that I feel can be improved upon (image 9). After modeling his entire body, I've come to notice that his head looks a little fat and the size is too big for his body. I actually caught this proportion issue earlier in my three-view basic shape model, but now it's time to address it. I've made distinct design choices about what I think is making his head look a bit too big and have made those adjustments. At this point I've modeled nearly 90% of Bleep and will make all the adjustments to his body that I think are necessary and then move on to my favorite stage… detail.

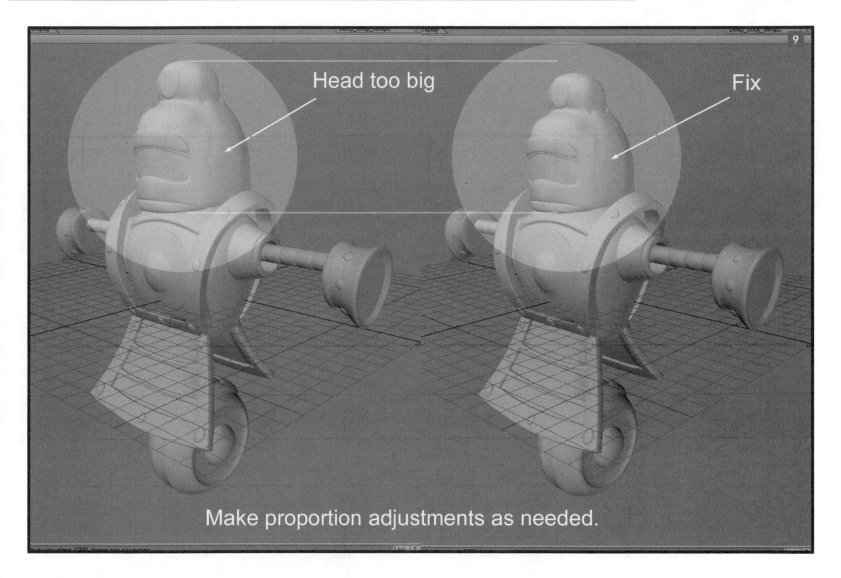

Head too big

Fix

Make proportion adjustments as needed.

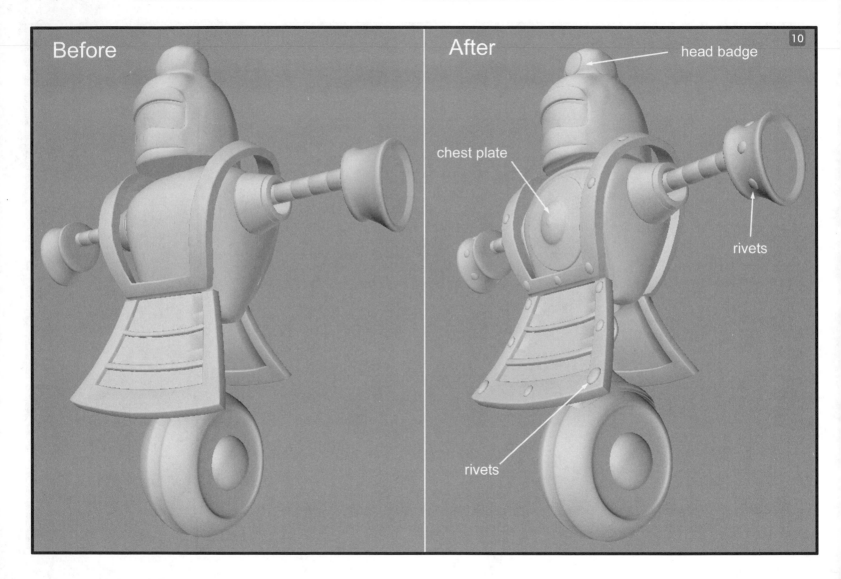

Detail

To me, detail is like adding the whipped cream, chocolate syrup, and cherry to a sundae. Without all those goodies added at the last moment, we'd be left with just a plain bowl of ice cream. Detailing your 3D model is akin to this process because it is the final modeling stage wherein everything you have done thus far really comes together. I originally named this section "The Last 10%" because most designs look fairly incomplete until you add that last 10% of detail that really makes them pop. Talk about detail — Bleep has a ton of it. From channeled contours in his head to bristling armor plating with brass rivets punched into his exoskeleton. The suspension arm extending out of his upper body alone is chock full of so many details that I dread having to model those parts. I guess the real question here is, does every detail need to be modeled? The answer is no. Every detail should be divided up into three separate categories: modeled detail, color, and texture. Color and texture are covered in the following sections, but for now I'm going to focus on modeled detail. Some of the details that I need to model are rivets, armor plate, contours and extrusions, teeth, badge on headpiece, wheel detail, and hand detail. I've included before and after images of Bleep showing some of the model details I created (image 10). Detailing is just like the previous sections on contour and proportion; details are simply miniature model accoutrements that enhance your design. So take the time to model details with the same care and precision you would for the first 90%.

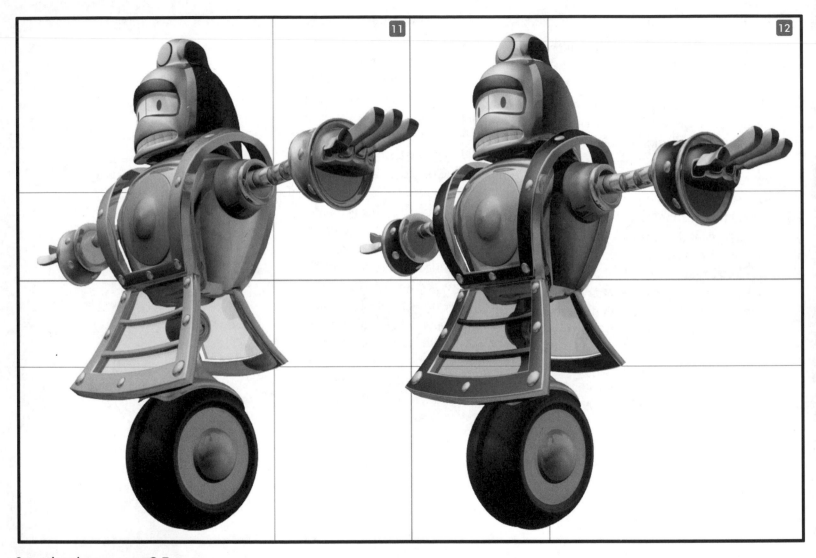

See color plate on page C-7.

Color

As you add color to any 3D model, you'll really start to see it come to life. Color is yet another dimension that adds contrast, depth, and character, and so becomes an additional design tool that requires careful application. As you apply your colors, there may be some very apparent design tweaks that weren't so visible during the initial modeling stage. Details and contours have a way of getting lost in the abyss of gray that is usually your default surface color during the modeling process. Sometimes I'll start to add color early to get a sense of proportion, detail, and overall design accuracy. There is no right or wrong way to add color; just choose a way that works in favor of the modeling process, as long as it helps to control your design accuracy.

In Chapter 6 I created a color palette and color comps of characters and backgrounds to serve as reference for this stage (image 11).

Using this color reference I've started to color Bleep. Coloring Bleep with his original color of gold looks really cool, but I'm getting this feeling that gold may be a little too much. What I mean is that by choosing gold as his color, I've inherited all of the presumptions that people make about objects that are gold. For instance the words precious, valuable, fragile, refined, forever lasting, and so on. Since I'm looking for an emotional response from the audience that is triggered by Bleep's aesthetic, I think the words valuable, refined, and forever lasting are great descriptions that match Bleep's character. I think the words precious and fragile indicate some sort of weakness and are words that I don't want associated with him.

I could change Bleep to a different color, or I could tone down the amount of gold on his body, but either way, whatever color I choose should add a feeling of strength and endurance. Looking at my example, you can see that I chose black as the color that would complement the gold of his body.

The emotional response to black is a feeling of boldness, strength, endurance, mystery, and darkness. As a master of espionage, his job is to lurk in the shadows and observe his subject until the time calls for a strike! The qualities of black that serve his character very well are strength, mystery, and darkness. Aesthetically, black now serves as a solid backdrop from which our gold is now just a decorative detail that adds a sense of refinement and value to his character. I've also created another level of contrast in his design by using gold underscored by large patches of black to give his design more depth and intensity (image 12).

Using your color reference as a guide, color your objects to get a feel for how they look in 3D. Are the colors you chose complementing your design or detracting from it? Is there a way to add small details of color to increase your object's depth and viability? Try to choose colors that add an emotional detail that will further increase your design's appeal.

Texturing

Texturing our 3D model is the final stage of detailing. Early on I chose some texture maps and have isolated them for reference. Using my ancient China theme, I would like to emboss detailing and calligraphy onto Bleep's body with the same care and attention to detail that you would see on a Chinese teapot or Ming vase. I think this kind of subtle detailing will really add to that feeling of value and refinement that the gold has done for his character. See my example of Bleep's chest. His chest is comprised of channeled contours that run around the front, sides, and back. His chest contains a large circular plate that is inspired by the large circular pieces of armor that ancient Chinese soldiers wore during battle. Those circular pieces of armor almost always had some kind of embossed detail or calligraphy, so I think the same should go for Bleep. I've created a Chinese-like pattern to use as a texture on this plate (image 13). Note the symmetrical iconic box-like details that just scream ancient Chinese art. I'm not only going to use this pattern on his chest plate, but I'm going to use it on his wheel and his hands as well. This repetition of design is akin to the kind of logo you would see repeated on a car, such as a BMW. BMW puts its logo on the front of the car, the wheels, the steering wheel, the stick shift, the rear fender, and even stitched into the seats. This kind of logo repetition reinforces the brand. In the case of Bleep, the iconic Chinese circular pattern reinforces his unique ancient Chinese design.

See color plate on page C-8.

The Power of Sublety

Another interesting thing about ancient Chinese design is that at first glance, you get hit with a wow factor. Like wow, that Ming vase is really beautiful (image 14). Even at a distance, the vase has such an iconic silhouette that you see and feel its appeal immediately. Then as you get closer to the vase you start to discover its beautiful colors and patterns that cover every inch.

With closer examination, you begin to see that each of those patterns has been hand painted and contains incredibly small details of pattern and texture. The wow factor has shot up 1000% because at first glance you had no idea that a vase like that could have so much detail.

It's all about subtlety and is very closely related to creating a focal point within a composition. At first glance, you understand the scene, on second glance, you notice more detail, and on third glance... wow! I didn't see that at first, but I like it!

Okay, as for Bleep, this kind of first glance philosophy is really important. At first glance we catch Bleep's overall silhouette and aesthetic, and on second glance we see some of the bigger details like his chest armor, brass rivets, and headpiece details. I want to include some subtle detail that can only be seen when you're really close to Bleep. See my example of Bleep's chest (image 15). I've taken the liberty of embossing every square inch of his chest with a very iconic Chinese graphic. It's not very apparent at first, but once you see it, it provides yet another level of detail and depth that makes Bleep's design more interesting and appealing.

See color plate on page C-9.

BGs

Backgrounds are another textured element necessary to any 3D animation. In the case of "Feed the Dog," our mountain vista with forest is most definitely a textured element. This is simply achieved by creating an image of the mountains, forest, and sky that can be texture mapped onto a large polygon in the background (image 16).

At this point, I have a bunch of objects that need texturing, so I'll follow the aforementioned process on each one of my designs until I've completed my list.

Finalized 3D Model

At this point I've done all the detailing and design tweaks I possibly can before going into animation. Perhaps there are some things that I can improve upon in the way of posing and expressions, but for now I'm pretty happy with Bleep's final design. Now that we've come this far, you can really see how the initial inspiration, research, design, and translation have influenced my final 3D model. It goes without saying that this kind of design application can be explored and delineated to the very last pixel on your screen, and for what we are learning, this kind of straightforward, "design it on paper first" philosophy is going to improve your work as a designer for the rest of your career.

3D Animation

If you need to learn the technical side of animation like character setup, visual effects, modeling, and the like, there are plenty of other books that teach those concepts at length. I'm not here to teach you all of those things. My focus is on teaching you to use your storyboards as a guide for scene composition, flow, and graphic impact.

Stick to Your Boards!

This section is going to teach you how to use your storyboards for compositional reference during the animation phase. We did all this work on our storyboards in Chapter 7 and now it's time to use them. I chose scenes 6 and 25 because I feel they encompass many of the design techniques that I'm trying to convey during this section on scene composition and execution.

Scene 6 is a medium to close-up shot of Bleep strangling The NCER from behind. The first thing I do is pull in my pre-scanned storyboard panel with this scene number. I load it up in the background of my animation program and then import any and all models that relate to this scene. Those 3D models would be Bleep, The N4CER, and my correlating background. Once loaded into the scene, I place my characters and the background in alignment with the storyboard. They may not match exactly, so use your best judgment. (image 17).

The opening of my composition from the storyboard feels a little too close to the characters. I'm taking into account that my camera is going to slowly push into a close-up of Bleep's face, so I want to allow enough room for that camera move. My solution is to pull the camera back a bit, effectively opening up my shot and giving us a little more breathing room for the push-in.

That's it; all the characters are in their proper position, I've articulated their limbs, heads, and expressions to coincide with my storyboard, and I have achieved a decent composition that feels designed and graphic. At this point, I will reference my camera and timing notes from my storyboard and fully animate the scene. As for lighting and rendering, that will be covered in the next section. For now, just focus on scene composition and fluid animation.

Scene 25 is a wide shot of Bleep with The N4CER in the foreground. Once again, I load in my corresponding storyboard panel, characters, and background, and then complete all the animation (image 18).

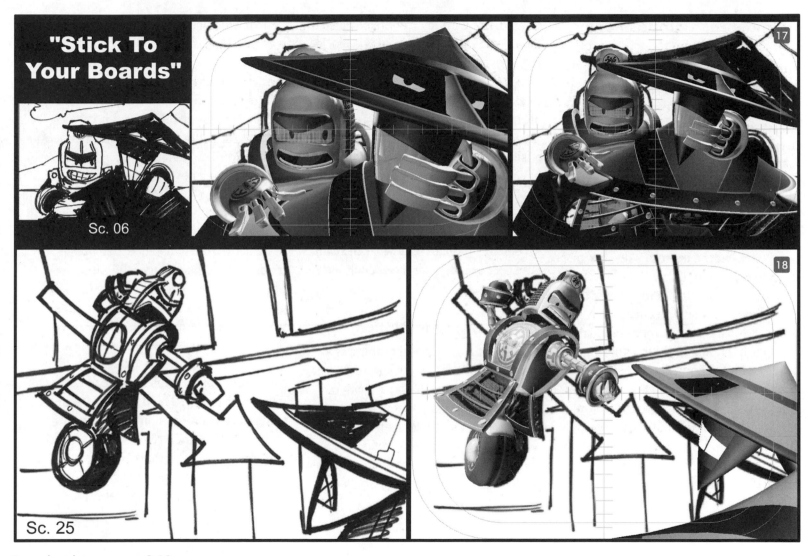

"Stick To Your Boards"

Sc. 06

Sc. 25

See color plate on page C-10.

Animate for Composition

It's important for me to point out that during the 2D phase of design, there is a lot of cheatin' goin' on! We know that drawings can misrepresent what really happens in a 3D world, but how can we use this cheatin' technique to our advantage? It's akin to the old lesson of don't build it if you don't have to. For instance, if you only see a character from the waist up for an entire show, why spend time building legs? Only build for what the camera sees, because nobody is going to know the difference.

This goes for compositions as well. Sometimes you have to cheat your scene setups to match your composition. With that in mind I am going back to scene 25 to show you an example. Scene 25 has Bleep flying in the air and The N4CER in the foreground. In order to get such a low dramatic shot on Bleep, I had to lower the camera very close to the floor. In this case, The N4CER is supposed to be lying on the ground, but with my camera so close to the floor, The N4CER would be blocking our view. The solution is to lower The N4CER through the floor in order to execute my composition. My example clearly shows how this was done (image 19). In other words, scene composition is king — no matter what you have to do, cheat your shots so they look their best. Don't get caught up in real-world details like having objects perfectly arranged or fully modeled. Model and animate only what the camera sees; as long as it looks cool, then that's all that counts.

Who's Going to Notice?

Who's going to notice that there is a rivet missing off that background structure? Who's going to notice that your character only has 10 teeth instead of 20? Although it still looks fine, who's going to notice that your reflection map doesn't match your background? Who's going to notice that you misspelled "Lawn Moower for Sale" on that sign way off in the distance? Who's going to notice that there are a bazillion different scenarios that require this question? The only person who will notice these details is yourself and others involved in your animation project. The audience is completely oblivious to these kinds of details. If they never knew it existed, then they'll never know the difference. Don't spend lots of extra time modeling contours and details that are only going to be seen from a distance; use image maps and the like to give the same effect. I've seen people actually model grass blades in a scene where the grass was only visible from a distance. If you have a close-up of grass, model a few feet of grass and then use a texture map for the rest of the grass that recedes into the distance. The most important thing here is to focus on composition and animation, then review your animations in real time. If there's a slight aesthetic mistake but it doesn't stick out like a sore thumb, then let it go.

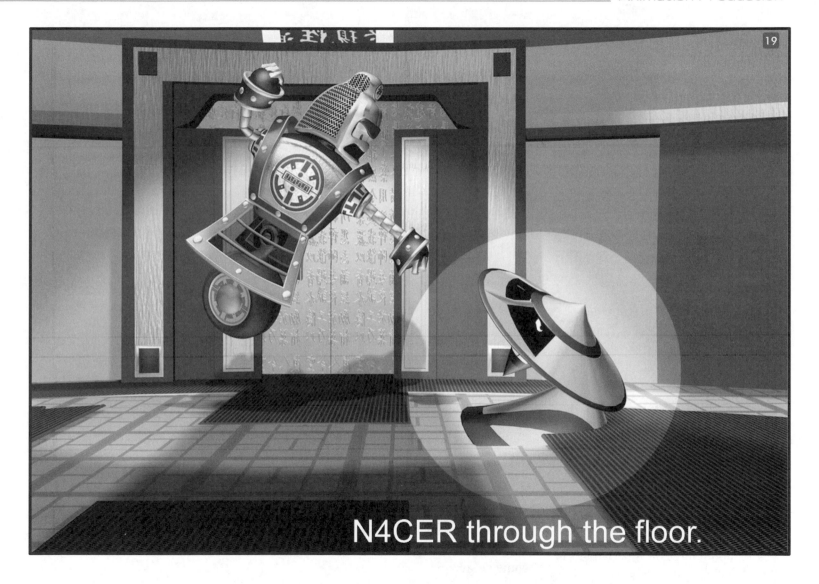

N4CER through the floor.

Lighting

Here we're going to use some of the lighting techniques we've learned in previous chapters, such as contrast, value, warm and cool lighting, and opposite colors. Although we've already colored our characters, adding subtle levels of cool and warm light and contrast with shade and shadow will add another dimension of focus and depth to our animation.

Contrast

Using contrasts in value is the most crucial component of proper lighting. Basically focused on light and dark only, we want to create a graphic, contrasted scene that establishes our focal point and creates an easy first read. It's as easy as saying, should my background be light or dark? This is basic stuff we covered in Chapter 2 on value. Scene 6 of "Feed the Dog" has Bleep strangling The N4CER in the foreground and a wide mountain vista in the background. Since this scene takes place during the day, the mountain vista is fairly light in value. My characters should be lit so

they contrast with the background, which means they need to be dark in value. How can I make these objects dark if it's the middle of the day? With shade and shadow. What affects shade and shadow? Light. Light intensity and direction is what will affect the shade and shadow of these characters. In this scene, the sun is behind our characters, giving us an opportunity to silhouette them against our light background. See my example (image 20).

Panel 1 has no lighting at all and our characters are in almost full silhouette. This has created great contrast, but we need to shine a little light on this scene to open it up. What I mean by open up is to use light to reveal details and such.

Panel 2 indicates a backlight of high intensity, which is our sun. I've also used the natural cast shadow to create nice graphic shapes on our characters to give more visual interest to the scene. Our characters are still fairly dark, so we need an indirect light source to open them up so we can see some detail.

Panel 3 indicates bounced and reflected light, which as you know is light that comes from an indirect light source like the sky, ground, and even other objects. I'm using the reflected light of the sky and a bounced light from our wheat field to reveal my characters' details, like their faces, hands, eyes, etc. This is a huge improvement over the last few panels; now our characters are really starting to look good.

Panel 4 indicates the final composition and, as you can see, it is a huge improvement over panel 1. Our composition has good contrast and our focal point, Bleep strangling The N4CER, is clearly delineated within the scene. To polish off this shot, I added a little bit of ambient light, about 5%, just to lighten up the characters a bit.

There are a lot of things to consider during the lighting phase in addition to good contrast. How about warm and cool lighting?

No light

Sun light only

Sun, reflected and bounced light

Sun, reflected, bounced and ambient light

See color plate on page C-11.

See color plate on page C-12.

Warm and Cool Lighting

I've got good contrast going in my shots, but another thing I'd like to point out is the attention to warm and cool lighting. In Chapter 3 we discussed the different variables of contrasting warm and cool colors. Warm coloring or lighting is usually indicative of something closer to camera, while cool colors or lighting is indicative of things in the distance. In the case of scene 6, my mountain vista background is already cool in color, so I used warm lighting on my characters to give depth to the scene. Scene 25 has a warm/cool color scheme as well and can be seen in my example (image 21).

Rendering

As far as rendering goes, there are a lot of different ways to do it. You can render all of your objects together at one time, or you can render your objects separately. I guess it really depends upon your situation, but rendering objects, reflections, shadows, and backgrounds separately gives you a huge amount of control over their value, color, and focus. For instance, scene 6 of "Feed the Dog" has my two main characters, Bleep and The N4CER, in the foreground and a wide mountain vista in the background. If I wanted to I could render my characters and background separately and then reassemble the shot in a compositing program like Adobe After Effects. Once I'm in the compositing stage, my background and characters will be on separate layers. At this point, I could blur out the background to give more depth, add warmth to my characters by using a color filter, etc. These kinds of quick effects like blurs, grain, coloring, contrast, etc., are far more difficult and time consuming to achieve in your 3D package than in a 2D package. Use 2D compositing programs to your advantage and separate your scenes into distinct layers not only to decrease render time, but also to give you more control over the look and focus of your scenes.

The next chapter talks a bit about some of these composite techniques, where they should be used, and how your work can benefit from them.

2D Shortcuts for 3D

Use Traditional Design to Save on Render Time

Let's say that you have a character in the foreground and a cityscape in the background. You can either model and render an entire city (lots of render time), or you could use an image of that city as a background element instead. Using a 2D approach to creating environments, textures, lighting, and reflections can save you a ton of modeling and render time.

Environments

An animated environment can add an incredible amount of depth and richness to your animation, but it can take an awful lot of time to model and takes an even longer time to render. I would say that if your camera is moving down a street or through an environment and you need background objects pushing past the camera, then the scene would require you to build those objects. On the other hand, if your scene has very little movement or the environment is

merely a simple element that falls second to the real focal point, like a close-up of two characters, then you can get away with a single image as your background.

There are three straightforward methods for creating an image that will replace an entire 3D background. The first is to paint an image, like a matte painting, cartoony background, or silhouetted environment. This method is used all the time in sci-fi movies, animated films, and video games. The three original *Star Wars* movies used matte paintings in many scenes that required extensive environments like those on the Death Star, Cloud City, and Endor, just to name a few. The paintings looked so realistic that they were able to take the place of elaborate sets that were needed to convince the audience that those environments really existed. As technology has allowed for digital paintings, many matte painters now mostly do their painting in a computer program like Alias Sketch, Photoshop, or Painter. Regardless of the method, creating background paintings for films requires some pretty good artistic skill, but I would say give it a shot; you never know until you try.

The second method of creating background images is to actually find an image that you like and then alter it for your own purposes. For example, scene 6 of "Feed the Dog" uses a background image of a wide mountain vista (image 1).

This original background is an unaltered stock photo that I found on one of the photo stock sites such as Getty Images, Image After, and Dreamstime.com. It's perfect for my concept, but what if I wanted to change that background to something a little more customized.

Sometimes you can't find a stock photo you like, so the solution is to find a few images that contain the subject you're looking for and then piece them together. For example, I wanted to change scene 25 to something a little more stark and void of detail, so in my search I found some great shots of Mount Fuji, a wheat field, and a sky element, and then stitched them together in Photoshop to create a custom background that I liked. I then took that final Mount Fuji image, mapped it to a single polygon, and inserted it into my shot (image 2).

Again, this stitching together of images is a great way to customize your backgrounds and textures.

Stitch images together to create final

Original BG

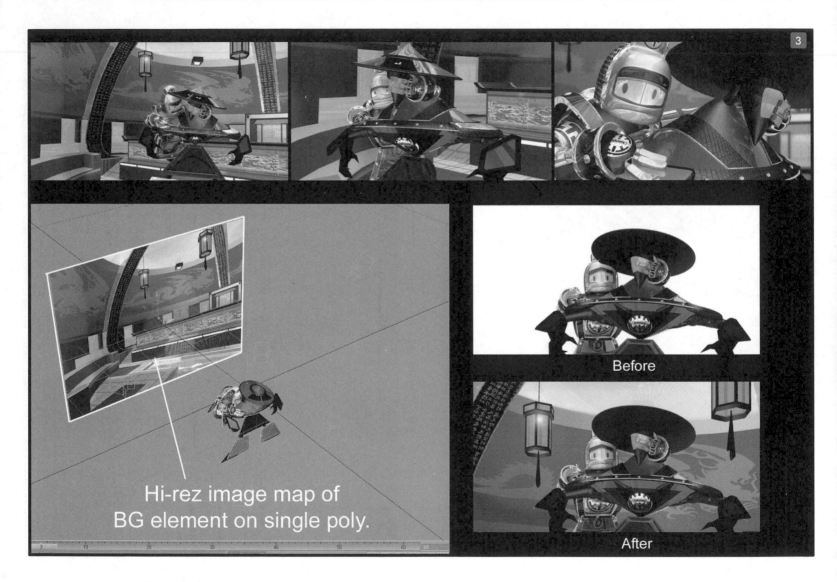

Hi-rez image map of
BG element on single poly.

Before

After

My third method of 3D environment replacement would be to prerender your environment without any characters or objects of focus in the scene. For example, let's say that you have four shots that require the same background element and each shot varies from wide to medium to close-up. Prerender your environment from the proper angle as a high-resolution wide shot, then map that image to a polygon and put it in its proper place within the scene. By using this method, you've effectively eliminated four full environmental renders (image 3).

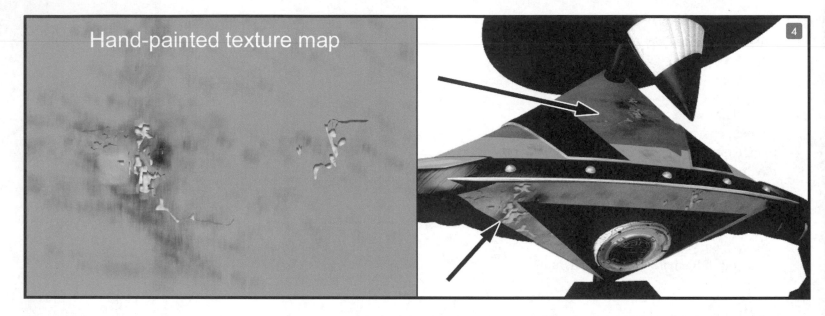

Hand-painted texture map

Textures

I've seen more people try to use the latest plug-in or procedural to produce a texture that could easily be hand painted than I even want to mention. It was always a no-brainer to me that using hand-painted textures not only gave a more stylized look, but were incredibly accurate to your vision. For example, I wanted The N4CER's chest plate to not only look battle scarred, but I wanted it to look chipped, rusted, and beaten. Using a paint program, I created a hand-painted image of his chest, giving it the war-torn look that I was going for. It not only looks exactly like I want it to, but it also adds another level of depth to The N4CER's aesthetic.

It goes without saying that this method can be used in a million different scenarios, so my job is to point it out as a viable method of texturing that gives you added control over design and saves on production time. Other texturing examples include a hand-painted vase, an old rusty door, a battle-scarred spaceship, a unique wall texture, a fabric pattern, metallic walls, or a blue sky with clouds.

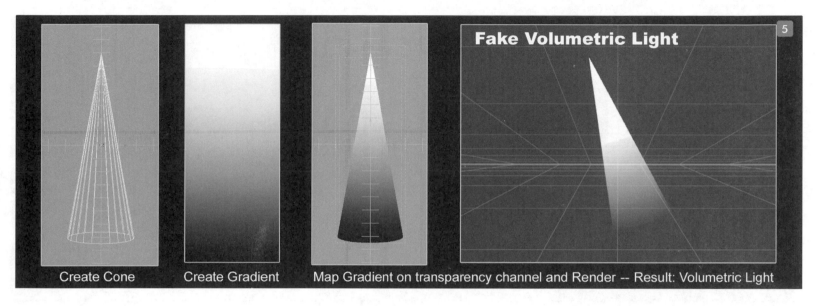

Create Cone | Create Gradient | Map Gradient on transparency channel and Render -- Result: Volumetric Light

Fake Volumetric Light

Lighting

Lighting is another big culprit with render-intensive volumetrics (which is used to create a visible light ray as if dust were in the air) and can get totally out of control. The two places that use 2D techniques for lighting are faked volumetric lights and fake reflected lights.

First let's talk about faked volumetric lights. This trick is about the oldest in the book (not this book, but probably the first book on 3D tricks). I like it because it's not just good for saving render time, but its application can be used in almost any environment. See my example (image 5).

First create a 3D model of a cone and give it a surface name of "Light." Go into your paint program and create a gradient image ranging from pure black to pure white. Now apply that gradient image to the transparency channel of your cone's surface, like in my example. The result when you render will look like a volumetric spotlight. I've used this cheat for all kinds of models needing a faked volumetric, like star-shaped lights, laser beams, jet engine glow, and fake fog in the distance. Some 3D programs can create this kind of gradient without having to use an image map; just follow the same guidelines, but instead create your gradient in the transparency channel and you will have an instant volumetric light!

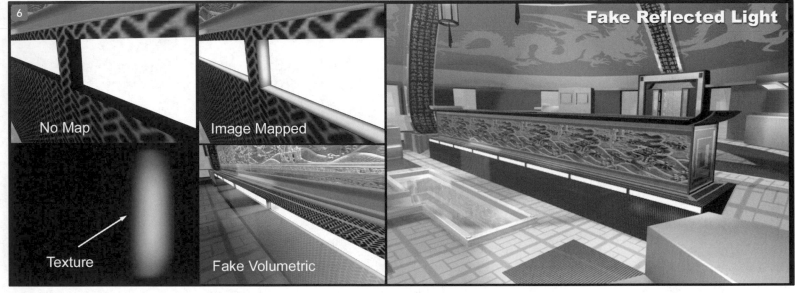

No Map

Image Mapped

Texture

Fake Volumetric

Fake Reflected Light

See color plate on page C-14.

The second lighting fake is the fake reflected light. Most 3D programs have a few lights to choose from, like the spotlight, distant or sunlight, area light, and linear light. I do 99% of my lighting using spotlights and distant lights, and rarely use a linear light or area light. Why? The answer is render time, plain and simple. Although linear and area lights cast more realistic shadows and are more versatile than cone lights, the render time is outrageous. See my

example for an explanation of this technique (image 6).

Bleep's kitchen/living room area has recessed linear lights all over the place. They look cool, but what you are seeing is merely a white polygon with a 100% luminance. In reality, that recessed light would not only be emitting light, but it would also be reflecting light into the metallic bezel that surrounds it. In order to achieve the reflected light in the bezel, I could place a linear light

near that surface, or I could paint a custom image map to fake the reflected light effect. Panel 1 indicates no reflected light around the bezel, just a bright white polygon. Panel 2 indicates reflected light around the bezel that was created by a texture map as seen in Panel 3. As seen in Panel 4, if I wanted to take it a step further, I could add a fake volumetric light in the shape of a rectangle, giving it more visual interest.

I first used the aforementioned techniques in combination back in 1999 during the production of *Thumb Wars*. The goal for me was to build a huge hangar bay in which all the Thumbellion Finger Fighters were housed. I spent many days on the model and created a ceiling full of truss work, flush-mounted neon lights, and dozens of volumetric cone lights, each adding a touch of atmosphere and design.

For the long neon lights, probably 60 of them were not even real lights but paintings. I actually painted each light, its bezel, and the reflected light and then texture mapped that image, repeating it several times.

I then used the fake volumetric cone light to spotlight each ship, adding even more depth and atmosphere. Before *Thumb Wars*, I had spent many hours drawing reflected light in environments and on objects, so it's second nature for me to want to add that kind of extra touch. Again, this was a solution that addressed long render times and the desire to add extra details like reflected edge lighting to my shots.

Look for design opportunities like the ones I found during the Thumbellion hangar model and it will pay for itself in good design aesthetic and short render times.

Hard Reflection   Blurred Reflection Map   Soft Reflection

See color plate on page C-14.

Reflections

The blurred reflection map trick isn't really a 2D paint trick but more of a realism trick that can save you loads of render time. A lot of standard 3D renders use reflection maps that are very sharp and lack the soft transitions that make a reflection look real. In certain cases sharp is good, like in glass, chrome, and car paint; in others like rough metal, frosted plastic, and rough tile, a softer reflection looks better. Blur your reflection maps for surfaces that require a soft reflection. This is easily achieved by taking your reflection map image into a 2D paint program, blurring the image to your own requirements, and then using it in the reflection map channel. You'll really notice the difference. See my examples that show the difference between a sharp reflection map and a soft one (image 7).

Here we are yet again adding another level of depth and aesthetic to the designs. 2D paint tricks like faked reflected light, faked volumetric light, soft reflections, and single image environments are fantastic for getting good results quick and saving a ton of render time. Scrutinize your work and look for those opportunities that allow for a more creative 2D approach to problem solving.

Composite for Effect

There are a heck of a lot of approaches to adding effects like blurs, glow, lens flares, smoke, and grain to your animations, but after many years I've come to the conclusion that nobody does it better than 2D programs like After Effects, Digital Fusion, Combustion, and Illusion. These programs allow the user to add simple special effects quickly and effectively without facing the long render times that a 3D program would require in order to achieve the same results. In my opinion, there are a few effects that you should just plan to make happen in a 2D program and not waste your time in 3D, so I've put together a short list of candidates and a quick explanation of their use.

Blurs

Use blur effects to soften up backgrounds or foreground elements. They are also good at softening up really grainy images or blemishes in an image.

Fake Depth of Field

In order to achieve this kind of effect in 2D, simply render your foreground and background elements separately and put them into separate layers. Blur only one layer, let's say the foreground, then slowly blur the background and at the same time blur the foreground. Make sure your transitions are in synch and it should look pretty good.

Quick Backgrounds

Let's say that you haven't fully decided on a background image and want to test a few with your 3D foreground elements. It may take quite a while to render each one, so do what I do — render out your foreground object as a separate element first, then save it out with an embedded alpha channel, like a 32-bit Targa file or a QuickTime file. 32-bit TIFFs work as well and will give you a fully transparent background you can see in Photoshop. Once you have your foreground element rendered, then you can composite it with any background you choose in order to previsualize how it will work within the context of your scene.

This technique can replace the "BG image on a single poly" technique. For those of you who know how to track a 2D image to moving footage, you may find this a lot easier. I've included examples of scene 6 with multiple backgrounds so you can see the variety. (image 8).

Quick Backgrounds

Render foreground with alpha channel,
then add any background you choose.

Edge Blur

A slight edge blur is a great way to add a soft edge that better integrates your foreground objects and their backgrounds.

Motion Blur

Sometimes you don't have the time to render all the passes required for good motion blur. Separate the moving objects in your scene and then add adequate blur to their layer to fake this effect. Some 2D programs have motion blur plug-ins that save a lot of time and add that great effect at very little time cost.

Soft Render

Sometimes a 3D render can look too sharp, almost to the point that it looks too much like 3D, whereas film has a wide range of color and softness that gives each shot depth, emotion, and tone. Add a slight amount of blur to your scenes to help soften the image, making it look more like film and less like harsh 30fps 3D. In this case you'll need to add grain on top in order for it to look right, but it's worth this extra step.

Glow

There are many glow effects in 2D programs, like edge glows, bloom, and overall glows. They are much easier to achieve in 2D and are available in about a hundred different applications.

Lens Flares

The lens flare is probably one of the most overused effects in 3D. Unfortunately, most 3D lens flares are limited to only a few distinct looks and take time to set up properly. 2D lens flares have hundreds of variations and can be applied to anything from a streetlight to a laser cannon in a matter of seconds.

Brightness/Contrast

Sometimes rendered scenes lack the necessary depth and detail as there isn't enough contrast between the black and white areas. Just put your shot into a 2D program and use the brightness and contrast functions to give them that much needed depth. You'd be surprised how many shots need that extra punch.

Fake Depth of field

Edge Blur

Motion Blur

See color plate on page C-15.

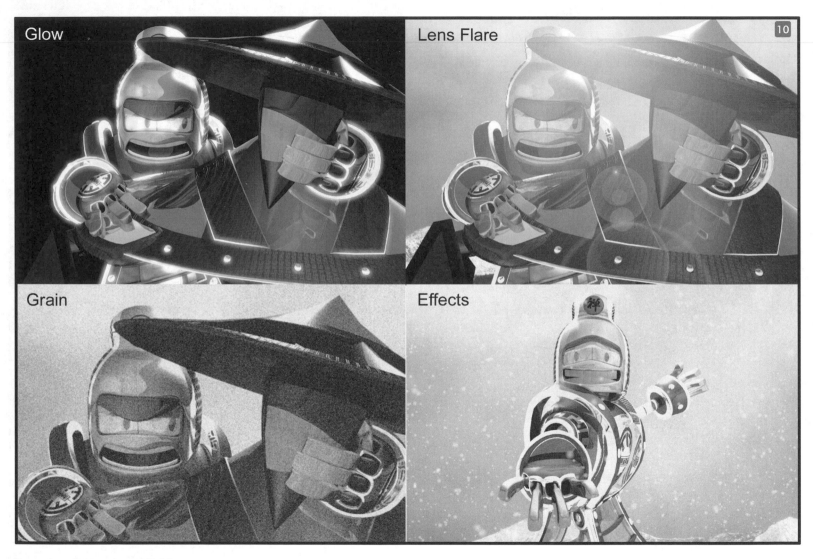

Glow

Lens Flare

10

Grain

Effects

See color plate on page C-16.

Color

Many 2D programs have an entire suite of tools dedicated to color that becomes an important ally in the war against the ordinary. The look of animations can range from incredibly bright vivid colors to soft, muted, and moody shots. How to get there is based on using an approach to color that is designed as well as purposeful. I talked a bit about opposite colors and warm/cool colors, but in this case we can go way beyond these studies to something more intricate and focused. For instance, a sepiatone shot is usually a monochromatic (one color) shot that uses brown for its overall tone. There are many variations on this theme, but there's no better way to get there than to use the hue and saturation tools found in a 2D program. Other applications of 2D color tools include overall hue shifts, specific color channel manipulation, monochromatic shots, and saturation adjustment. Experiment and enjoy.

Grain

Most anything shot digitally or on film or videotape will have some kind of grain in it. Since most 3D renders don't have grain in them, you need to add grain in one of two ways. 3D programs have plug-ins for adding grain, but they're very limited in the variety of grain you can choose from. 2D programs, however, have grain tools that allow for endless combinations of grain amount, shape, size, color, etc. To me, adding grain is the last tool in your design arsenal before you ship off your animations as final. Use it sparingly though, because too much can become distracting.

Chapter Eleven

Execution

Introduction

We're now coming up to the final stages in the design and animation process. At this point we've taken design and applied it to our story and produced some animation. Some of that animation has been rendered and some has not. Either way, our goal would be to finish up our animations and put them together into a short. As you will read in this chapter, a finished animation is not our goal; rather, the goal is to use design first and walk away from this book with the tools of design that will make you a better designer/animator. Read through the next sections with careful analysis and use them to improve not only your work, but the work of others.

Critique Thy Work

Most people feel the word critique has a negative connotation, but in our case, constructive critique or constructive criticism is a positive action. Critique is a foundational stage of project development that must be applied to every step of the design and animation process.

Critique, as it applies to you, is an honest evaluation of your design work that offers suggestion, praise, and solutions that will better your project.

Critique of your work can be handled in a couple of ways. Self-critique is simply observation that offers solutions.

For instance, if your dark object is getting lost in the shot because it's on a dark background, then critique would tell us, "We need more contrast!" Adding contrast is the solution to that problem, but is it considered the entire critique? No. The entire critique is based on evaluating every detail of your shot. For example: Is the animation good? Is the lighting good? Does the scene have good flow? Are my designs enhancing the scene or detracting from it? Is that light too bright? Is the composition tight? Is the color good? It goes on and on. A good critique should not only point out the flaws within your shots but also the positive attributes that make your animation good. There's no way to learn what you are doing right if you don't point it out. I was always taught to start a critique with a positive comment. I always look for the best attributes of a design or animation first, then look for the attributes that need improvement. For the positive attributes, note them and apply the same sensibility and design choices to future projects. For areas that need improvement, do a little problem solving by offering solutions to the problem, then apply those solutions.

A good constructive critique is the most honest moment during the design process. Be honest with yourself and your work; otherwise, you're fooling nobody. For example, I get demo reels and portfolios sent to me all the time by animators looking for work. The first thing I do during my critique of their work is to evaluate their level of honesty. Does their level of work match their resume? I've seen cover letters that say, "Highly skilled animator who is a perfect fit for your company... etc., etc." At this point, that kind of bold statement has set me up with a very high expectation. If the work on their demo reel doesn't match the statement "highly skilled animator," then I can only assume this person has never had an honest critique, or others have falsely led them down the wrong path. As a director, I don't want to work with anyone who doesn't know their own skill level and how they fit within the context of my productions. Those with

less skill admit they have room for improvement and display a thirst for that knowledge. The opening statement on their resume might look something like, "Confident entry-level animator looking for a position to learn and grow with your company... etc." I find that kind of attitude refreshing and if I can lend a hand to help that person achieve his or her goals, then great. To me, complete honesty is the only way to improve yourself and to help others. Critique is not about taking things personally but about honest evaluation of your work that leads to helpful solutions that than lead to a better execution.

You can either critique your work alone or you can ask others for their opinions. Who you ask is very important. If you ask your friend to critique your work and that person is an accountant, then you're more or less asking "the man on the street" for his opinion. That critique will be based more on personal taste and the rather simple likes and dislikes of the common viewer. Good stuff, but it's not the complete picture. To get the complete picture, ask a professional animator, designer, or director in order to get a critique based on experience. Other professionals have been down the same animation path over and over again and they know what works and doesn't work. Their critique can be extremely valuable just based on what kind of experience they bring to the table, but like all critiques, you should evaluate their suggestions and observations with the same scrutiny that you give everyone. Don't just run off and start changing things based on one person's opinion; ask as many people as you can to get a well-rounded critique. If many people agree that a certain portion of your animation could be improved, try to get a consensus on how and what your solution would be.

In the case of your animated project for this book, it's now time for critique. Make a list of the qualities about your animation that you like and the areas that you can improve. Be honest with yourself and ask the same of others, and you'll really have something to work with. If it feels right, then make those improvements to your work and go forward with your project. No matter what you do in life, there is always room for improvement. When you finally finish your short animation, there will be things you'll feel like you missed. This is a natural occurrence with any creative endeavor. I'm sure the filmmakers of *Shrek* have about a million changes they'd like to make in order to improve the movie, but the reality is, *Shrek* is finished, delivered, and gone and can no longer be changed. With any animated project, it will soon come to an end and the only hope you have is that like *Shrek*, your project will

encompass almost everything you wanted to achieve. Critique never ends, but your projects will, so choose the improvements that you think make the biggest or best difference for the project at hand and then move forward, feeling confident and satisfied.

Delivery

Delivery is what fuels the production train, and without it, animation production would never get done. The amount of tweaking, testing, ideation, and application is endless, so the only thing that keeps that in check is a definitive delivery requirement. That requirement could be a delivery date, a percentage of completion, or a simple animation test. Either way, understanding your delivery requirements and sticking to them is the difference between success and failure.

For our little project we only had one delivery requirement. In Chapter 6 our delivery requirement was defined as, "...if things go the way they should, by the end of this book you will have an outstanding foundation from which you can create your own animated short." As far as I'm concerned we've nailed that delivery requirement. I feel confident that together we've created a great foundation of design and learning that can be utilized not only on your current project but on future projects.

Completing "Feed the Dog" is going to require continual setup, color, texture, animation, render, and 2D effects until I reach the last scene. After all the scenes are rendered, I would import each shot into an editing package like Avid, Final Cut Pro, Adobe Premiere, or even After Effects to get my first glimpse of my story in action. This stage is the first time you see how your story flows together and requires a keen understanding of flow, pacing, and transitions. Again, using a good constructive critique, I will make design decisions about shot length, composition, flow, and aesthetic cohesion based on what I see at this stage. If I need to make some changes, I will. I'll then reimport those shots and replace the old ones until I've finished the last one.

If I feel my story flows together well and I've achieved all my design goals, then the only thing left to do is to add music, dialogue, and sound effects.

Editing, dialogue, music, and sound FX are all part of post production (after animation production), and are disciplines that take just as much time to learn as animation. If you don't know much about how these processes fit within an animation production, there are plenty of books that will explain their roles. Adding music and sound FX makes a huge impact in how your animation looks and feels and I can only encourage you to discover this for yourself and apply it to your work. All in all, the more you learn about each facet of the animation pipeline, the more your work will benefit from the collective contribution of each production skill.

Execution

We've now arrived at the end of our project. In this short book, I've done everything I can in order to convey the importance of using design first. The traditional design techniques that you learned in Chapters 2 through 10 should be reflected in your final animation and the work that you do from here on out. Value, contrast, lighting, color, tension, flow, proportion, contour, perspective, gesture, inspiration, research, presentation, character, story, storyboards, textures — all are integral and crucial phases of using design first. With time, these techniques will become second nature and your ability to use them will effectively increase. I'm just looking for you to pick up the pencil first before touching the keyboard... it's my only request.

If you decide to execute your short animation, do your best to keep focused on the goals at hand: composition, flow, and aesthetic. Each scene should be able to stand on its own as far as design and animation are concerned, but the entire project should work as a whole by utilizing the qualities of aesthetic, tone, and story that make it a single piece.

As for "Feed the Dog," my only goal at this point is to utilize my design material to finish my animation and use the power of observation and critique to improve my final project. I've put together a collage of images that have resulted from the design, modeling, and animation process of "Feed the Dog." There were so many phases to this design process and so many hurdles I had to overcome, sometimes it's really cool to see how much you've accomplished. As I analyze these images, I can't help but feel excitement, confidence, and satisfaction that my role as a designer has been fulfilled. Your education, experience, and observation are the best tools for learning design and its application in the work that you do. Working to develop your drawing and design skills, spending more time modeling and animating, and asking questions of experienced professionals on how to improve your work are all invaluable educational tools. Treat every day as a day of discovery and try to see something new in the world. Keep asking questions and stay focused on your goals. Soon your design eye and observational skills will collectively improve your worth as an animator and for the rest of your career you will have the most powerful and important weapon in the animation arsenal — design.

Bleep's Design Process

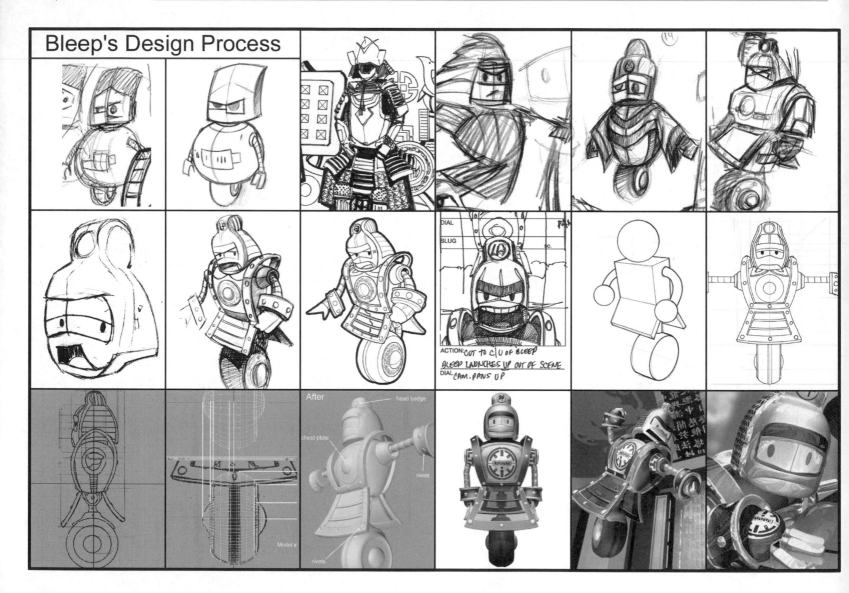

ACTION: CUT TO C/U OF BLEEP
BLEEP LAUNCHES UP OUT OF SCENE
DIAL CAM. PANS UP

After
head badge
chest plate
rivets
Model i
rivets

Industry Tips

Introduction

Some of you have never worked in an animation studio before and consequently have a lot of questions about how to get hired. There are so many variables that go into increasing your chances for getting hired it would be impossible to list them all. There are some tried-and-true ways of getting considered for a job, so the first place to begin would be to understand what studios are looking for. Once you understand the way a studio operates and how it chooses candidates, you can capitalize on this knowledge by creating your portfolio and demo reel to fit its needs. It goes without saying that not all studios nor candidates are the same, so focus on your skills first and then find a studio that matches your interests.

What Studios Want: "Calling All Designers!"

Animation is a business and because it's a business, money is the driving factor. Making the most money in animation falls under a very complex set of circumstances, unique to each studio. They all function based on one thing in mind: creative is king. Those studios and individuals that create the stories, characters, and concepts for the animation world are considered the most valuable component to the industry. There are varying degrees of creative contributions, so where you fit into that picture is up to you.

Your role at a studio is to help it create a product for sale. Studios want animation professionals who have a profound creative impact on their final product, because a better product means happy clients, which means more sales. To qualify for a job, studios look for at least three things: a good work ethic, team player, and applicable creative work. There are all kinds of positions available — from entry-level animator to producer — but the more traditional art techniques you have in your skill set, the more likely you are to have creative input within the pipeline. If you have something unique to add to the production that gives it more value, then you are more valuable to the production. Those who drive the creative vision ultimately have the most control and creative freedom. Each contribution to the project is equally important, so it all depends on where you see yourself within that environment.

Most companies function on an agenda that is based on the known.

As in, they know what their customers want and the quality of work they expect from their employees. Through the experience of building their business, they've carefully constructed a pipeline that works best for them, so knowing your company's pipeline and how you can fit in will make you a valuable commodity to its team. Every studio functions differently, so taking the time to understand the product a particular one creates will put you ahead of your competition. The product created can vary from high-end visual effects to simplistic animated kids' television shows. This gets into choosing a good studio that you feel not only reflects your creative goals but becomes a place for learning, opportunity, and growth.

How to choose the studio you'd like to work for is just as crucial as getting the job. This can take research, but can be as simple as going to a company's website. Take time to examine the work to get an idea of what level of experience the company is used to. When applying for a position, understand there should be a thread of commonality between your animation work and the studio's projects. It doesn't have to be a perfect match, but you should be on the same wavelength. For instance, if you have cartoony animation on your reel, apply to a cartoony animation studio. If you're good at compositing, then apply to an FX house that does a ton of compositing. Like design, finding a studio that matches your own criteria takes research. Once you've found what you like, do your best to prepare your work and present it in the most professional and favorable light.

Demo Reel Do's and Don'ts

In general, most animation projects are very specific and require a quick turnaround. Studios are looking for animation professionals who can fulfill those requirements, so in order to compete, your demo reel must show off your strengths. Everyone has a talent, so if your talent is lighting, then have your demo reel reflect this talent and highlight this skill on your resume. Studios want a quick read, like, "This person says he's good at lighting… and look, the demo reel reflects that." Get it?

The Harsh Reality of Demo Reel Submission

Your demo reel is your representative and it should look its best from every aspect. You wouldn't wear a pair of jeans and a ripped T-shirt to a formal dinner, so why would you send an unorganized, undesigned demo reel to a professional company? Many things count toward making your demo reel a success. The first is that your demo reel should catch someone's attention almost immediately. Your best work should be the first thing on your reel. Most studios rarely have the time to sit through an entire demo reel unless they really, really, really like the work. For instance, an animation director at a very large studio told me that if he's not interested within the first five seconds, then he tosses the demo reel. Sounds pretty harsh to me, but that's the reality of the situation: your demo reel is nestled among hundreds of other candidates. If your work doesn't get noticed right away, you're out.

How to Improve Your Chances of Getting Hired

Now that we've discussed the realities of this situation, let's discuss how to improve your chances of being noticed. First of all, any music, graphics, and sound FX you add to the mix will count for you or against you, just as much as the demo reel content itself. If you add music, sound FX, etc., a director or producer will start scrutinizing your ability to edit and properly add sound to your demo reel as well as the content you're showing. For first-timers, adding that kind of complexity like an edit with great music, proper transitions, and sound FX is incredibly complex and if it's not executed with precision — you're out. My suggestion is to keep it simple and straight to the point.

First, start off your demo reel with a well-designed title card containing your name, skill set (modeler, animator, etc.), and contact information that is no longer than three to five seconds. Then launch into your animation. Your title card can be an animated graphic with a cool reveal. Watch MTV or Comedy Central to get an idea of how to reveal graphics quickly and effectively; nobody does it better than those two. Besides, after reading this book, you should have the skills to research, design, and execute a kick-ass title card with no problem… so don't disappoint me. As for music, choose a piece that doesn't overwhelm your visuals, like smooth ambient grooves or something, not hardcore industrial death metal. Your edit should be very basic, cutting from one shot to the next, while every once in a while throwing in one of your better animations just to keep the interest of the viewer. At the end of your reel, finish it off with your second best piece of work and then cut to your title card. Done. Your demo reel should be no longer than two to three minutes.

Include a shot by shot breakdown of your demo reel with an explanation of the shot and what your contributions were. For example: "Red car skidding out — design, modeling, and animation." This short list will give the viewer an accurate description of your abilities and contributions.

Your resume should be well designed, organized, and to the point, using a custom-designed letterhead. Your cover letter should be short and to the point; don't get too much into the big speech, "I thank thee for the chance opportunity to allow my contributions to accurately address thy needs as a blah... blah... blah...." As I've said before, be yourself. Write a letter that's honest, personable, and denotes research, like, "I did a lot of research about your company and I like the project you did for Fox entitled *Whatever.* I noticed that you do a lot of 3D character animation and my demo reel has good examples of my character animation work... etc.... etc...." Remember that you're trying to get noticed for your unique qualities and skills. There's no better way to get noticed than through a thoroughly researched and honest cover letter.

Your demo reel should be either DVD or VHS format. Repeat the use of graphics from your letterhead onto the cover of your demo reel to give the entire package a cohesive, professional appearance. Remember, your demo reel is your representative; it should look its best and deliver a clear concise message about who you are without you having to be there.

Demo Reel Returns

Why don't most studios return your demo reel submission with a letter? The reality is that most studios are inundated with demo reels and don't have the time or resources to answer every demo reel submission with a letter. Consequently, your reel ends up on some big pile waiting to be reviewed. Some studios take the time to send you a form letter thanking you for a submission, but that doesn't help much because it doesn't give you any real understanding of what they think of your work. The answer to what they think is very subjective. Just because you didn't hear anything from the studio doesn't mean that you're out of the running. In fact, demo reel submission and job hunting is mostly a waiting game. The studio is waiting just as much as you are, but as soon as that project lands... look out, they're on the demo reel hunt. The big dig through the VHS pile begins. If those producers were just awarded a car commercial, they will be mostly interested in demo reels with cars; if they get a trailer with photoreal compositing, they will be mostly interested in demo reels with photoreal compositing. That's why I stress focusing on your strengths and showing them off in your demo reel. As you gain more experience, the variety of work on your demo reel is going to increase, thereby making you a much more versatile candidate who gets the job. It's something to work toward, but variety and versatility within your reel are key, because the content on your reel must match the immediate needs of a studio in order for you to get hired.

How Long Should You Wait?

There's really no answer to that question other than what feels right to you. I would personally wait about four months before sending a new reel and would make sure that it has new material on it. That gives you some time to produce more animation, gain some experience, and give the studio a chance to get some new projects. It's all a huge waiting game, but the beauty is if you get hired, you're in for good, because you'll not only have professional work on your reel, but new contacts within the biz that help keep you employed.

All in all, getting a gig working in animation is an amazing experience, because you're getting paid to do what you love. I feel the most important aspect of my professional career is that it's not a job, it's a lifestyle. I choose to design, animate, and produce because I love it… it just so happens I get paid. So in conclusion, do your best to be unique, work harder than the next guy, and always be honest about your work.

Index

2D
drawing, 219
shortcuts, 273-289
vs. 3D, 214-215
3D animation, 264-267
3D model,
coloring, 255
final version, 263
texturing, 256-258
scanning, 230-231
3D modeling, 236-237
3D vs. 2D, 214-215

A

animation, 1
animator, 2
artist, 2
asymmetry, 72-77
audience, defining, 122-123

B

backgrounds, 262-263, 284-285
creating in 2D, 273-277
basic shapes, 8-9
blur effects, 283

bounced light, 22-23
breakdown, 155

C

camera positions, 206-209
cell phone project, 120-121
defining audience, 122-123
defining concepts for, 132-137
presentation for, 138-140
research for, 124-131
character, 146-148
development, 148-149
clients,
feedback from, 140-141
working with, 120
colors,
adding to 3D model, 255
applying palette, 181-182
comparing, 183
cool, 60-67
creating palette, 179-180
gathering reference, 179
in 2D, 289
opposite, 56-59
primary, 57

secondary, 57
selecting, 179
warm, 60-67
composition, 40, 201
concept,
defining, 132-137
presenting, 138-140
construction, 11-12, 108-111
connecting, 112-113
contour, 80-85, 247-249
contrast, 32-33, 39, 68, 268-270
cool colors, 60-67
cool lighting, 271
core shadow, 23
coverage, 192
critique, 86-87, 291-293

D

delivery requirements, 294
demo reel guidelines, 299-301
depth of field, faking, 283, 287
design, 1, 4-6
direction, 156-158
exploration, 160-163
theme, 100-101

types of, 88-89
vs. story, 184
design material, scanning, 230-234
designer, 1-2
detail, adding, 252-254
dissolve, 203-205, 208-209

E

edge blur, 286-287
effects, adding, 283-289
energy, 80-84
example projects, *see* cell phone project
and "Feed the Dog"

F

fade, 205, 210-211
"Feed the Dog," 143
  Angus character, 168-170
  applying color palette, 181-182
  Bleep character, 164-167, 222-225,
    228-229
  creating color palette, 179-180
  design direction, 158-159
  design exploration, 160-163
  gesture drawings, 174-175
  inspiration for Angus character, 152
  modeling Bleep character, 236-263
  refinement of sketches, 176-177
  screen direction, 198-199
  script, 185-190
  selecting colors, 179
  story, 153-154

story breakdown, 155
storyboarding, 193-195, 202-204
  The N4CER character, 171-173
  timing, 212-214
flow, 48-51, 198-200
focal point, 44

G

gesture drawing, 91-93, 95, 174-175
glow effects, 286, 288
grain, 288-289
graphic design, 41
grays, 60, 62

H

halves, modeling in, 240-243

I

illustration, 7
image maps, scanning, 232-233
imprinting, 94
indirect light, 22
individuality, 102
inspiration, 96-97, 150-152, 156
  applying, 99-101
  finding, 98-99

K

key light, 22
KISS rule, 114-116

L

lens flares, 286, 288
light,
  bounced, 22-23
  indirect, 22
  key, 22
  reflected, 22
lighting, 20-31, 64-66, 268-271
  creating in 2D, 279-281
line convergence, 34-35
line drawing, 13
line thickness, *see* line weight
line weight, 18-19

M

modeling in halves, 240-243
motion blur, 286-287
motivation, understanding, 116

O

observation, 6, 86-87, 250-251
opposite colors, 56-59

P

perspective, 34-35
primary colors, 57
primitives, 10
  using, 11
proportion, 68-71, 244-247

R

reference material, gathering, 124-131
refinement, 107, 176-177
reflected light, 22
    faking, 280
reflection maps, 282
reflectivity, 30-31
render time, tips for decreasing, 216-217
rendering, 271
research, conducting, 124-131
rough sketching, 102-108
rule of thirds, 78-79

S

scene numbering, 195
screen direction, 198-200
secondary colors, 57
shapes, basic, 8-9
shot breakdown, 192-194
silhouette, 19
simplicity, 114-116
sketching, 7
    rough, 102-108
soft render, 286
still life drawing, 36
story,
    breakdown, 155
    creating, 153-154
    goal of, 1
    influence of visuals on, 184
    inspiration for, 150-152
    vs. design, 184

storyboarding, 192, 196-197
storyboards,
    scanning, 234
    timing, 212-214
    using as reference for animation,
        264-265
studios, 297-298
style, 5, 156
subject matter, selecting, 144-145
subtlety, 259-261

T

tangents, 52-55
tension, 46-47
textures,
    adding to 3D model, 256-258
    creating in 2D, 278
thirds, rule of, 78-79
three-view basic shape drawing, 222-226
    using as reference, 238-239
three-view orthographic drawing,
    219-222, 227-229
timing, 212-214
transitions, 84-85, 202-205

V

value, 32-33
viewing angle, 14-15
volumetric lights, faking, 279

W

warm colors, 60-67
warm lighting, 271

Design First

for 3D.com Website

Access new images, updates and cool merchandise...

...If you like **Design First**, then you'll love what's on this site.

goto---www.designfirstfor3d.com

About the CD

The companion CD contains images and a test animation related to projects in the book, along with all the images from the book.

The CD will auto run when you place it in your CD drive. In the screen that appears, click Hi-Rez Images to see additional images and Video to see the test animation. (You will need QuickTime to play the video.)

To access the images from the book, use Explorer and select the Book Images folder.

Warning:

By opening the CD package, you accept the terms and conditions of the CD/Source Code Usage License Agreement.

Additionally, opening the CD package makes this book nonreturnable.

CD/Source Code Usage License Agreement

Please read the following CD/Source Code usage license agreement before opening the CD and using the contents therein:

1. By opening the accompanying software package, you are indicating that you have read and agree to be bound by all terms and conditions of this CD/Source Code usage license agreement.

2. The compilation of code and utilities contained on the CD and in the book are copyrighted and protected by both U.S. copyright law and international copyright treaties, and is owned by Wordware Publishing, Inc. Individual source code, example programs, help files, freeware, shareware, utilities, and evaluation packages, including their copyrights, are owned by the respective authors.

3. No part of the enclosed CD or this book, including all source code, help files, shareware, freeware, utilities, example programs, or evaluation programs, may be made available on a public forum (such as a World Wide Web page, FTP site, bulletin board, or Internet news group) without the express written permission of Wordware Publishing, Inc. or the author of the respective source code, help files, shareware, freeware, utilities, example programs, or evaluation programs.

4. You may not decompile, reverse engineer, disassemble, create a derivative work, or otherwise use the enclosed programs, help files, freeware, shareware, utilities, or evaluation programs except as stated in this agreement.

5. The software, contained on the CD and/or as source code in this book, is sold without warranty of any kind. Wordware Publishing, Inc. and the authors specifically disclaim all other warranties, express or implied, including but not limited to implied warranties of merchantability and fitness for a particular purpose with respect to defects in the disk, the program, source code, sample files, help files, freeware, shareware, utilities, and evaluation programs contained therein, and/or the techniques described in the book and implemented in the example programs. In no event shall Wordware Publishing, Inc., its dealers, its distributors, or the authors be liable or held responsible for any loss of profit or any other alleged or actual private or commercial damage, including but not limited to special, incidental, consequential, or other damages.

6. One (1) copy of the CD or any source code therein may be created for backup purposes. The CD and all accompanying source code, sample files, help files, freeware, shareware, utilities, and evaluation programs may be copied to your hard drive. With the exception of freeware and shareware programs, at no time can any part of the contents of this CD reside on more than one computer at one time. The contents of the CD can be copied to another computer, as long as the contents of the CD contained on the original computer are deleted.

7. You may not include any part of the CD contents, including all source code, example programs, shareware, freeware, help files, utilities, or evaluation programs in any compilation of source code, utilities, help files, example programs, freeware, shareware, or evaluation programs on any media, including but not limited to CD, disk, or Internet distribution, without the express written permission of Wordware Publishing, Inc. or the owner of the individual source code, utilities, help files, example programs, freeware, shareware, or evaluation programs.

8. You may use the source code, techniques, and example programs in your own commercial or private applications unless otherwise noted by additional usage agreements as found on the CD.

Warning:

By opening the CD package, you accept the terms and conditions of the CD/Source Code Usage License Agreement.

Additionally, opening the CD package makes this book nonreturnable.